From the bylanes of Delhi, Agra & Jaipur

Ronald Vivian Smith

Vitasta
LET KNOWLEDGE SPREAD
www.vitastapublishing.com

Published by
Renu Kaul Verma
Vitasta Publishing Pvt Ltd
2/15, Ansari Road, Daryaganj
New Delhi – 110 002
info@vitastapublishing.com

ISBN 978-93-86473-47-9

First Edition 2019
Third Reprint 2023

MRP ₹595

Editors: Kanagam King, Papri Sri Raman
Sketches by Tony Smith
Cover and layout by Somesh Kumar Mishra
Printed by Vikas Computer and Printers

Dedicated to my dear friend Pran Nevile,
doyen of stories of the British Raj,
and to his wife Savitri,
an iconic entity.

Contents

Foreword

Ronald Vivian Smith has been Delhi's most faithful and constant chronicler for nearly six decades. In column after column and essay after essay, he has introduced his readers to sights and sounds not to mention people and places that we would have remained blithely unaware of, not the least because many of those sights and sounds, and people and places have been sacrificed at the altar of urban renewal. They live only in Smith's prodigious memory and, by extension, through his indefatigable writings.

Were it not for Smith Sahib and that treasure trove that is his memory, we would have been *mehroom*, bereft, of the story behind the Pir of Bachon ka Ghar, or the New Year festivities at Ludlow Castle, or who was the Thakur's Sleek Beauty, or what's the mystery behind the Owls for Slaughter, or what and where is the Hell on Dunghill. It is these and scores of such tales that find mention in this book. Saved from being lost forever, given the short life newspaper columns have, and especially in the age before the internet when old articles never made it to the archives, collections such as these acquire great significance.

Having walked the streets of Delhi since he first came to live here in 1961, Smith knows Delhi's past better than anyone else. And not just the city's parks and tombs and serais and mosques, he knows the gossip and legends that spilled over in its streets, the whispers that once floated down its lanes and bylanes, the stories he once heard either directly or from those who had, in turn, heard them from older denizens of Delhi. His history is not culled from dusty history books or air-conditioned reference rooms. Instead, it is distilled from the city's heat and dust, its scents and sounds. When mixed with dollops of piquant humour and a generous world view his version of history is, in a word, humane.

Smith speaks as he writes. Reading his columns, and I must say I have been an avid reader for years and, still, read them faithfully at every opportunity I get, I still find myself charmed by the easy intimacy to his writings about the past. He sounds like a chatty but prodigously knowledgeable and wise family elder. He has been answering all our questions about our city, questions we wouldn't know who to ask, whose answers we are unlikely to find in conventional books of history. For instance, what is '*Masihi shairi*'? Which is the fort with the 'weird' history? What is the secret of '*purani haveli*'? What is the 'legal eagle's odyssey'? What was a Delhi Christmas like in the 1890s? More importantly, how was New Year's eve celebrated in 1857 after the siege and slaughter of the spirited Indians?

It is these and other micro-histories that paint the small picture, like Jane Austen's proverbial two-inches of ivory, that add nuance to our understanding of the city that so many of us are happy to call home. Like the city flaneurs, the word being derived from the French noun *flâneur*, means 'stroller', 'lounger', 'saunterer', or 'loafer' Smith's seemingly aimless ramblings over six decades have yielded a rich crop of memories: vivid, colourful, detailed, graphic to the point of photographic recall. The painter with the pen, the urban explorer, the connoisseur of the street, R V Smith is all this and more. May he live long and continue to enthral us with his word pictures for many years to come.

Rakhshanda Jalil
Commentator & Litterateur
December 2018, New Delhi

A Castle Old And Grey

I never see a castle
That is gaunt and grey and grim,
But my thoughts at once go backward
To the past so misty and dim.

If I climb the broken stairway,
Where the stone is smooth and fine,
I hear a rustle and whisper,
And footsteps in front of mine.

Only the grey old castle,
Of crumbling stone and lime,
Still stands to speak of the ages,
And the iron footsteps of Time.

—Alexander Anderson

with article on Queen Victoria's dal

The Dal's Lament

'YEH mooh aur masoor ki dal' One of the pulses that became the favourite of Queen Victoria, who liked its soup and lent her name to it so that it became famous as *Malika Masoor*. No wonder the snub that not every mouth could savour masoor dal

has held good ever since it seems. Now this dal is selling at 100 rupees a kilo, while arhar dal, which once formed part of the poor man's daily meal, is touching Rs 230. *Ghar ki murghi dal barabar* (a domestic hen is just as cheap as a dal) is an old saying. But now it seems to have been reversed because even chicken is less costly than arhar dal. Incidentally, moong-ki-dal was known as *Badshah Pasand* as Bahadur Shah Zafar was fond of it and chana dal as *Tote-ki-dal* as it was cheap and fed to parrots and pigeons. Moong is now Rs 112 a kg and chana dal Rs 80.

What actually happened to make dals expensive? The bad monsoon is cited as a reason, though the truth may be that pulses are being hoarded by unscrupulous traders and the government faces the jibe whether this was what the much-vaunted *Acche Din* slogan meant. Forgetting the political nitty-gritty, one would like to delve a bit more into history. Biblical Esau sold his birthright to his twin brother, Jacob for a pot of dal. Birbal taught Akbar a lesson by cooking *masoor dal khichri* on a slowly burning fire, while Cleopatra blossomed on Egyptian pulses (now being imported). When Edward VII succeeded Victoria, an Urdu poet composed a verse with twenty-one blessings on the emperor but since Edward did not reign long enough the blessings were diverted to his son George V, who came to India for the Delhi Durbar in 1911-12. Each blessing ended with *Elahi Salamat rahe Badshah* (Oh God, may the king remain safe). A blind man, Lucas born in the same year as Jawaharlal Nehru, was one of the few who could recite the twenty-one blessings by heart in a highly emotional voice. Ashraf Mamu, eccentric as he was, would knock at a house at random and demand rotis. When they were offered to him he would tell the housewife or maid to remove the top and bottom rotis. He would then take only the ones in between to eat with dal cooked by him in the porch outside an abandoned house. Whenever anybody called him *Mamu* (maternal uncle) he would let out a volley of abuses. But if addressed as *Chacha* (father's brother) he would lapse into nostalgia about the visit of George V. *Wah beta, yaad hai, badshah salamat aaye the, kaise mithai bati thi* (remember how sweets were distributed when the king came)!

Abid Bhai never entered his ancestral Nizam's haveli, but cooked dal in an outside verandah. He had been an Excise Commissioner, who went about mounted on a horse, until he fell in love with a courtesan. When she ditched him, he lost his mind. His wife also left him while Abid Bhai went about with a policeman's baton in hand demanding uncooked dal at certain houses only.

But coming back to Lucas, besides recounting *Badshah-ki Barkatein* with a bowl of *Keoti dal* (mixed pulses), he was also noted for reciting a long-forgotten poem, *Dal-ki-Fariyad* (The Dal's Plea, but actually lament). It started off with the words,

Ek ladki bagharti hai dal
Dal kehte hai
Main kabhi hare-bhare kheton main lehrati thi

A girl was seasoning the dal. The dal said, I once swayed in the breeze in green fields and then went on to lament that one day the dal crop was harvested and a cruel contractor came and took away the pulses, which he locked up in a godown and sold at high prices when the demand was great.

The dal then tells the girl, 'Alas, what a day has come! After frolicking in the fields today I am boiling in a pot on a roasting fire and you are adding to my misery by giving me a *baghar* (*tadka,* twang with ghee and cut onions) to make me tastier to the palate'. The girl hears the dal's lament and bursts into tears as its plight has hit a tender chord in her heart. She stops applying the tadka and sits down to write a poem on what the dal had gone through. It was so touching a poem that it came to be known as *Dal-ki-Baghar* instead of *Dal-ki-Fariyad*. Those who think that only slaughtered animals, fish and table birds (like chicken) feel pain and that dal can be safely consumed may have second thoughts on hearing its *fariyad*. Ashraf Mamu, Abid Bhai and Lucas are long dead and probably no modern book contains Dal-ki-Fariyad but some old-timers still cannot forget the lament, more so now when dal prices are skyrocketing not because Hollywood actresses have learnt to relish dal-chawal!

Cabbages And Kings

SHAB-e-Barat last week and *Ganga Dussehra* before it were a reminder that *puri-halwa* tastes better with slices of *kakri-khira* (cucumber), though the Mughals preferred the pickle made of the two. They were also fond of *bandgobi* (cabbage) which brings one to the rhyme of *Cabbages and Kings*, which Rudyard Kipling probably had in mind when he wrote, 'The tumult and the shouting dies/The Captains and the Kings depart'. Kipling couldn't have known at that time that it would apply so famously to the euphoria created by the Delhi Durbar of 1911, when an overwhelmed George V and Queen Mary returned to England and the relieved rajas and maharajas to their principalities. But centuries before Lewis Carroll's *Alice in Wonderland,* Shah Jahan had come out with his own Cabbages & Kings-like tribute to the kakri and the *tarbuz*, just as eloquent as what the Walrus said to the Carpenter 'of many other things':

Pahuncho na iski hargiz Kabul dare ki kakri
Na purab aur na paschim khubi bhare ki kakri
Na Chin ke pare ki aur na bhare ki kakri
Dakhin ki aur na hargiz us pare ki kakri
Kya khoob naram-o-nazuk is Agre ki kakri…

The Emperor was sold out on the qualities of this variety of cucumber. Whether it was sweet or bitter, *kakri* was the ultimate reality for him like the Day of Judgement.

About water melon the poet Nazir substantiated to say:

Kyon na ho sabz jamurand ke barabar tarbuz

Karta hai khuskh kaleje ke tai tar tarbuz
Dil ki garmi ko nikale hai yeh aksar tarbuz

(The water-melon is large as the Jamurand fruit. It nourishes the dry liver and often gives relief from heartburn.)

Ramesh Chandra Sharma, a noted historian, has mentioned this in his paper published in the *Journal of Historical Research*. The early Mughals liked vegetables to be cooked on a slow fire with mutton. But potatoes and tomatoes were conspicuous by their absence, probably because they were not grown then. Besides his revelation of Shah Jahan's love for the kakri and tarbuz, Prof Sharma mentions the *Chronicles of the Pathan Kings of Delhi* by Edward Thomas (1871) to underline the importance of oral history, eating habits and 'the evidence furnished by coins, inscriptions and other antiquarian remains of the times of the Sultans of Delhi and Akbar the Great'. He goes on to say that the coins of Sikandar Lodhi struck in Agra were not as fine as those made in Delhi, which had been temporarily discarded by him and his son Ibrahim. The succeeding Mughals, Babar, Humayun, Akbar and Jahangir also preferred Agra.

Kakri, according to local lore, grew in abundance near the now extinct *maqbara* of

Shah Jahan's mother, Jodhabai, wife of Jahangir and not of Akbar as per popular misconception. The latter's own consort, though also a Rajput princess of Amber, is identified by only her title of 'Mariam Zamani'. One wonders if Shah Jahan and Mumtaz Mahal munched kakris in the Agra Fort on summer afternoons during their courtship. Incidentally, a good *kakri* year signifies the birth of more girls but less mangoes – and vice versa. Mumtaz, says Professor R Nath, gave birth to eight sons and six daughters, dying after delivering her last child – a short-lived girl, Ayesha.

Discarding his ancestor's love for Agra, Shah Jahan built Shahjahanabad 'and Delhi reclaimed its proud position of being the traditional royal seat of Islam in India', asserts Dr Sharma. But that was after the building of the Taj Mahal, whose masons were served *arhar dal* and *roti*, with *petha* as a nourishing sweet dish. The kakri and tarbuz they could get from the banks of the Yamuna and eat to their heart's content. The emperor embellished with marble his red sandstone buildings, which were of two kinds – religious and secular, says Dr Sharma. The latter, ignoring the Islamic injuction, were decorated with animal, bird and also human figures, besides flowers and fruit.

Kharbuze-ka-Gumbad, though built in Tughlak times, fits in between. The *kharbuza*, interestingly, was the favourite fruit of his great-grandson, Jahandar Shah.

Outside the Red Fort you can sometimes still hear the vendor's cry comparing kakri to the celebrated beloved Laila's fingers or the ribs of her lover Majnu. The tarbuz and kharbuza of Yamuna bank, however, bask in the glory of their *shirin* and *lazzat* (milky sweetness and exotic taste) as though echoing Shah Jahan's tribute.

The Old Fogies' Club

THE yesteryear *mehfils* at the *Deori* in a downtown Delhi *mohalla* were replete with witty conversations that still tickle the mind. Four old men, Salaman Sahib, Tommy Sahib, Webb Sahib and Harry Sahib had a sundowner between 7.30 and 9 pm while recollecting recent and past events, like Colonel Nasser's stance on the Suez blockade or Pandit Nehru's soft corner for Edwina Mountbatten.

Salaman, with curled-up hair like Kaiser Wilhem II, was always dressed in a half-sleeve shirt, khaki knickers and stockings reaching up to his knees, worn with brown shoes. He spent the forenoon and early evening sitting in a balcony in the Red Light area watching the world go by or giving advice to dancing girls who came seeking it and handing out *tawiz* amulets for curing *Paari-ka-Bukhar* (malaria). 'Is this your handwriting, like a child's!', he admonished me when I went to get rid of my fever and was asked to address a letter to piano-maker Henry Sahib in Ahmedabad as his own hand shook.

Salaman Nana returned home for lunch, rested and then went back to the Shehar as he used to refer to it. If his family members asked him to attend a court hearing or take a grandchild out, he would reply, 'Beta, you know I have to go to Shehar'. That was excuse enough. So nobody bothered him. At the mehfil he spoke little but whatever he said was treated as golden words of wisdom. As a bachelor he had spent his early life as an Urdu teacher (once as tutor to poet Josh Malihabadi) while supporting his elder brother's widow and children. He often came out with pithy comments, like the one on his only sister: *Bua tau har ped ki chayya letin hain* (Bua is a person fond of resting in the shade of every tree on her path). This was said with regard to her habit of frequently changing church membership – Catholic to Protestant, to Seventh Day Adventist, to Pentecostal or Free Church. His Jacobian family had a history dating back to 1857, when his father Joseph Sahib, *Karinda* (overseer) of a Nawab, used to look after the zamindari. Once Munshiji, as he was known, had to face a gang of dacoits. The gang had to return empty-handed as Jacob Sahib had got wind of the impending dacoity and vacated the house, leaving his wife and children at the house of the *khansama* while he, along with other servants, sat atop a tree to keep track of the happenings, armed with swords that sometimes flashed dangerously as it was a rainy night with lightning and thunder.

Tommy Sahib was a descendant of the Montrose family, one of whose branches produced the Urdu poet Benjamin Montrose 'Muztar', pupil of Ustad Daagh Dehlvi. When Daagh died in Hyderabad in 1905, Muztar commented:

Ek Daagh tha so who bhi tau Muztar guzar gaya

Ab baqi bacha hai kaun Hindostan mein.

(Now that Daagh is no more, there is no other poet in India).

Tommy Sahib had combed-back curly hair and flaring nostrils like Salaman and his eyes were just as red as his, but he wore a shirt and pyjamas while staying with his socialist niece, Vicky and her vivacious daughter as the only surviving male of the family. He too was a fount of knowledge.

Webb Sahib also dressed like Salaman Sahib, but with a *sola topi* on his head, hair parted like Edward VIII (Duke of Windsor after abdication). A Sufi at heart, though a hereditary member of the Church of England, he spent Thursday nights at some dargah and the next day would relate his experiences at the mehfil. *Kya sama tha—kya chiragh roshan they, aur beech raat ko paak sheyeh ghoomti nazar ati theen* (what an atmosphere created by qawwalis, and as the earthen lamps burnt past midnight one could almost see the souls of the blessed hovering around). The other wisemen present nodded in agreement with remarks like *Raat hi ko tau shabab ata hai, jab chiraghon ki lau jati hoti hai aur raina jawan hoti jati hai* (the nocturnal ambience is set when lamps burn low and, paradoxically enough, the night gets younger).

Harry Sahib, who had been Superintendent of Railways in Rewari, had his own tales to tell. His father had been a general of the Maharaja of Jaipur and had taken part in wars among Rajput chieftains and then in Afghanistan. Harry Sahib's eldest son, Ronnie was a veteran of World War II, having fought against Rommel's Desert Legion, and younger son, Harvey an RAF bomber pilot and later personal pilot of the Maharaja of Cooch-Behar, father of Maharani Gayatri Devi.

The family ancestors had served as *Sirdar*s of Jaipur State since the early eighteenth century. Harry was also fluent in Urdu with a great sense of humour. One of his sons was having a quiet smoke one day when he suddenly walked into the room. The boy hurriedly put the cigarette into the cane chair cushion. 'Mind, mind don't burn your bottom', Harry said with a sarcastic laugh. The son didn't know which way to look.

Listening to these old-timers was an experience of a lifetime. They are all dead, of course (Salaman Sahib in May 1954 when Roger Bannister broke the four-minute mile race barrier). The Deori in which the mehfil was held has now become a godown, where one sometimes wonders if their spirits are still around, discussing *Aap biti ya jag biti* (what befell them or the world), especially on Thursday, when people light joss-sticks in memory of the dear departed.

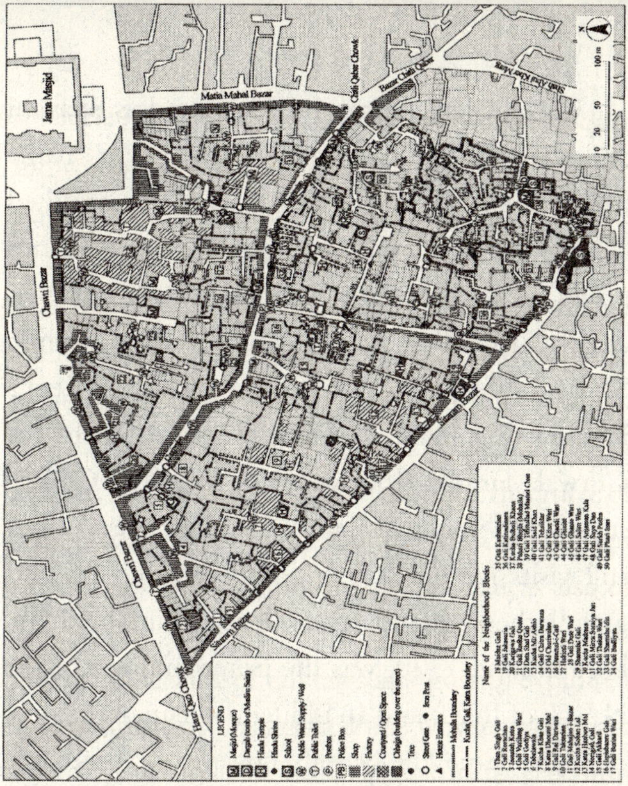

Space Formation and Transformation of the Urban Tissue of Old Delhi, India - Scientific Figure on ResearchGate. Available from: https://www.researchgate.net/Formation-of-Kucha-Gali-and-Katra-and-Distribution-of-Urban-Facilities-in-Old-Delhi_fig1_245440835 [accessed 12 Nov, 2018]

Tales Kuchas-Katras Tell

WHEN Shah Jahan moved his capital from Agra to Delhi he introduced *kucha*s and *katra*s in Shahjahanbad too. These were named after famous people or after the trades and professions pursued there.

Kucha Ghasi Ram, whose landmark is Bhavani Shankar's *Namak Haram-ki-Haveli*, got its name from the astrologer whom the emperor consulted before venturing out of the city or even to various places in it, so Ghasi Ram became his trusted adviser, according to Mahabir Shankar Mathur. The eighty-eight-year-old former resident of Kucha Khushal Rai (named after a medieval Rai of the Gurwala family) from where St Stephen's College started off, now lives in Mayur Vihar Phase-1 but still visits his old haunts. Mathur Sahib says his grandfather's grandfather, Dewan Buddh Singh, born around 1770, was the prime minister of the Nawab of Jhajar and an influential man of the time of Shah Alam. The Nawab, however, was executed in the aftermath of 1857. Noted for his exquisite collection of coins right from the time of Akbar to Queen Victoria, her grandson, great- grandson and after, Mathur is quite an authority on Old Delhi with his rupee, anna, paisa, cowrie, damari and dhela tales.

Kuchas (actually koonchas) retain their history in name only as the original inhabitants are either dead or have left to live in modern colonies. Kucha Lattu Shah is named after a saint associated with *lattoo*s or spinning tops, but why it is not known. Kucha Ustad

Hamid is the place where one of the master architects of the Taj and Lal Qila lived. Kucha Rehman, according to Haji Mian, was actually named after Raja Ramrai Mall and is a corruption of the name. Kucha Dilwali Singh, in Ajmeri Gate, is named after the maternal uncle of Guru Govind Singh, who was attached to the court of Bahadur Shah-I, eldest son of Aurangzeb, who as Prince Muazam ascended the throne in 1707. Dilwali Singh was the one who introduced Guru Govind to the emperor and they formed a close friendship. The consorts of the Guru, Mata Sahib Devi and Mata Sundari lived in the *kucha* till the time of the invasion of Nadir Shah in 1739, though Dilwali died in 1708. The ladies then went away to Mathura. They returned after normalcy returned to Delhi and built the gurdwara in Mata Sundari Road.

Kucha Chobdar was named after the bodyguards of Shah Jahan and his decendants. They were the flag-bearers and spear-carriers. Later the kucha was inhabited by dealers of chobas (nails) and other hardware. Kucha Mahajani in Chandni Chowk was so named because of the *mahajan*s or *seth*s who were bullion merchants and moneylenders to the latter-day Mughal emperors.

Katra Shahenshah and Katra Nawab were

named after two nawabs of the Nizam who built their mansions here. Kucha Sakka, better known as Sakka Gali, was where the water-carriers or *bhisti*s stayed. Few of them survive as most of the younger generation has taken to other professions and the bhistis (traditional water carriers) are hardly found jingling their *katora*s (copper cups) in front of the Jama Masjid. There was a time when they filled up their *mashaka*s (waterskins) from a well near Hare Bhare's shrine and offered water to wayfarers but refrigerated water spelt the doom of their profession.

Kucha Baghwala was adjacent to the garden laid out by Jahanara Begum, Shah Jahan's daughter, off Chandni Chowk and has now become Gandhi Park. Kucha Pandit was the domain of the Brahmin pandits, where the author of *Twilight in Delhi*, Ahmed Ali lived before moving to Karachi in 1947. Kucha Patiram is named after an astrologer-cum-vaid who so pleased a Mughal emperor that he named a locality after him. Katra Nil is the historic fabrics and goods market. Bazaar Sitaram was the abode of the Kashmiri community, where Haksar haveli was the most prominent building and where Jawaharlal Nehru got married to Kamla Kaul on 8 February 1916. Kucha Dewan Singh is named after a nineteenth century dewan or vazir. Bilaqi Begum's kucha in Dariba is named after a famous begum of her time. So also are the kuchas of Bibi Gauhar, Kutbi Begum and Fateh-un-Nissa Begum. Katra Zinat Mahal in Lal Kuan is named after Bahadur Shah Zafar's queen, whose mahal is now a rabbit warren and badly deteriorated. Kuchas Brijnath, Chaudury, Hira Lal, Aqil Khan, Mir Hashim, Sakhanand (the royal astrologer) and Maulvi Qasim are also named after dignitaries of their time, just like Katras Lucha Singh, Dinanath and Mohan.

All in all, the kuchas and katras tell tales of times past, many of which have been forgotten, due to the absence of a written history, leaving behind a veritable puzzle for the researcher and historiographer, as the young group on a UNESCO project have slowly come to realise. The problem is that few old-timers are around to play the role of a *dastangoi*, as rightly observed by octogenarian coin-collector Mahabir Shankar Mathur, passing his time in drab Mayur Vihar. It is devoid of colourful history, except for the vanished peacocks that graced the area long after 1803, when the British won the Battle of Delhi against the Marathas, purportedly fighting on behalf of Shah Alam.

Legends & Facts Of 1857

THE Uprising of 1857 was a watershed in India's history as it marked the end of the medieval era and the beginning of a new one, the dawn .of the modern age. That was also the time when legends and superstitions played a big part in guiding the destinies of both the British and the Indian contestants. The late Lala Hanwant Sahay's grandfather had heard in Chandni Chowk that if the new moon came right above the ramparts of the Red Fort its moat would be filled up with the blood of the *Firangis*, but if the blood made its way to the Yamuna and polluted the river the British would win back what they had lost.

Hanwant Sahay was one of those held for conspiracy in the Hardinge Bomb case of 1912 but by then his grandfather was dead. The Maulvi of Faizabad, Ahmadullah Shah, who had made the prophecy of the new moon, had done so not in Delhi but in the main market of Meerut, where *Sab lal hoga* slogans in crimson dye were daubed on walls and stables.

To counter Sir Charles Napier's assertion that if he became Governor General, 'Christianity would become the State religion as Providence had entrusted India to England', the Maulvi had called upon Muslims and Hindus to combine and protect the land of their forefathers. His deep-set eyes and fierce mien had the desired effect when he bluffed the sepoys in Sadar Bazaar, Meerut that the Queen's Rifles had been ordered to disarm them. With loud shouts of *maro firangi ko* the sepoys ran to the cantonments and set the bungalows of the British ablaze. Colonel John Finnis, a veteran of forty years, who tried to stop them, was shot through the head. He was the first of many victims killed in a bloodbath that started on Sunday, 10 May and lasted till the following day when the sepoys left for Delhi.

On the way they saw a *nilkanth* (bluejay) flying towards their destination and the Hindus among them shouted, 'There goes Lord Shiva's sentinel to guide our way'. Soon after a white-bearded fakir was sighted sitting on a mound, reciting the *kalma*, which the Mussalman soldiers took as a propitious sign. However the fakir was disturbed in his recitation by a king cobra, with its hood raised, threatening to strike him. The Pathan sepoys picked up stones to kill it, but their Brahmin and Rajput comrades forbade them, saying it too was a sign of Shivji's blessings to the cause. The alarmed fakir suddenly stood up, with his *chimta* (tongs of bent iron) and the snake, taking fright, slithered away into the thicket.

At least that was the tale heard by Virginia Maguire from Tommy Martin, who himself heard it from a fellow-lieutenant while they were on their way to Jhansi, where the Rani was hesitating between challenging the British or accepting their terms for the annexation of her kingdom.

Much later Martin was rumoured to have set fire to a haystack in which Laxmibai had taken refuge after losing the Battle of Gwalior to Sir Hugh Gough. Martin claimed it was the Rani who had requested him to do so when he pursued her on horseback and was on the point of throwing his spear at her. 'Stop, young man', she had said, 'instead of the spear just throw that flaming torch into the *khalyan* and take the treasure hidden in yonder mound'. Only God knows if it's true but Martin became immensely rich after the battle and settled down in Agra to lead a retired life, recounting the legend of Laxmibai's gift to friends over evening drinks. But the fact remains that the Rani was killed in battle and did not die of suicidal burns.

Another legend is that Bahadur Shah Zafar was determined not to lead the rebel sepoys, who had promised him the wealth of India to fill up his depleted coffers, but a dream made him change his stance. According to his private secretary, Jivan Lal, the King was told in a vision by his grandfather (Shah Alam) that the time had come to undo what had happened at the Battle of Plassey 100 years ago and that he should lead the rebellion. But at eighty-two Bahadur Shah hardly slept at night because of a persistent cough and dreams had long ceased to be part of his sleep. However the royal hakim Ahsanullah Khan told the King not to be misled by detractors and think twice before siding with the sepoys. It was his queen, Zinat Mahal who later convinced him to support the freedom fighters.

Whenever 11 May comes around people in the Walled City talk about these incidents as though they took place the day before. Like the sheet of blood seen in the sky in 1856, stretching from Agra to Delhi, which must have been as unnerving as the recent tremors that struck both cities, such legends liven up the dull days of May despite its suffocating heat and the dust raised by the bulldozing of the Gordon Highlanders' memorial site at Badli-ki-Sarai... the shin bones remarkably intact.

Yaarian Of Yore

WHEN the film *Yaarian* was making waves in Delhi, septuagenarian Shujat Mian's mind went back to *yaarian* (friendships) of old times that have not dried up and vanished with the passing away of the *yaar*s (buddies). For how can one forget Shaan

Elahi, Hamid Sethi and Nawab Shauqat, whose affair sent Chawalwala Nawab to the gallows? A big *yaar* was Farooq Mian, who smoked English Manila cigars, bought from the then exclusively modern Habova Stores in Agra. The person who fetched the full box for him got a princely Rs 5 in the 1950s, plus one cigar to be smoked away from prying eyes, lest it was reported to the elders.

Chotte Mian was a *Nawabzada,* the youngest of three brothers, of whom *Fazlu Mian* (Thinnie) was the eldest and *Fatthu Mian* (tall and flabby) or *Manjle Mian* the middle one. He and Bade Mian didn't smoke but liked having snacks at forenoon and again after tea-time and then while playing patience before dinner, in which Chhote Mian too sometimes joined. Farooq Mian also had a great fondness for hunting, along with his friend, Rajinder Singh (Raja). The two usually went in a discarded Army weapon-carrier for *shikar* to Gurgaon at night and Fazlu Mian often accompanied them. Once they entered a Reserve Forest and when a guard stopped them, Chhote Mian asked him in his grandliloquent style why the gate had not been opened despite clear instructions to the Forest Ranger. 'Don't know Sahib', said the non-plussed guard. 'Go get the keys from him then', replied Mian. The guard went running to carry out the 'order'. But as soon as his back was turned, Raja backed his vehicle and knocked down the gate. The party then drove through the forest in search of game. When not engaged in such quixotic exploits Chhote Mian would find it difficult to pass the time. While Fazlu Mian went looking for the washerwoman behind their *kothi* and Fatthu Mian kept gazing at an open window for a glimpse of the girl who lived on a top floor, Farooq Mian would put on his fancy flowery kurta and, along with chums like Munne Bhai and Chunnu Bhai go to a popular cinema house for fun. All three brothers are dead but what *yaar*s they were and Shujat can never forget them. Raja is still around, but good boy Khalil, who had joined Habib Bank, died young to the regret of many.

Mota (fat) Masood used to come from Firozabad to pursue court cases in Tis Hazari. He was fond of eating and litigation. When there were no more cases to be fought, he filed a suit against his younger brother which kept him occupied till his death. But people have not forgotten him since he never ate alone and always invited whoever was around to join in for a free bite, no matter how costly the stuff. Akbar Mian was a great lover of cards and when not minding his shoe shop in Ballimaran would spend his time playing rummy. He won sometimes in night-long sessions, smoking cigarettes all the time and sharing dinner with friends. Sayeed Bhai, a lawyer, joined him sometimes and when he returned home late at night, his wife, a reputed beauty, would refuse to open the door and he had to spend some hours stretched outside on an easy chair. His father was the one who would alert the Begum Sahib saying, 'Sayeed has gone with Akbar Mian and wherever the latter goes there's bound to be gambling'. Sayeed Bhai's great friend was Sayeeduddin, who was unfortunately killed. And who can forget Abid Bhai, who had lost his mind after an affair with a courtesan and was always enquiring about *Mujras*?

A true chum was Karim Beg (great-grandson of Munshi Abdul Karim, Queen Victoria's Urdu teacher). In a tiff over a girlfriend, daughter of a famous Bishop, he shot another student in the college hostel. Even the ingenuity of the reputed Barrister Nuruddin Ahmed (thrice mayor of Delhi) could not save him and he was sentenced to life imprisonment but was released for good conduct after ten years. He married and settled down but fell from a parapet while cleaning a house window and died. Mirza Arshad Baig (Ladle) was the handsomest bloke of his time and half the college girls were after him, but he had all his affection reserved for his closest friend Marris though his mother misconstrued the friendship. Ashok Bhai, who was known as Devanand, is still around with his imitation puff and so is Qadir Mian. However, Kailash Bhai, who sang soulfully, especially the song, *Jane woh kaise log the jinke pyar ko pyar mila*, with his eyes closed, is no more. Also gone is Wajid Mian, who looked and acted like Ghalib. There is also no trace of Sahir Bhai, who became a veterinary surgeon and began to be called 'Municipality' whenever he came from his dispensary near Arab-ki-Sarai. He was a timid chap, too shy to even give an enema to a horse. Some others are settled in out of the way colonies in Delhi, making the west Nizamuddin oldie moan, *Yaaron ne itni door basai hain bastiyan* (alas friends have settled down so far away). Still these *yaarian* cannot be forgotten and sometimes Shujat Mian gets up in the middle of the night shouting, 'Cyril shoot the damn crocodile'. It's only when the good wife calms him down that Shujat goes back to bed again, muttering, *Kya yaar the aur kya yaarian* (what friends they were and what friendships).

* Some names have been changed.

The Black Shirt

ONE often sees strange characters in streets, bazaars or in courts, hospitals, police stations, in a church, mosque or temple. One remembers a tall thin man with a leering look, wearing a black shirt over narrow pyjamas who stood out as more unusual than any in faded butler shoes with weird rings on his fingers. One saw him at namaz in the local mosque and during Christmas at midnight mass he was seen standing right at the end of the church nave with those who had come in late or were reluctant to sit down in the pews. Wearing a serge coat over his trademark shirt, he received Holy Communion last of all. Incidentally, not everyone gets it unless he is a bona fide Christian (a Catholic in this case) as priests can easily detect an imposter. One kept track of the man and found that he lived alone in the *Qasabpura* (butchers') *mohalla* and was very fond of one particular boy whom he fondled and tried to lure in other ways too while chewing a paan indolently. But the ten-year-old sensed something wrong and avoided him as best as he could.

The man, whom nobody seemed to address by name, disappeared after some years. Who was he – a spy, CID man or just a queer character without any ostensible means of livelihood?

There was another person in white full-sleeved shirt and black trousers, with salt and pepper hair combed back, who also had an air of mystery about him. Someone commented that he was a Freemason who attended the Lodges in Janpath and Qudsia Garden. Addressed as Jagan Uncle by some, he seldom spoke and was never seen with his wife and children. A nosy parker brought word that he had been a Grandmaster in the old Madras Lodge and later settled down in Delhi. Whenever one met Jagan Uncle one felt a chill down the spine, especially after the late Father Monthu whispered one evening that the man must have been taking part in secret rituals at midnight in which the Eucharist was desecrated and sometimes a nail driven through it.

When one asked a Freemason friend about it, he pooh-poohed the priest's assertion as a fanciful allegation. 'There is nothing of the sort done at what actually is a fraternal, philanthropic organisation which borrows some rituals from the Old Testament of the Bible and does no jadoo-tona', thundered the offended friend. However, Father Monthu also claimed that one day he caught a woman who after receiving the sacrament quietly wrapped it in her shawl. He followed her out of the church and asked her if she was a Roman Catholic. The woman nodded. 'Then why did you not consume the Eucharist?' he enquired. The woman said that she wanted to give it to someone seriously ill at home who couldn't come to church.

'But if you had told me about it I would have gone and given her the sacrament myself', said Father Monthu. Since the woman had no answer to that, the priest literally forced her to swallow the Host at the church porch and warned her not to repeat her sacriligeous action. By the way, there are no women Freemasons here.

One wonders if the man with the black shirt also used to do what the woman had done but with greater caution. Was he a Mason or member of some satanic club or a magician who tried to misuse the sacred Host? He posed as a Christian in church, a namazi in the mosque, a Shiva bhakt in the shivalaya and a Panth devotee at the gurdwara. He was spotted at the Parsi temple in Bahadur Shah Zafar Marg too. And, wonder of wonders, he sometime played a role in the Daryaganj Durga Puja and also occasionally acted in the Ramlila. One Id-uz-Zuha he definitely visited a house in Ballimaran to slaughter a sacrifical goat and took the skin after pocketing the fee. 'Who the hell was he?' One asked the old sacristan Francis. 'I only know', replied Francis, 'that his name was Sultan and he sometimes appended Masih and Singh to it'. Sultan was allegedly discharged as an orderly for sexually assaulting the young son and daughter of an officer and jailed for seven years under Section 377 of Tajirat-e-Hind (IPC), after which he worked in a Freemason Lodge until he was turned out as a fraud. Thereafter his earnings came from Satta gambling as he had the knack of predicting the New York Cotton Market's opening and closing (Khulta-Bandh) future quotations, disclosed Bacchu Bhai, an ex-*Kurk-Amin (*bailiff). Both he and Francis are long dead and probably Sultan too but one hasn't met a *har fun maula* man like him again. The bluff and bluster surrounding him refused to end even after it was confirmed years later that he had been an Officer on Special Duty (OSD), extraordinary and plenipotentiary, of the World War days!

Tailor Tales

TAILORMASTER tales can be interesting. When did the first tailors come into prominence? It should have been in the days of Genesis after Adam and Eve were driven out of paradise dressed only in skins. Adam is believed to have lived

930 years and Eve for over 800. So their children may have been better clothed because of the progress of human ingenuity despite the rhyme, 'When Adam delved and Eve span/Who was then the gentleman'! In Christ's days garments were stitched for the privileged few who could afford more than one in a lifetime. But Christ had only one which too was given away in a draw of lots after his crucifixion. That it became a prized possession as 'the Robe' is another story.

Earlier in the Ramayana and Mahabharata days dhotis and shoulderwraps wouldn't have needed tailors. However during the Delhi Sultanate the tailors were mostly Central Asian, though there were some local tailors too. The garments of the ruling class were tailor-made, the poor were not so fortunate. Housewives stitched their clothes and those of neighbours also to add to the family income. So the Darzin made her appearance. She was herself very poor and a latter-day poet portrayed her plight in this verse: *Dukhtar-e-darzin ka seena dekh kar/Ji mein aata hai malmal doon*. The shair was not above the charge of using a double-entrende. On the other hand, his wish to give *malmal* (cloth) to cover up her breast could obviate the hint of a massage.

Now for the Darzis, they too were poor and led lives of penury but were an important part of society all the same. Hardships made some of them eccentrics. There was Toori who had taken to smoking charas and sometimes got his measurements all wrong. But in more lucid moments could stitch some of the best clothes. Then there was Masterji who became mad after his wife eloped with someone younger. Masterji left his tailoring shop and went about with just a razor blade, a needle and thread, altering shirt collars at people's homes. He was pretty good at it and sometimes lapsed into reveries. Pointing to his palm where two lines incredibly merged into a birdlike image he would say, 'This is *chidya*, Sheela's *chidya* and she gives it to anyone she likes'. Sheela was his wife's name and that was Masterji's way of getting back at her.

Joseph Gabriel was a school tailor who stitched khaki uniforms for Anglo-Indian boys. He got very little for his labours but could still be magnanimous. Once an orphan boy was sent away from class by the lady teacher as he was wearing a torn shirt. The boy's tale of woe touched Joseph Darzi's heart. He collected all the *kattarn* (cloth clippings) he had and stitched a new shirt for the boy. Though it took him till midnight to do so he went home a happier man and didn't mind eating a cold, tasteless supper and his wife's grumbling. Unfortunately both died in the plague that struck Delhi and Agra in the first decade of the twentieth century.

Then after Bhuddhi Master and Master Mehboob, there was Balloo the tailor who stitched memsahibs' clothes while visiting the Civil Lines bungalows. Sometimes he was helped by Mrs Whelpdale and Mrs Saldhana, two seamstresses of St Xavier's School tailoring department. He sat in the verandah with a Singer machine and as he worked on it told old tales to enliven his task. Incidentally, Mohd Umar & Sons, CP tailors stitched Jawaharlal Nehru's *sherwani*s and *achkan*s. Once when Lal Bahadur Shastri was asked to proceed to Kathmandu in cold December, Nehruji told him to take two sherwanis from his house since Shastriji didn't have much of a wardrobe.

The tailors of the Metiabruz area of Garden Reach in Calcutta, who have been carrying on their profession from Mughul times, through the Nawabi days and the British period to modern times, have their counterparts in Lucknow, Agra and Delhi. Moghul tailoring, which began in the days of Babar and Humayun, influenced Agra and later Lucknow, from where it spread to the Nawabs of Bengal in the decadent period of the Moghul Empire.

That was when the sherwani craze had already begun to spread in preference to the traditional *angarkha* of the old courtier. Tailors began to learn new fashions and by the time of Bahadur Shah Zafar's downfall the poets of Delhi had begun to parade the streets of Chandni Chowk in their well-cut sherwanis. Of course, they couldn't vie with the *Banka*s, whose long moustaches and romantic gait was the envy of even the tie-collared British.

And then came Nawab Budhan, the dandiest of the nawabs whose sherwani cut was the cynosure of all eyes and led to immediate imitation. It was the tailors who flourished at the expense of the well-dressed and their ways became arrogant to the point of exasperation. But the tailors and their clients were redeemed by the onslaught of western fashions and 'London trained' tailors sprouted everywhere. Those who viewed the change in fashions with dismay set up a chorus of *Charkhata* (clothes cut on all four sides). But this phase too passed and the tailor's goose still rules the fashion world.

Lutyens' Architectural Wonder

THE ambience of New Delhi is such that few cities can compete with it. Lutyens and Baker designed a Capital that hardly lacked in anything, except for a Red Light area. This was because it was thought that shifting the brothels from Chawri Bazaar to

GB Road would also serve the purpose of those from New Delhi who sought the company of dancing girls. In a new publication, Pran Nevile, former diplomat, historiographer and an old Delhiwallah, observes: 'The oldest profession continued to thrive during the Raj. There were well-staffed brothels in Bombay, Calcutta and other main cities and cantonments frequented by British civilians and soldiers.'

Be that as it may we have come a long way from then. Now it is the auditoriums that people go to, to watch music, dance, films and variety programmes or to the Malls. Many of the buildings that host these shows are in South Delhi, which bears the stamp of Lutyens and Baker. The architects had planned on a long-term basis. Though India International Centre, Habitat Centre and Ghalib Academy may not have been their handiwork they are part of the extension of the same thought process.

Had Raisina Hill (Rāyasīnā Pahārī) not been cut down, New Delhi might not have come up at its present location. The earlier plan was to build a new city in what is called North Delhi, around Kingsway Camp, where the Durbar of 1911 was held in the presence of King George V and Queen Mary. It was there that the king announced that a new Capital would be built so that the seat of power could be transferred back to Delhi from Calcutta.

This was done because the plan was to make it an extension of the Mughal capital, which was abandoned after the War of Independence in 1857 when the last Mughal emperor Bahadur Shah Zafar was exiled to Burma and in his place the British started ruling from Calcutta, where they had set up their first fort-factory in the seventeenth century. It later became the headquarters of their East India Company, with smaller fort-factories in Bombay and Madras.

The return to Delhi was perhaps in keeping with the old adage, that though Delhi had been uprooted and destroyed or deserted many times, in course of time, it sprung back since the time of the Kaurvas and Pandavas over 3,000 years ago when the two rival families fought the Mahabharata war and the subsequent despoliation of ancient Delhi. However the descendants of the Pandavas held on to a part of Delhi and eventually the Chauhans and Tomars came into power, with Lal Kot becoming the citadel of Prithviraj Chauhan. That was in Mehrauli, where after Prithviraj the Sultanate period rulers also had their seat of power.

But slowly it began to be shifted towards present day New Delhi, with Firozeshah Tughlak building his Kotla and then the Sayyid and Lodhi dynasties holding sway. Incidentally, what is now South Extension still has the monuments of the Sayyid period and the Lodhi Garden area those of the Lodhis. This was the matrix on which Lutyens and Baker worked to plan their New Delhi as a garden city with 24-hour water supply and no power cuts. Gole Market and Connaught Place were the fashionable shopping centres. Then there were clubs like the Imperial Gymkhana Club, exclusively for British civilians and military officers, Chelmsford Club for Indian officers, eminent professionals and civilians and Talkatora Club (now Central Secretariat Club). The most popular meeting places (unlike the present day India International Centre and Habitat Centre) were India Coffee House in Queensway (Janpath) or the United Coffee House in Connaught Place (CP)

Tongas were the main mode of conveyance as there were no taxis or auto-rickshaws, both in Old and New Delhi. The Gwalior Northern India Transport Company was the only private bus service. Once a woman managed to get into the bus but her husband was left behind. She started shouting for him and a considerate lady conductor stopped the bus and called out, 'Husband, husband, aiye aiye' much to the amusement of the commuters. There was also a trolleybus from the CP Outer Circle to Tis Hazari. The constant watering of the lawns of Lutyens' bungalows and those on the Central Vista to Talkatora gardens, Lady Willingdon (Lodhi) and other gardens kept the underground water level quite high. The Ridge area on the west of Reading Road (now Mandir Marg) was a vast hilly track (incidentally, it was here that Nathuram Godse did target practice before he shot Mahatma Gandhi) where the sahibs went for horse-riding. However the Delhi Imperial Zone (DIZ) area was the best maintained. 'Nestling under neat foliage it was a pure garden city, a city within the city of New Delhi' where the Indian staff of the Imperial Secretariat stayed in well-designed quarters cooled with *khas tatti*s in summer by the bhistis. The places for recreation were the cinemas – Odeon, Plaza, Regal and Rivoli, that showed only English films. The leading restaurants were Davicos, Wenger's and Piccadily with fancy ballrooms. These served only English dishes and liquor. No Indian cuisine was allowed in CP's Inner Circle 'as the smell of Indian curries was supposed to pollute the refreshing atmosphere of the place'. The only exceptions were Laxmi Restaurant and Madras Hotel in the Outer Circle, later joined by Nirulas. With no congestion on the roads, no population explosion and pollution-free air life must have been surely carefree in those days!

It is worth noting that Lord Hardinge, the Viceroy who was overall in charge of the planning of New Delhi, had suggested to Lutyens and Baker that they should build a city which would showcase the old and the new. One can see the Jama Masjid from Connaught Place as a result. The red sandstone used for the prominent buildings like the Viceroy's House (now Rashtrapati Bhavan), North and South Blocks and Central Secretariat was in keeping with the style of the historic buildings of Shahjahanabad of the Mughals.

Raisina Hill was chosen as new constructions over it could be seen from far away even in Old Delhi. The roads were made wide and spacious with fountains and shady trees that added to the ambience. Stone columns were erected as lamp-posts and architectural patterns were copied from the buildings in Jaipur and Agra to make the new city look like an extension of the one built by Shah Jahan.

Lutyens had spent a lot of time in surveying the

surroundings of Delhi so as to incorporate some of the salient features of Mughal and pre-Mughal Delhi. His attempt was to fuse both Muslim and Hindu architecture, along with examples from the edifices of Greece, Rome, England and France to present a unique synthesis that would be a modern day wonder. And so it is, for New Delhi can vie with any city in the world because of its magnificent layout and eye-catching constructions.

If one stands at India Gate one can see the broad, tree-lined avenues that attract both people and film makers. Even foreign tourists are enamoured of the site. For those who have watched the Beating Retreat ceremony and the Republic-Day parade coming down Rajpath the creations of Lutyens and Baker dazzle the senses.

When The Past Beckons

SOME times things seen and relished years ago come back to mind like a pleasant picture that cannot be erased. Here's one such experience worth repeating: There is a railway line just behind Brar Square over which (I recall) passed a passenger train late in the evening. There was complete darkness over the track, with only the engine light to pierce it. One went close to the track and waited for the train to pass by. A lot of bushes were in the way, but once one had braved a few scratches, one was in a position to observe the almost empty compartments and the man who drove the train.

He was a gaunt chap who must have started driving steam engines a long time ago. His arms were covered so one didn't know if they were tattooed with all those fancy illustrations of fairies, snakes, love-hearts and a cross in a thorny creeper. His face was expressionless (did he ever smile?) and his eyes seemed to penetrate the darkness, like the engine light. He looked like a solitary man. Perhaps there was a jack assisting him, shovelling coal into the engine, his muscles standing up to the task, and black soot covering his face and the dirty rag on his head. Those times are past now. The driver doesn't need a jack to keep the engine running and the merry fire burning to build up the steam. The two were forever making tea on it in those days. Not now because of electric traction.

As the driver buzzed by in his engine one saw a man standing in a compartment thinking of when he'll be home. Perhaps his wife and children awaited him, perhaps not, for the wife may be busy preparing a frugal dinner and the children sleepy and hungry. The father who was taking a train ride was a fruit seller. You could make that out from the empty basket he carried. Did he sell bananas or oranges? Apples must have been too costly for him and one couldn't imagine him selling papayas. Could it be that nobody awaited him at home, for he might have been one of the many who form Delhi's floating population and whose families are in the nearby towns?

A group of labourers were sitting in the next compartment, chatting way in the congenial atmosphere after a hard day. They did not look dog-tired though. Long practice had taught them to conserve their strength. In the next compartment sat a group of men who must have been working in some office. They were playing cards, with not a care in the world it seemed. The files and the paper work, the boss's retort were forgotten. The second last compartment had a jean-clad youth, humming a song and, then as the guard's cabin passed by, one was left alone in the darkness.

That train brought back memories of an Anglo-Indian boy called Denzil. He was a jack on the Western Railways, which had one of the best hockey teams in the 1950s, with players like Saxbe. Denzil, fair, stout, handsome, with a big puff mounted on his side-parted hair, had a rich store of stories which he related whenever he came home to his adoptive family in Ludlow Castle Road, as he was an orphan brought up by the nuns.

One rainy evening, as Denzil sat sipping his coffee, he got into the mood to relate some of his experiences. This one occurred on the stretch between Jaipur and Phelera. 'It was a winter night', he said, 'when the driver of the train Sunny Vibert was going at a very fast speed to make up for the time lost because of delayed line clearance at Bandiqui. Suddenly Sunny saw a girl in white walking in the middle of the track – and what was even more surprising was that she was leading a cow right in the direction of the steam engine. The time was ten past midnight.'

Sunny was bewildered and pointing out the unnerving sight to his jack, applied the brakes with full force. But by that time, the engine had run over both the girl and the cow. As the night express came to a screeching halt, Sunny and Denzil jumped down to see what remained of the two trespassers. They expected to see a grisly sight but what they saw was more perplexing. There was no sign of the girl or the cow, though they looked all around and the guard too joined them in the search. 'Weird surely', said Denzil, finishing the coffee in one gulp. 'We later learnt that a village girl and a cow were run over by a train some years ago on that stretch and ever since that spectre sometimes disturbed drivers hurrying on their way to Phelera.' We don't associate such yarns with diesel engines, which do not wail like the old steam ones. Do we?

Incidentally, the wail of the steam engine could be heard for miles around and woke up kids and grown-ups alike. Poonam Devi got up in the nick of time to prevent a robbery in her house in Sarai Rohilla on hearing the whistle of an engine. On 1 January 1866 Old Delhi first heard the wail of a steam locomotive when the first train arrived just at the dawn of New Year's day. But now in the din of so many confusing noises we surely are living in less romantic digitalised times.

Kothi Meena Bazaar - Agra

THE launching of the Prime Minister's Awaas Yojana-Gramin from Kothi Meena Bazaar was another reminder that medieval times can sometimes curiously merge with the present. The *kothi* actually was the residence of the Lieutenant-

Governor of the North-West Province of which Agra was the Capital for some years before Allahabad became the seat of power of the British administration. That was the time when Delhi had been relegated to being just a *parganah* of Punjab Province. The Lieutenant-Governor of the North-West Province controlled the area almost up to the outskirts of Delhi at a time when there was no Haryana and the Lat Sahib's writ ran well beyond Hodal. One may ask why the place was known as Meena Bazaar *kothi*? The reason was that the grounds of this kothi, situated near Shahganj, were temporarily used to hold the weekly Meena Bazaar when Shah Jahan's entourage was on the move to Delhi and elsewhere. The name stuck when the British took over.

Kothi Meena Bazaar was one of many Raj-day bungalows which, along with erstwhile State guest houses like Gwalior House, Bharatpur House, Kota House, Dholpur House and Jaipur House, vied for prominence in the social milieu of the time, along with the Metcalfe Testimonial.

Halingar Hall of the Martin family was the home of T B C Martin (Munna Baba) built by his father (a hero of 1857) and where he lived for many years with his wife Blanche till he moved to the Cantonments and the hall was taken over for government use, as part of the civil courts. Halingar Hall in its heyday was the meeting place for Anglo-Indians of Delhi and Agra. The Delhiwallas came at the weekend by train to take part in cultural activities, dances and tombolas that preceded grand dinners with Gracie Bibi presiding. The Alexanders from Jaipur and some families from Bandiqui, Dholpur and Alwar were also among the participants after the return of Major James Alexander from the Afghan War.

Not far from Halingar Hall was the Fantasia of JF Fanthome, Hony Magistrate and chronicler of the 'Mutiny time' events in Delhi and Agra. His descendant F J Fanthome, who died some years ago in Dehradun, was an Anglo-Indian leader of Delhi whose cousin is an MLA in Uttar Pradesh. After the death of J F Fanthome, justly famous for his book, *Mariam - A story of the Indian Mutiny,* (which was adapted for the film Junoon, starring Shashi Kapoor and his wife Jennifer) Fantasia was taken over by YWCA for some years until it was eventually sold to a business family at a time when a lot of old bungalows were being disposed of by the Church Missionary Society. Among these were the ruins of the Scottish Church and attached cemetery. The site was bought by Dr B M Sarkar whose nursing home now occupies the place.

Fantasia at one time was the celebrated location where British and Anglo-Indians congregated. A number of marriages were also held there with brides being taken away to Delhi nursing nostalgic memories of Fantasia and the life they lived in its vicinity.

Would it surprise some to know that 'a missionary named Sophia Bland was the godmother of every child born of the union of Delhi-Agra families between 1885 and 1900?' According to journalist-historian Thomas Smith, St Paul's Church, built near Fantasia by Governor James Thompson in 1855 was once the site of the old garden of the Dutch factory. He says that in 1618, Van Ravesteyn, who headed the Dutch mission, managed to get the necessary concessions from Emperor Jahangir and established a Dutch factory in 1621. Its first head was Woutier Heuton, who was succeeded on his death in 1623 by Francis Pelsart, who was unfortunately shipwrecked later off the coast of Australia. Thomas Smith goes on to say that in 1854 when the foundations of St Paul's Church were being laid the tombs of Justin Offley, chief of the English Merchants who died in 1627 and John Drake who died on 5 March 1637, were among the six discovered and removed to the church cemetery.

The English and Dutch merchants, it may be recalled, mainly operated between Delhi and Agra and John Drake was shot when he resisted being coloured during Holi while on his way back on horseback. With his sword Drake had managed to keep the riotous villagers at bay until one of them shot an arrow from behind a tree that struck him fatally. The Dutch factors in Delhi were among those who attended his funeral and were permitted to mete out punishment to the accused villagers.

It is worth remembering that not only Shah Jahan but also his daughters, Jahanara and Roshanara, were fond of the camping site for the Meena Bazaar while on the periodical move to Delhi (120 miles as the crow flies) where Shah Jahan was building a new city, Shahjahanabad. When the Red Fort came up the emperor was particular in having a Meena Bazaar built in it on the lines of the one in the Agra Fort. And among the features added by his daughters was the one of the sale of glass bangles, which they so much enjoyed when the Chudiwalis from the rural areas of Shahganj came to sell their colourful assortment of chudis to the princesses. Perhaps the Prime Minister may not have been aware of this when he launched his Awaas Yojana at Kothi Meena Bazaar. But it is not improbable that some of the descendants of the bangle-sellers may be among the beneficiaries of the housing scheme 400 years later.

The Jaipur Mummy And The Pharaohs' Curse

THE curse of the Pharaohs! It takes one back to 1946 and the Albert Hall museum in Ram Nivas Garden, Jaipur, for the first encounter with an Egyptian mummy. Those were the days when exasperated grandmothers warned children that if they did not behave themselves their *mumiai* would be taken out. The word meant something terrible until one grew up and learnt that it was of Persian origin from which the word mummy has been derived. To *take out the mumiai* meant taking out the fatty matter from the body in preparation for embalming. The children of today are spared the infliction of the word but in the ears of an older generation it still has an ominious ring.

The Jaipur mummy is that of a woman or rather a girl, Tutu and has been on display for many years now. It belongs to the latter dynasties when the corpse was laid out with the legs stretched out as opposed to the earlier crouching position. The sleeping posture, when the mummy was laid on the side, came into vogue some 5,000 years ago from the VI Dynasty onwards. The embalmers took seventy days to prepare it, during the course of which except for the heart, the other internal organs like the liver, lungs, stomach and intestines were preserved in a separate parcel.

From the XVII to the XXI Dynasties the bodies of the kings and queens were so well-preserved that they have survived to this day. Among the well known ones are those of Ahmosi I, Tethnosis I and III, who conquered Syria,

Amenophis III, Amenophis IV, the heretic king, Seti I, whose son Rameses II is the most famous. Seti's mummy, supposed to be the best preserved, was displayed in Cairo Museum after being kept away from public view for fourteen years.

The mummy kept in Jaipur gave birth to many superstitious beliefs like the visits of a mysterious Egyptian woman to the flower-beds of the Ram Nivas Garden at the dead of night. Some claimed to have seen the apparition by moonlight. This belief was common in Egypt where the internal organs were associated with the god Osiris, the *bai* (soul) was thought to outlive the *khat* (body). But *ko* (life) still haunted the neighbourhood where the body was kept and became the spirit that ate the offerings made to the mummy by the Ko or hereditary servant who passed on his mantle to his male heir.

The exhumation of mummies is considered by some to be sacrilegious with its attendant curse. The early explorers who found the mummies are all believed to have died violent deaths. The mummy in Jaipur was also considered to have a curse attached to it. Popular belief associated it with a princess who had fallen in love with a shepherd and been ostracised until her rehabilitation after the death of her lover. But she died soon after and was mummified. How the belief came to Jaipur is not known. Perhaps it was picked up from some other tale and gossip did the rest.

According to Yaduendra Sahai, a former director of the museums in the City Palace and Jaigarh Fort, the mummy is actually that of a young priestess of the time of Rameses the Great. It was presented in 1881 to Sawai Madho Singh on behalf of Brugsch Bey, curator of the Cairo Museum by Sir G Birdwood and Dr T H Andley who was also the curator of the Jaipur Museum, which has a special section for Egyptian antiquities. Albert Hall, in which the museum is housed, was designed by Sir Swinton Jacob and completed in 1886 by Maharaja Madho Singh, whose predecessor had started its construction in 1876 to mark the visit of the Prince of Wales. Built in the Indo-Saracenic style, it is a marvellous piece of architecture and has been renovated now.

What was the curse attached to the mummy? 'the destruction of those who sought to display it'. The end of the princely State is cited as an example. But isn't it rather far-fetched? Madho Singh also tried to get a mermaid for the museum from the Dholpur ruler but failed. And that brings one to the question whether such strange creatures exit or are mermaids found only in the imagination of poets and daydreamers? One should think so, for where else but in legends will one find creatures, half-fish and half-woman who sing under the stars and sometimes lure fishermen and sailors to their doom. But a picture taken by an American tourist in the Indian Ocean some time ago seems to point to the existence of mermaids all right. The mermaid was unfortunately dead or it would have surely made a fascinating exhibit.

Irshad Hathiwala, animal supplier to the erstwhile Dholpur State, used to claim that a former raja had a mermaid and a merman over hundred years ago. The female used to sing to the male when the moon was up and there were no attendants near the special tank built for them. Hathiwala is long dead but the story sounds more credible now that someone has been able to photograph the legendary creature. The mermaid not only sang but also wept at their capitivity. Whether the merman also shed quiet tears is not known, but when in a happy mood the two made amorous advances and the female would even rub her mouth against the male's. The raja loved them for they were his prized pets and spent a lot of money on their upkeep. He showed them to special visitors, including the Viceroy and other rajas and maharajas. After a few years the two died one after another in quick succession. The mermaid because of some illness and the merman of a broken heart, leaving the raja, a sadder and perhaps wiser man. Hathiwala continued in the raja's service long after this. His knowledge of animal behaviour had made him a much admired figure and he was in great demand during the shooting season. But came 1947 and the riots that followed ended the career of Irshad Hathiwala. Not only that, he lost his all including his eyesight, and had to flee to Agra for dear life.

In later years one saw him as a pathetic figure wearing a dirty sherwani and an oily cap, holding a stick in one hand and resting the other on the shoulder of a young boy as he made his way to the Nawab's kothi. He was forever asking people to draft petitions to the Crown on his plight. Later he used to carry about an impressive list of personages, including the President and the Prime Minister. But none of his letters brought the expected reply. Days turned into months and the months into years when an envelope with the Ashoka emblem embossed on it arrived at his home in the old quarter. It promised token compensation all right but Irshad Hathiwala had already gone to the happy hunting grounds.

Coming back to the story of the mermaid, the one photographed by the American was amazingly like a woman, except that its upper half resembled that of a fish but with long hair that looked pleated like a pigtail. If one were to cover the face, the 'legs' and the torso could, from a distance, attract any prying male and make him believe that a young beauty was basking on the beach. The mermaid was obviously some kind of fish, akin to a dolphin. The body, if one remembers aright, was deposited with the Fisheries Department but whether it was preserved is not known.

However one still possesses the rare picture, which in a way is a reminder of the long forgotten Hathiwala and his tales of strange animals, birds, reptiles, mermaids and mermen and the two specimens in Dholpur, one of whom sang to the other when the moon was up and it was time to forget the bitter tears of their captivity. Hathiwala tried to settle down in Jaipur but couldn't for lack of patronage.

The 'Sigheh' Of Joe Nash

IT was a dull morning in February 1965 with clouds hovering in the sky over Barakhamba Road and very little light coming from the open window, but a cool breeze was blowing and upsetting the papers on Joe Nash's table. Suddenly Joe heard a scream and ran towards the newsroom, getting out of breath in the process. Only 20-year old Shima Sharma was inside as she was the morning duty sub-editor in the English newspaper. Her clothes were on fire. Joe took off his long coat and threw it around the girl, forcing her to the ground and beating out the flames with his hands. Shima stood up slowly, a pathetic sight with huge gaps in her clothing. Her neck was red and Joe was sure there were burns on other parts of her body too. He was more concerned about her than his own injured hands. 'What happened?' Joe asked. 'I was switching on the heater when there was sparking and the next thing I knew was that my clothes were on fire', she replied.

Joe thought that the best thing was to take the girl home in the office car. Shima's mother was horrified on seeing her coming back in such a state. 'I'll take her to the doctor', said Mrs Sharma, 'he is just around the corner'. Joe thought that was the signal for him to leave.

Joe Nash was an Anglo-Indian Chief Sub-Editor, a bachelor who lived in Rajpur Road. This was the third time he had saved Shima's life. The first time was when she slipped during an office Christmas Day picnic to the Taj Mahal. They had caught the train at New Delhi station and got down at Agra Cantonment. The party of six headed to the monument through Shahjahan Garden (the erstwhile Macdonald Park). There were three girls and three men, including Joe.

The Taj is a glorious sight on a moonlit night, almost like a part of heaven. But on a winter morning it had a rosy hue which was no less exciting. 'How beautiful' remarked Shima. As she said so, a hurrying photographer bumped against her and she lost balance. Joe caught hold of her hand but she went over the narrow marble balustrade near the eastern minaret. With all his might he tried to pull her back but lost his balance too. The other two sub-editors leapt forward and caught him by the waist. Joe found the weight on his hands too much while Shima kept crying 'Save me, save me'. He thought that both of them would fall to their death 50 feet below. But just then the two other girls, Reena and Rachel, held his legs while the young men, Gopal and Robin tugged at Joe with all their might and he in turn managed to pull up Shima to safety 'My God, I nearly died!' exclaimed an exhausted Shima. Joe replayed the scene in his mind as he sat at his desk after returning from Shima's house.

The second time, he remembered was when Shima fell into the river while dancing on the Yamuna pontoon bridge during another outing and Joe once again saved her. Two days after the office fire incident Shima's father called him up with the request that he should make it convenient to visit his place on the coming Sunday evening.

When Joe went there he found Shima and her parents anxiously waiting for him. 'Come, come', said Mr Sharma, 'We want you to go though a symbolic wedding with Shima as you have saved her life thrice. But because of religion, caste and a 12-year age difference the real union of you two is not possible. In any case, we have already chosen a husband for her. But you have the first right. After the ceremony you will have to set Shima free from her obligation. This is known as Sigheh or temporary *nikah* in the Middle East but we in India have our own version which has been practiced on rare occasions, like even marriage to a tree.'

Joe heard what was said and though quite bewildered nodded in agreement. A pandit was called and he asked him to put on a dhoti-kurta, kept ready by the Sharmas. Joe went to the bathroom and put them on rather awkwardly. When he returned he found Shima dressed up as a Hindu bride waiting for him. The pandit said, 'You can take your bride of the evening to another room but mind this does not confer conjugal rights on you'. He then tied a part of Joe's dhoti to Shima's embroidered saree, keeping the knot loose deliberately. Joe bolted the door of the side room, lifted up Shima's ghoonghat and kissed her. 'You are my love', he said, holding her passionately and kissing her again. He then made her sit on his lap and played with her tresses. 'Shall we go now?' asked Shima. 'Wait a minute', he answered biting her lips and cheeks.

As they walked back into the drawing room, Joe noticed that Shima's parents were eyeing them curiously. 'Was it done as I had said', enquired the Pandit. They both nodded. 'Now (he said to Joe) that you have been symbolically wedded swear that you will forego your right to cohabitation with Shima. Also, will you again come to her aid whenever the need arises?' Joe shook his head in agreement. The Pandit threw a few drops of water on him and Shima and untied the knot to signify separation. Joe stayed on for dinner but did not relish it and left soon after. His lady-love did get married to a Brahmin engineer and Joe remained a bachelor till his death in 1998. But some years earlier by a curious circumstance he had to discreetly donate his sperm so that Shima (thanks to a visiting US Specialist) could conceive as her diabetic husband had been rendered sterile. A strange story no doubt and not readily believable too but Joe Nash used to swear that it was true. If Shima is alive she must be a grandmother now!

* Some names have been changed.

The Many Splendoured Monuments Of Mehrauli

THE Archaeological Park in Mehrauli is the site of many a monument and the abode of history. Every lane and stone in it is historical, for here flourished many kings, princes, princesses, vazirs, generals, warriors, saints and mendicants. Prehistoric tales associate Mehrauli with the descendants of the Pandavas. Later it saw the building of Quila Rai Pithora which bears witness to the glory of Prithviraj Chauhan. But after the Rai's defeat in the second battle of Tarain at the hands of Mohammed Ghori, Qutbuddin Aibak made Mehrauli his capital and the Slave kings who followed him continued to rule from there. Then the Khiljis took over and monuments like the Qutub Minar, Alai Darwaza and Alai Minar of Alauddin took shape. The Tughlaq built their own capital nearby and the Sayyids and the Lodhis also left behind their grand creations.

The Mughals too built monuments there as they were great devotees of the saint Qutbuddin Bhakhtiar Kaki after whom the Qutub Minar is named. Near the post office in Mehrauli is a rugged, nondescript building that gives the impression of a fortress, a small one, which marks the site where Banda Singh, the famous Sikh warrior, was executed by emperor Farrukhsiyar. Now more than 250 years after Banda's martyrdom a shrine has been built to his memory.

Semi-divine females or yoginis have been an integral part of Indian folkore. These women were naturally beautiful and had voices which could charm the listener.

A temple dedicated to yoginis is said to have existed in Mehrauli which legend says was built by the eldest of the Pandava brothers, Yudhishtir. It was after them that the part of Delhi not covered by the imperial city of Indraprastha was known as Yoginipura. The temple of yoginis is now referred to as the Yogmaya or Jogmaya mandir. To its north is Anang Tal, a tank said to have been built by Anangpal or Anandapal, son of Raja Jaipal, who was defeated by Mahmud of Ghazni. Anangpal also built a sun temple close to the Yogmaya mandir but of this no trace remains.

When Taimur the Lame camped on the bank of Hauz Khas in 1398, his historian Sharfuddin Yazdi remarked that the place was not only a good retreat, but worthy of respect for its creator, whom he wrongly thought was Firoz Shah Tughlaq. The tank was actually built by Alauddin Khilji, who reigned from 1296 to 1316. Firoz added to the complex. One heard the song, *Jab shaam dhale aana, Jab deep jalen aanaa* sung by Yesudas in that setting at sundown many years ago and the echo is still heard deep in the heart even in the present mundane surroundings of Hauz Khas.

Viewing the tomb of Iltutmish from inside one instinctively looks up at the sky, for it is roofless. It is believed that the Slave emperor, who ruled from 1210 to 1235, had asked his beloved daughter Razia not to get him buried under a roof, though there are some who think that the roof caved in during an earthquake. It was subsequently repaired by Firoz Shah Tughlaq.

The tomb of Jamali-Kamali is a riddle of sorts. Sheikh Fazalullah was a noted poet and saint who lived through the reigns of Sikander Lodhi, Ibrahim Lodhi, Babar and Humayun. He died in 1536, exactly ten years after Mughal rule had been established. His romantic bent of mind found expression in poetry which was highly appreciated and because of this young Fazalu went about with his head high in the air. One night Fazalu paced the green grass up and down as the hours went by and at last saw a form approaching through the trees. Thinking that his beloved had come he bounded forward and caught hold of the figure draped in a robe. But on parting it found to his surprise that it was an old man who looked like a *dervish*. Since that night his life changed and he became a hermit himself.

The tombs of *Dadi-Poti* (grandmother and grand-daughter), on Hauz Khas Road, constitute a legend. Who were these two personages who, despite being nameless, are still remembered by people? Were they members of some royal family who were waylaid by ruffians and eventually lost their lives? The graves seem to date back to Lodhi times, which means they are several hundred years old. During that period graves built on a platform were of people belonging to the nobility.

A palace shaped like a ship, that's Jahaz Mahal in Mehrauli. The mahal is located on a corner of Hauz Shamsi and is believed to date back to the Lodhi era. It was built as a retreat for the emperor in the summer months when the heat and dust of Delhi made life uncomfortable, even for royal families. Or was it a resort for pilgrims? At that time too the capital had many shrines of Muslim saints where people came not only from all over India but also abroad – Turkey, Iran, Iraq and Arabia to pay homage.

The proverb that a saint of a distant country attracts more admirers held good here too and it was only natural for the ruling dynasty to build pavilions and rest houses for the pilgrims and their horses or caravans. It was considered not only a work of piety, but also a social obligation and, as a result, the city developed, with more buildings coming up. Not only this, it also created employment for many, though there was no population explosion at that time.

One is impressed by the rectangular courtyard in the centre, the arched chambers at the sides and an arch which gives the impression that part of the palace was a mosque. There are blue tiles in the pavilion which leads to the gateway and the monument has square towers or *chhattri*s at its corners. It is a romantic building and forms the backdrop of the annual *Phoolwalon-Ki-Sair*. While it is Lal Quila and Qutub Minar one thinks of, when one thinks of Delhi, a place not many know of is the Mehrauli Archeological Park.

In the shadow of the Qutub Minar lies the grave of Alauddin Khilji, forgotten and neglected. There is no dome over it also and no inscription either to proclaim the greatness of the man who, despite the advice of his fat *Kotwal*, styled himself as the 'Second Alexander'. The sultan couldn't have dreamt that 700 years after his death his monument would be so forlorn as that with a mongoose living on it.

Begampur mosque like Khirkee Masjid is among the seven built during the reign of Firoz Shah Tughlaq by his Minister, Khan-i-Jehan Junan Shah, a man of deep religious conviction in a despotic age when faith played a big part in the affairs of state and piety had to be displayed like an emblem on a shirtfront. The mosque has a huge courtyard with cloisters at the sides. The corridors have a row of windows and gates on the south, east and north. The name Begumpur suggests it was built in memory of a Begum. Yet it is not always so. Take the case of the Arabic Sultana. One night the Sultana dreamt that a torrential stream was emanating from between her thighs in which a multitude of men and women were bathing. The next morning she told her husband about it, and the Caliph summoned all his wise men to interpret the dream. Many tried but failed, and then an old man unravelled the meaning thus: the stream was the Caliph's wealth, and the multitude was the zeal of the faithful waiting to participate in it. Hence the Sultana had to build a canal and a mosque to make her dream come true. She did so and became a religious woman after that. That's how the Mehrauli Archaeological Park unravels the past.

History in a Pillar

INSIDE the Noida golf course is a stone pillar set up in 1916 by the British to mark their victory in the Battle of Delhi on 11 September 1803. The place where the battle was fought is now known as Patparganj. According to a news agency report, it has not been popularised as a tourist attraction because if it is declared a heritage site the increase in the number of people visiting it will cause problems in the maintenance of the 18-hole golf course. Interestingly enough it was the Noida Authority that retrieved the Victory Pillar in 1989 when it was hidden by wild bushes and weeds. It was spruced up to make the inscription readable again. The restoration of the pillar to public view must have made General Gerard Lake (who led the British forces) turn in his grave, though the pillar was set up 108 years after his death.

Lake entered Delhi after capturing Agra the previous year in 1802. He was the most successful East India Company general until his failure to capture the near-impregnable fort of Bharatpur which however, fell to Lord Combermere in 1826. After the siege was broken, the first trooper to enter the fort was Antonious Joanidies (later known as Sir Anthoy John), a Greek soldier of fortune who went on to establish the once reputed chain of John's Mills after amassing wealth in diamond trade. Under his descendants one of the mills was set up in Delhi too at the initiative of Sir Edwin John. To come back to the first Viscount, Lord Lake, the hero of three continents died in London, five years after his path-breaking Delhi victory, on 20 February 1808, aged sixty-three. Born in February 1744, he fought in the American Revolution War, French Revolution, Irish Rebellion of 1798 and the Anglo-Maratha War of which the Battle of Delhi was a part. Earlier when he took Meerut, Lake met Begum Sumroo and in an ecstatic moment planted a kiss on the cheek of the legendary chieftainess of Sardhana. The Begum's Muslim troops took offence at this but with great tact she calmed them down, saying it was the 'kiss of a padre to his repentant child'.

Like that there were many battles of Delhi, starting from 1191-92, which included the ones fought between Mohammad Ghori and Prithviraj Chauhan, the one of wits between the Mongols and Alauddin Khilji, Taimur's rout of the forces of Mahmud Tughlaq at Loni, then the three battles fought at Panipat between Babar and Ibrahim Lodhi, Akbar and Hemu (not counting the Karnal skirmish between Mohammad Shah and Nadir Shah, the Persian invader) and the Maratha confederacy and Nadir's successor, Ahmed Shah Abdali. Though referred to as the battles of Panipat, they were really fought for the possession of Delhi and as such linked with the fortunes of this imperial city. In all these battles (save the first one between Prithviraj and Ghori) the invaders were victorious, though Alauddin succeeded in chasing away the Mongols camping below the very walls of Delhi by not losing his nerve.

However the only 'Battle of Delhi' recorded as such in history is the one between Scindia's Marathas and the British. The Marathas pretended to fight on behalf of the Mughal emperor, though Shah Alam himself was wavering between support to the two parties as he knew that he was caught between the devil and the deep sea.

To quote from Percival Spear's *Twilight in Delhi*, The British Governor-General, 'Lord Wellesley's object was to secure the prestige of the Mughal name without any admission of its superior authority; Shah Alam's to maintain the imperial pretensions at the cost of any conceivable practical concessions. Lord Wellesley's agent was the British Commander-in-Chief, Lord Lake, and his agent in Delhi was Sayyid Reza Khan. During July and August Shah Alam's letters wavered between appeals for help (against the Marathas who had made a virtual prisoner of him, keeping him in a golden cage as it were) and complaints of his treatment by the British as the fortunes of war ebbed and flowed.

On 27 July, 1803 Wellesley, in a personal letter, assured Shah Alam that if he accepted the asylum which he had directed Lake to offer, then every respect and degree of attention would be shown to him and his family and 'adequate provision will be made on the part of the British Govternment for the support (ease and comfort) of Your Majesty, your family and household'.

But as Spear also thinks, the Governor General's assurances were those of a forked tongue for, besides promising respect, dignity and personal security, he wanted Lake to 'urge Shah Alam and the heir apparent Akbar (later Akbar Shah II) to reside at Monghyr in Bengal' (now in Bihar). However Sir Charles Napier, the conqueror of Sindh under the apology 'Peccavi' (I have sinned) was of the view that the emperor should be sent to Fatehpur Sikri, Akbar the Great's deserted capital, which was closer to Delhi and hence perhaps more acceptable to the blind emperor.

Shah Alam asked for British support on 29 August and on 1 September under French dictation, had announced that he would take the field against the British, 'whose invariable custom it is, in whatever country they are allowed to reside under fixed stipulations, speedily to seize upon that country'. Despite this assertion he welcomed Lord Lake five days after the general had won the battle.

As for the battle itself, there was not much to it. Despite the heroics of their French commander and his small band of compatriots, it turned out to be more of a skirmish, with the Marathas (more used to guerrilla warfare) failing to carry the day. The freewheeling local soldiers of Delhi, who had raised the cry of '*Deen Dean* (Faith) and come out to give battle to the pork-eating infidels' from the gallis and mohallas of the city with antique swords, spears and matchlock guns, were the first to retreat.

The women of Delhi, the able-bodied men who had stayed at home, the emperor, his son and begums in the Red Fort waited for some miracle to happen but their hopes were belied and the British finally put their seal on Delhi, which was to last till August 1947. British tourists who come to pay homage to their ancestors who died in that battle and on 19 September, when the Firangis retook Delhi years later, in the war of 1857, somehow miss visiting the 'Victory Pillar' in Patparganj. Probably they were not aware of its existence earlier but now that the spotlight is back on it they may well start visiting it on the anniversaries of the battle, with Raj historian, Dr Rosie Llewellyn-Jones who usually leads such parties between September and November almost every year. This may be cause for dismay for the Noida Golf Course Authority as, according to PTI, Tee No 16 is located right on the steps leading to the pillar, the inscription on which reads: 'Near this spot was fought on 11September, 1803 the Battle of Delhi in which the forces of the Mahrattas commanded by M Louis Bourquian were defeated by the British Army under General Gerard Lake.' A ball lofted by a golfer may well fall on the Tee, hitting the head of someone examining the memorial is the main cause of worry for the Noida Authority.

Lake Of blood

A strange story one heard from the shikari Cyril Thomas is worth narrating. During the World War II years his cousin Lieutenant George had come on leave from Dehradun (where he guarded Italian prisoners in the concentration camp) and went hunting and fishing near the Khooni Jheel on the northern Ridge in Delhi. He couldn't find much game, except for some rabbits and ducks, which he thought would come in handy for making Christmas roast. The fish somehow were not biting the bait because of the shallow water. But just then he saw a deer coming into view. This was surprising as antelopes did not frequent the *jheel* area. He aimed his army rifle and fired a shot which definitely hit the deer but still it bounded away, with the hunter in hot pursuit. It was getting close to twilight but George was intent on not letting his quarry get away. He entered a thicket by following the trail of blood left behind by the animal – and there it was at last. As soon as George came closer, with his gun ready for another shot, the dear took the form of a *Firangi* woman and asked him to stop which, he of course did, more out of fear than anything else.

A speaking deer was the last thing poor George had imagined. He stood rooted to the spot, with his hand too paralysed to use the rifle. 'Don't come here for a shoot ever again', said the deer-woman, 'because if you do you won't return alive. I am the guardian of the place ever since my death at the hands of the rebel sepoys of 1857 whom I, an unmarried girl, was trying to escape after my parents were shot. They killed me too but before leaving a bearded Maulvi among them tied an amulet to my arm, saying, "After dying you will live on as a deer for some hours every week and take care of whatever animals roam about the jheel". He left after sprinkling some water on me.' Then the deer-woman cursed George, 'You have wounded me and the pain is intense and I don't know how long it will last but since it is my dual existence I cannot die again. Instead you will suffer for this misdeed well beyond X'mas that you were hoping to celebrate. And another thing: Don't ever marry or you will not live long after it'. She then took on the shape of the wounded deer again and limped away into the jheel, the sound of splashing water confirming to George the passage the wounded deer-woman had taken.

When George returned home he was burning with high fever despite the cold. Cyril was surprised at the state in which he was and asked him how he had become so ill suddenly. It was then that George told his story. Cyril laughed at first, saying he must have got drunk on the shoot. But his cousin's deteriorating condition and the game he had bagged made him think that probably there was some truth in the yarn.

George was bed-ridden till 6 January, the day Christmas ends and most of the time in a delirium, in which he mumbled that the deer-woman was taunting him and warning him to keep away from the jheel and never try to enter wedlock but remain single like her. After his recovery George was a changed man. He did not go to the jheel again and was grateful that he had recovered in time to resume Army duty. Cyril Thomas died in 1992 and George a few years earlier as a retired Major noted for many an affair, but whether it was because of the fear of the deer-woman or his own disinclination to wed, he remained a bachelor all his life. And one more thing: whenever he went hunting or fishing he made sure that he had a companion with him – just in case the deer-woman accosted him again. With this sort of weird reputation no wonder Khooni Jheel is given a wide berth after sunset by people in the know.

Firoz Shah's Legacy

POLICE accosting a Maulvi in a forest bordering the Bodyguard Lines of the President's Estate should cause little wonder. Ghazi Norool Hassan, say reports, was found living in an alcove of the Ridge área along with his son, claiming to be the caretaker of a *mazar*. This shrine is supposed to be very old and in keeping with the legacy of the reign of Firoz Shah Tughlaq. A large part of Delhi was forest area in the fourteenth century and this helped the emperor to indulge in his favourite past-time of hunting. Right from Mehrauli to North Delhi there is evidence of the Sultan's hunting lodges where he sometimes rested at night too. While in North Delhi he built an observatory, besides a hunting lodge.

On the Ridge near Karol Bagh is the ruined gate of Bhuli Bhatiyari-ka-Mahal. Though Sir Sayyid Ahmed Khan thought it was a distortion of the name of a nobleman, Bhu Ali Bhatti, there are not many takers for this assertion.

Historian Ishwari Prasad says that Firoz Shah was a pious man, despite being an orthodox Sunni who illtreated the Shias and non-Muslims. But at the same time he was generous and not fond of shedding blood, like his cousin and mentor Mohammed bin Tughlaq, whom he had succeeded. Firoz was a great devotee of dervishes, many of whom flourished in his empire. One of them probably was the Pir Sahib of the place where the Maulvi was found living secretly for forty years. The forest area of which the shrine is a part, had many other *dargah*s which were demolished when New Delhi was built. Raisina Hill was also covered with a forest where wolves, leopards and hyenas were found. So a Forest Ranger's bungalow was set up there. In later times this bungalow became part of the Sacred Heart Cathedral and now after renovation, is known as Maria Bhawan.

Some old mosques still exist in nearby areas which may date back to Tughlaq times. For that matter the place where now stands Gurdwara Rakabganj was also a jungle once in which during Aurangzeb's time lived a contractor, Lakhi Singh of the Mughal court. When Guru Tegh Bahadur was beheaded on the orders of Aurangzeb, there was a violent storm, taking advantage of which Lakhi Singh and his eight sons (who had come on horses and bullocks) took the body away, while the Guru's head was taken away by a man named Jatha. Lakhi Singh drove all the way from Chandni Chowk to the forest where he lived and putting the body in his house set it on fire to avoid suspicion. Later Gurdwara Rakabganj came up there.

But to come back to Firoz Shah, the number of mosques and dargahs that were set up in his reign rivalled the inns, gardens and hospitals. He is said to have laid 1,200 gardens around Delhi and the nearby areas. In each of them a sufi found refuge. The Sultan lived up to the age of ninety, the longest living ruler of Delhi after Aurangzeb. He was so generous at heart that even while laying siege to a city he would often turn back on hearing the cries of women in distress and suffering from the pangs of hunger, along with their children. Even while on shikar, Firoz Shah would pay obeisance to saints who had set up abode in his empire. Many of them were helped by him to set up *khankah*s or hospices, and when they died the Sultan was always ready to build a mazar for them.

Once while visiting a dervish he was puzzled on seeing a goat and a *tendua* (panther) lying in the courtyard of the jungle abode. Seeing his amazement at the sight the dervish told him that in the royal darbar this may not be possible but in his khankah the goat and the panther could lie side by side, forgetting their enmity.

When the British built what is now President's Estate, they reclaimed a lot of forest land in which wild animals roamed. But still a lot of the area acquired by Lutyens and Baker was left as forest land. The mazar of which Noorol Hassan claims to be caretaker is only one among many hidden away from the public eye. Don't be surprised if in course of time the mazar becomes a regular shrine with an annual *Urs*. But, for this the history of the mazar and of the saint buried there would first have to be determined. Until then Ghazi Noorol Hassan can continue to be caretaker of the legacy bequeathed to him by Fakhruddin Ali Ahmed. The late President himself preferred to be buried outside the New Delhi Jama Masjid, opposite Parliament House, where once the heart-broken poet Hasrat Mohani of *Chupke, chupke aansoon bahana* fame had made his bachelor's quarters.

Ghostbusters & Victims

GHOSTBUSTERS were in the news after the death of Gaurav Tiwari, CEO (Chief Executive Officer) of the Indian Paranormal Society. It is pertinent to remember that the tragedy took place in Sector 19, Dwarka, which is not very far from the cemetery and crematorium developed in Sector 24. His mysterious death has been attributed to suicide by self-strangulation at a time when he was under great stress because of what he claimed was a negative force that was opposing him.

One recalls that many years ago an Afghan staying in the Jama Masjid area after fleeing his country following a blood feud was found dead, sitting in his chair and looking up at the ceiling with a weird expression that reflected intense horror. Khan Sahib was an old man and one who was greatly interested in the supernatural, which often kept him occupied till late at night. His death was a mystery that was never solved. Some thought his hereditary enemies from Kabul were responsible for it but most residents of the area were convinced that it had something to do with ghosts and spirits. The Maulvi Sahib who sold perfume in Matia Mahal market and acted as an exorcist too was convinced that supernatural forces were to blame.

The second incident was that of another old man, popularly addressed as *Maama* (maternal uncle) who was found naked beside the nude picture of a weird deity with an *aarti* lamp still burning in his hand (something unusual for a Muslim). Maama was a bachelor, who used to dress in sherwani-pyjamas and slowly cycled about wearing a *turki topi*. The expression on his face was also one of intense horror, as though he had seen some ghastly sight.

Sheikh Farooq, who never worked since he was the son of a nawab, was famous for calling up spirits of the dead. On a visit to Karachi when he was holding a séance he (sic) conjured up the spirit of the singer Saigal. On the apparition's reluctance to answer his questions, he uttered some abusive words. Soon after whenever Farooq went out, a black dog would follow him. He got perturbed and his favourite medium told him that he had offended the singer and unless he apologised he might have to pay with his life. He did as told and the dog stopped following him.

Back in Delhi Farooq Mian was holding a séance and those present were his close friend, Kunwar Sahib, noted shikari Cyril, Chunu Khan and two boys, Maxie and Marris. The inebriated Kunwar said, 'Call the spirit of the young lady doctor who committed suicide some months ago and I'll meet her under the peepul tree in your kothi compound for a romantic rendezvous'. The spirit did not come but a voice was heard from the garden saying, *Aaja bahar aur dekh kya hota hai* (come out and see what happens). The Kunwar got up as if to answer the call but Farooq Mian admonished him, telling him about his own experience in Karachi. 'Never be rude to spirits', he cautioned.

Amir Rajpal, who used to stay above a famous shop in Connaught Place, went to the Martyrs' Cemetery in Agra where he intended to spend the night in search of the paranormal. Just before midnight he saw a chilling sight, screamed and fainted with fright. Luckily two chowkidars and a caretaker of the cemetery, who lived near the gate, came running and revived him. Rajpal lived many years after that but never forgot the experience about which he wrote in *Sun Magazine*.

Satyajit Ray contributed a story, *Anath Babu's Terror* for an anthology of ghost stories edited by Ruskin Bond, in which he related the tale of a man he met on a train to Raghunathpur. Anath Babu was keen on visiting the house of Haladhar Datta, which was supposed to be haunted. After he and Ray had inspected the haveli, Anath Babu decided to spend a night there all alone. He had been a renowned ghostbuster who collaborated with Prof Norton of England and wrote many articles on the paranormal. In the morning when Ray went to the house with some tea, he found

Anath Babu sitting on an easy chair, his eyes transfixed on the ceiling and a horrible look on his face which was reflected in his fear-stricken eyes. The veteran ghostbuster had met his end the same way as the owner of the mansion, Haladhar Datta many years earlier.

As Eliphas Levi, nineteenth century authority on the paranormal put it: Ghosts do not kill. They can't because they are dead entities but they can instill horror, so much of it that it can cause death due to cardiac arrest. In local parlance this is termed as *dehshat se dil phat jana*. That nearly happened in the case of an orphaned boy's aunt whose mother had died while giving birth to him. The boy used to long for her at night. One night he was more than usually insistent, causing his aunt to come running to see what he was up to. What she saw made her swoon. But on recovering she found a bottle in the boy's hand and milk in it was that of a human mother which, believe it or not, he drank till the age of three. But his aunt died suddenly one evening and the cause could not be ascertained though some said she had seen her dead *bhabi*.

Sheikh Farooq commented that the expression *Bhootni Ke* did have some basis after all. His sudden end in Karachi not long after in a way confirmed the belief that ghostbusters too are not immune to fatal consequences arising from actions which could be influenced by uncanny forces or whims. Gaurav Tiwari's death may also be one such case.

The Red Fort Trials

WHEN November approaches old-timers' memories of the Indian National Army (INA) trials of 1945 are revived. They were held in the Red Fort and continued up to May 1946 at the adjoining Salimgarh. Trials in the Red Fort actually began in the Mughal days since the time of Shah Jahan when the Dewan-e-Am was the venue. Aurangzeb continued them and so did his successors. Muhammad Farrukhsiyar tried his uncle and ex-emperor, Muizuddin Jahandar Shah (son and heir of Bahadur Shah I).

Muhammad Shah Rangila held some frivolous trials, among them was the one held after the shoesellers' riot of March 1729 at Chandni Chowk in which the tooth of his beloved courtesan Nur Bai was broken when someone threw a stone at her palanquin while she was on her way back from the Red Fort. The sentence was that the culprits were to provide shoes for a year to the royal harem. But the courtesan's tooth unfortunately could not be replaced in an age when tooth transplants were a long way to becoming a reality.

Probably the colourful emperor liked the gat-toothed smile of his beloved, with the gap making it even more coy. His son Ahmed Shah and queen Qudsia Begum were tried too and while the former was assassinated, his mother spent her life sans power in the Suhagpura or widows' quarter in the fort. Shah Alam was tried, blinded and deposed temporarily by Ghulam Qadir Rohilla in 1788. And his grandson, Bahadur Shah Zafar was deposed after trial by the British and sent into exile in Rangoon.

Some eighty-seven years after that the British again held trials in the Red Fort. Those who have seen the son et lumiere show at the fort will remember the hubbub when the scene of the Indian National Army men's trial was enacted. Among the defence counsel were Sir Tej Bahadur Sapru, Bhulabhai Desai and Jawaharlal Nehru, a briefless lawyer until then. Sir Naushirwan P Engineer was appointed counsel for the prosecution.

According to Wikipedia sources: Among the ten court martials held, the most celebrated was the one of Shahnawaz Khan, Prem Sehgal and Gurbaksh Singh Dhillon, three officers of the British Indian Army who were taken prisoners-of-war in Malaya, Singapore and Burma during the Second World War. They had, along with a large number of officers and men, joined Netaji Subhas Chandra Bose's Indian National Army and fought for it side by side with the Japanese forces. The three were charged with 'Waging war against the King Emperor' and murder and abetment.

The second of the ten trials was against Abdul Rashid, Fateh Khan and Shinghara Singh. In the light of the public unrest during the first trial, with the Congress and Muslim League joining forces, the charge of treason was dropped but the three defendants were sentenced to deportation for life. The sentence was, however, not carried out under public pressure and Field Marshal Claude Auchinleck, Commander-in-Chief of the Indian Army, was forced to release them. But rumours that some of the INA prisoners had been executed in the Red Fort refused to die down.

Zahooruddin Qureshi, then a young man, disclosed in the 1960s that he and several others used to go and stand as close to the fort as they could to see the comings and goings of the two dozen defence counsel and senior military officers. The flags of the Congress (Trianga with Charkha) and the one of the Muslim League, green with the crescent moon and star on it, were seen fluttering on the roadside trees and slogans of *Larke lenge Hindustan* and *Ek Nare Taqbi* were heard even as the police charged at the demonstrators. But after the verdict was delivered the tension simmered down.

During the trials Mir Mushtaq Ahmed, later Chief Executive Councillor of Delhi, used to carry a chair and paste anti-government posters on the walls not only in Old Delhi but also as far as Connaught Place. He was arrested for this. Mir Sahib, who died a few years ago, would talk about those days with great pride, saying that he and some others would go behind the fort and shout slogans against the British. There was no Ring Road then and gypsies who used to camp there in the open space were also persuaded with a few rupees to shout *Qaumi nara*s. Another protestor was Hanwant Sahay, who was sentenced to seven years imprisonment in the Hardinge Bomb Case of 1912 but continued to take part in the Freedom movement after his release. The trials were followed by mutiny in the Royal Indian Navy that spread from Bombay to Karachi and from Vizag to Calcutta. Then an Army mutiny took place in Feb 1946 in Jabalpur, besides revolts in Madras and Pune. In all forty-five men were tried for treason, though a large number were discharged.

Even after Independence there were trials in Salimgarh of those held on the charge of spying for Pakistan or China. Over thirty years ago the superintendent of the rotary press of a CP newspaper, Philip Ambrose, suddenly disappeared while on his way home from night duty. It was later learnt that he had been accosted by Criminal Investigation Department (CID) men and taken to the fort where he was detained for about a month and questioned about the Pakistani

High Commission men with whom he used to go far shikar. His torture included not being allowed to sleep, with a bright light being shone on his face all night. Philip was finally released as no charges could be proved against him. He resumed newspaper work and often spoke about his ordeal in the fort. Likewise Afzal Peshawari, a hotelier, was held and interrogated in the fort after explosions in the Jama Masjid area post-Independence. Now, of course, Salimgarh has become a Freedom Movement museum and the Army barracks cleared of troops staying in them. So naturally the Red Fort trials have ceased. But son et lumiere revives them alright every evening, especially so from November to May, making some believe that a torture cell still exists there.

Hell On Dung-Hill

A teacher who takes Catechism class on Sundays took her students to the landfill sites in Ghazipur and Burhari to give them an idea of how the hell fires burn as per common belief. Dante Aligheri had in his *Inferno* described the biblical Gehenna where Lucifer and his band of fallen angels had been thrown after they had revolted against God. John Milton in his *Paradise Lost* had also depicted the scene of eternal torture where the souls of the damned undergo punishment. Mrs Barboza showed the class boys and girls the dumps where refuse burns night and day and those who toil at the landfill sites who are almost like hell's angels. In the olden days when the population of Delhi was only two lakhs, dumping refuse was not a problem as it was not much considering the fact that there were no plastic bags and other containers of packed goods. Wholesalers brought them in gunnybags and the retailers sold the stuff to customers who came with *thaila*s, cotton bags or *gamcha*s and other cloth pieces to carry their purchase back home.

Now with so much waste generated because of paperwraps for both condiments and eats in a generation addicted to fast food and the amount of vegetables and meat consumed and wasted, along with dried up bouquets, loose flowers and garlands offered at the mushrooming temples or shrines and a lot of other rubbish, it becomes difficult to dispose it off in a very congested environment. No wonder the civic authorities are running short of landfill sites. The vans that come every morning to the colonies and mohallas with a recorded voice asking residents not to litter public places (to what effect?) give an idea of the tricky problem of waste removal. These vans dump the trash at the municipal *dalao*s from where huge trolley-trucks carry it away amid an unbearable smell. Imagine how it must be at the landfill sites?

And yet there are people who earn a livelihood by burning the refuse there, unmindful of the nauseating smoke which is emitted twenty four hours a day. During the Mughal days and also in the time of the Delhi Sultanate, Delhi's outer spaces were not congested and dumping refuse was no problem. First at Mehrauli and then in what is now Nizamuddin and Old Delhi the inhabitants just waited for the *methar* to come in the morning and take away the trash in a huge basket, along with the rubbish from the *sandas* or house lavatory. (In the Red Fort and Agra Fort Mughal lavatories were built on tunnels in which sweepers toiled daylong). He dumped the basket at an open space, away from the mohallas from where it was taken away in bullock carts, horse and donkey carts to the outskirts where the whole lot was downloaded and in course of time became manure. In the villages without toilets, it was defecation in the fields which generated manure. At a time when the people of western countries (where there were no methars or *metharains*) were throwing their night soil on to the streets unmindful of passers-by, or in the medieval Elizabethan house tanks dumped with perfume, sanitation facilities in Delhi and elsewhere were more systematic and one did not find so much night soil on the streets as emphasised by Bindeshwar Pathak of Sulabh who has made a historical study of the subject. The methars worked under the *Chungi-ka-jamadar* and 'Bum Police' of Shahjahanabad. Despite the kind of work they did, Sheikh Methars were not ostracised. After a bath they could even join in the namaz at the mosque, since most of them were Muslims. The others were cruelly branded as *Bhangi*s (those addicted to bhang as a solace for the drudgery).

Interestingly, a correspondent wrote this in the 1960s: 'Nizamuddin has many attractive features but the huge refuse dump on its outskirts (not seen now) lessens the appeal of the place for both the tourist and the Delhiwallah. The dump, which contains all the refuse of the Capital, has piled up into a hill which could pass off as Delhi's Gehenna. Vultures and kites hover over it, attracted by the carcasses which lie scattered all over. Like a medieval picture of hell.'

Sohna has been working on the dung-hill for years. He is a lonely man without a family, though he remembers that there was a time when he had one. But his wife died and the children drifted away and this was the job he eventually got. He smokes a bidi while busy and a *chillum* when relaxing, and through the tobacco haze he views the dung-hill with a kindlier eye. 'This hill provides us with our dal-roti. We are bound to it and have developed our own equation with the place', he says with a philosophical look. His companion Radhey once worked as a sweeper in the bungalow of an Englishman. He remembers his name, Bird Sahib. That was in the pre-1947 days when every compound had its own sweeper, living in a ramshackle hut at the corner. His daughter Phoolie died of cholera after eating an unripe water-melon one evening and soon after his blind mother also passed away. His wife eloped with her cousin and then came Partition which saw the Englishman depart. After that life had not been the same for him. The new owner of the bungalow, a brown sahib, engaged another sweeper and Radhey was left to himself and his *charas*. Later, he came to the dump and now works on it by fits and starts. There are several others like him, though not all of them are relics of a broken home. The kites and vultures that swoop down on the 'hill' seem to have become familiar with them, for together they constitute the morbid scene that is the dump. It is a place which gives a creepy feeling to even those passing by in a train. But how many of them know that like the Ancient Mariner, the outcasts who burn the refuse also have a tale to tell. Is it the same story at Ghazipur and Burhari?

*Names have been changed.

History Repeating Itself?

THE 30,000 saplings planted in Delhi by school children under a government scheme to replace the fast disappearing tree cover under the onslaught of modernisation with its concrete jungles is a reminder of history repeating itself. Some four centuries earlier Princes Jahanara, Shahjahan's elder daughter, planted as many saplings in the area that is still known as Tis Hazari. Now associated mainly with the courts complex, the place was a wide piece of land.

Camels, horses and even elephants could be seen at Tis Hazari in those days, besides bullock carts and various other animal-drawn carriages. Many traders also camped here, among whom were a sizeable number of Kashmiris. There were several shady trees below which the merchandise was kept while the animals and men rested. This gave the place the appearance of a goodsyard. Dogs, predatory birds and animals and also thieves and robbers were attracted to this camping ground for various reasons. The *Gujjar*s were specially feared because of the night raids made by them.

The armed men who provided protection to the caravans were not part of the police but retainers who were not particularly vigilant on the outskirts of Delhi. Petty thieves were let off lightly, but the Gujjars and others were dealt with severely when caught. Putting a robber to death was considered a legitimate right in those days. This served as a deterrent, but still robberies were pretty common, more so at the time when Qudsia

Begum, Muhammad Shah's wife extended the Mughal garden right up to the Yamuna bank a hundred years later.

How did Tis Hazari get its name? There are a number of stories, the most famous one being that of Baghel Singh, the Sikh general, who camped here in 1783 with 30,000 soldiers during the reign of Shah Alam II. Shah Alam was able to ward off the threat to his capital through the intervention of Begum Sumroo, the chieftainess of Sardhana, who pleaded on behalf of the emperor with all the oratorial skill and powers of persuasion at her command. Her effort earned her the gratitude of Shah Alam who gave her the honorific of 'Beloved Daughter'.

The invading force was pacified and departed after exacting several concessions and a big sum of money. Begum Sumroo went accompanied by her aide-de-camp Inayatullah and spiritual advisor Bishop Julius Caesar, along with bodyguards. Her critics however imputed her success to witchcraft and the 'magical shawl' she wore during battles and diplomatic assignments.

Another story would have us believe that 30,000 soldiers were always kept ready for action here during the times of Shah Jahan and Aurangzeb, but there is hardly any historical evidence to support this view. A more plausible story is that a begum who held a *mansab* of 30,000 had a garden here. Incidentally, Nur Jahan also held a *mansab* of 30,000, besides Jahanara. During the coronation durbar of 1911, the Maharaja of Udaipur (Maharana of Mewar) camped here and, it is said, entered the Walled City only after conquering a miniature Delhi set up at Tis Hazari to fulfil the vow taken by Maharana Pratap. According to historian Maheshwar Dayal, in the British days there was a railway passing by Tis Hazari.

However, one must appreciate the spirit in which the *havan* was held by the Indraprastha Nagrik Parishad. Men collected there on a hot May day, drew attention to the need for erecting memorials to the heroes of the freedom struggle who fought and died in 1857 and after. Among them the foremost name was that of Ramchandra Panduranga better known as Tatya Tope, the great general who drew envious appreciation from even the British. But Tatya Tope was never associated with Delhi or Tis Hazari. Here the spotlight was on Bahadur Shah Zafar, Zinat Mahal, Mohammad Bakht Khan, Hakim Ahsanullah Khan and others of lesser note and fame.

Unfortunately however, the only caravans passing by now are the convoys of trucks carrying goods to distant places inland and adding to the pollution and traffic congestion in the metropolis. The move to allow their entry only at night seems to be a step in the right direction.

Legal Eagles' Odyssey

PROFESSOR Dennis Pereira, M.A., LL.B., lived in the Civil Lines with his young wife, Sylvia. He was a rich man with properties in Goa and Bombay, which meant that he took life easy, though he sometimes dabbled in legal cases and off and on took English

Literature classes as a part-time lecturer in Delhi College, to which he went in his Ford car. While at home in No 8 bungalow he liked to entertain friends in the evening, many of whom came partly because of his entertaining company and partly because of the beautiful Mrs Pereira who didn't mind a bit of flirting. Among the regulars was the Thakur of Jat-ka-Nagla, near the Tundla-Agra Road, but the Thakur preferred to stay in Delhi in a house rented to him by a Nawab friend from where he came in a phaeton, sometimes with his wife Nalini, otherwise alone. They were a young couple with plenty of leisure, except for a nagging property dispute with the Thakur's sister Rajni.

Professor Pereira took a deep interest in the case which was being heard in the Dewani Kacheri at Agra by an Anglo-Indian Munsif magistrate, William Paterson. Before the final hearing he spent practically the whole night with the Thakur (himself a legal eagle) in helping to prepare the defence statement as the regular vakil had fallen ill. The next day they were at the court where the case was listed in the afternoon. Paterson was known as the *Ghantewala Munsif* because proceedings in his court began and ended with the ringing of a bell. So after the bell had been rung the magistrate said,

'Has the defence anything more to say before the court delivers its judgement?' 'Yes Your Honour', replied Professor Pereira (acting for the absent vakil), 'Thakur Rajendra Singh desires to make a statement'.

'Statements are as a rule not welcomed but considering the special circumstances of the case in which two reputed families are involved, the ends of justice would be met if the statement is made', said the magistrate. The Thakur bowed and began to read the note he and Pereira had drafted: 'Your Honour, the House of Jat is an ancient one. The first Thakur, Kunwarpal Singh traced his ancestry to the great Chhanghaji, who had killed a tiger with his bare hands. His son Jitendrapal fought at the Battle of Sikri. His sons and grandsons achieved fame and some were made Mansabdars by the Mughals. We fought the Punjab rebels during the reign of Bahadur Shah I. In Farrukhsiyar's reign we thwarted the Sayyids of Bara and harassed Nadir Shah on his way back from Delhi. We fought against Hafiz Rehmat Khan at the Battle of Mirankatra (23 April, 1774) and helped in the capture of his grandson, Ghulam Qadir Rohilla after he had blinded Shah Alam. During the "Mutiny" we fought shoulder-to-shoulder with the troops of Bahadur Shah Zafar. My father left the British forces in World War II and joined the INA and as a result we lost most of our jagir and what was left to us was consolidated by my foster father, Thakur Surendrapal Singh. I am his heir but now my sister Rajni Singh and her husband want to gain possession of all the property on the plea that I am an adopted son and she the sole heiress.'

'Anything more?' asked the court. 'The defence rests', said Pereira. The magistrate thought for some time and then said: 'Though a lot of what you said is irrelevant to the case yet the court salutes your eloquence. As far as the properties are concerned, Rajni Singh has a point (Rajni smiled) but taking into consideration the circumstances of the case we cannot deprive you either. Therefore the court rules that whatever is in possession of Rajni Singh is hers. You can retain the ancestral house and land attached to it if you give her the plot on which the farm is situated.'

Pereira and the Thakur held a whispered conversation before giving acceptance. The bell rang and the court rose. Professor Pereira and the Thakur returned to Delhi late in the evening but by that time Mrs Pereira's admirers had dispersed. The Professor's driver, Ram Singh had brought the car to the station and they drove to the Civil

Lines where they had a quick drink after which the Thakur went home in his phaeton to find that the Thakurani had delivered a bonny boy in his absence, heir to the estate he had managed to save after a legal odyssey. But not long after, Professor Pereira died suddenly. Some said he had been poisoned. His wife returned to Goa where she remarried, much to the annoyance of the Thakur who thought his old friend had been stabbed in the back. Pereira's pocket-watch (according to father's notes) is in Australia with one of his descendants while a great-grandson of Ghantewala Munsif, Fergius Paterson is a surgeon in a London hospital. As for the Thakur, his only grandson died of tuberculosis in Wazirpura, adjacent to the Dewani Kacheri (Civil Courts), while Jat-ka-Nagla came into international limelight in the 1960s when a wolf-boy, Parusram was rescued from a nearby jungle, like Atlanta of the Golden Apples and Romulus and Remus, legendary founders of the city of Rome.

Purani Haveli's Secret

IN the 1950s a Delhi college girl, who was injured seriously in a train accident near Mathura, was recovering from her trauma in Paharganj. She was greatly depressed and her cousin Sayeed Uddin made it a point to visit her regularly and cheer her up. One day when Afshan opened her eyes and saw Sayeed sitting near her bed, she asked him to tell a story to relieve her boredom. Sayeed, who was interested in the occult, scratched his head, trying to remember an article by a spiritualist he had read in an old issue of *Globe Magazine* edited by Thomas and Habib. Well here's the tale he related: 'A degenerate nawab lived in Purani Haveli in Kucha Tihar, south-west Delhi. Munne Nawab had inherited a good fortune from his uncle and with no close relatives, didn't bother much about how he lived. He did have a lot of companions who enjoyed nawabi hospitality. One day at a different venue one of them was suddenly taken ill at his sub-urban home near Beriwala Bagh. A doctor was called and after the young man, Ameer was better, the nawab sought leave and enquired if he could take an old pack of cards lying on the table that had attracted his fancy. Ameer was only too glad to oblige because his benefactor had hardly ever demanded anything from him. The nawab brought the cards and placed them on his bed. One night he gazed at each one for some time until he came to the Ace of Spades. There was something strange about this card and no sooner had he passed his hand over it, a beautiful woman stood in front of him with a queer smile and said "Whoever possesses this card possesses me."

'The nawab was taken aback. However he managed to recover his composure and ask the young woman to sit down. "How did you emerge from this pack?" he asked. "That is a long story", said the stately personage. "I am Princess Zamani, daughter of King Idris. While still a girl I was married by proxy to King Zuber, but ere I could reach his palace a wizard chief forced my palanquin bearers into his fortress where he tried to seduce me. But I resisted. Meanwhile Zuber, my husband, attacked the fortress. The day it fell, Zahur, the wizard, caught hold of my hand, threw me on a bed and ravished me. I pulled out his dagger and stabbed him in the heart with and then myself."

'"Oh, it was a gruesome sight. His blood and mine was spilt over a pack of cards. But before he died the evil man breathed a charm on one of the cards, entrapping me in it." The woman ended her story and lay down on the bed as though exhausted. Munne Nawab stared at her face,. She was the most beautiful female he had ever seen.

'"Zamani", he said, "I have fallen in love with you and would make you my bride". "That cannot be", she said, "but so long as you have this pack of cards I will keep you company in the wee hours when none else is around and the moon is not more than seven hours old", she replied. Just then the clock struck and Zamani was gone in a flash, leaving the quivering Ace of Spades, the symbol of death, on the bed. The nawab could scarcely believe his eyes. He wondered why Ameer did not know the secret because the pack of cards had been lying at his house.

'A few days later he held a party at which Ameer was also present. They drank late into the night and when the party broke up he asked Ameer to stay back. When they were alone he broached the subject. "Where did you get this pack of cards from?" he asked. A nervous Ameer stammered out: "Why, I picked it up from the Red Fort museum when I went there along with my cousin. I thought nobody would bother about such an old pack."

The nawab heard what Ameer had to say. Now he was certain that he alone knew the secret of the Ace of Spades. At the next new moon he waited impatiently after a good drink, the taste of which lingered till the clock struck the longed for hour. He passed his hand over the enchanted card and, lo, Zamani stood in front of him. Her dress was sky blue, and the diamond in her nose-ring shone like the evening star. "Where, have you been all these days?" he couldn't help asking. "In deep slumber – what you call death. But now that you have revived me, tell me what is that on the table?" "Oh, that is a packet of condoms", he replied in a matter of fact way. "And what are condoms?" the brown eyes of the princess gleamed. "Well, it prevents conception." "That's wonderful", said Zamani. "I wish we had something like that in our time. My father had many children from his concubines, though the queen, my mother, had just two – my brother and me. I must say that of all the things you people have devised over the centuries this is the greatest."

The nocturnal experience, which he faithfully recorded in his diary, was such that slowly the nawab lost interest in daily life. Zamani held all the pleasures and thrills. But when she was not around after the seventh-day moon, the nawab would just sit and brood. His servants got alarmed and a doctor was discreetly brought who examined him and diagnosed that besides symptoms of insanity he was also suffering from tuberculosis, and in urgent need of medication. And that probably prolonged his life. So the "affair", real or imagined, with Zamani continued and the last time she came she told him that it was to take him away.

Munne Nawab was found dead of cardiac arrest with the diary on his chest the next morning.'

But by the time the tale ended Afshan had fallen asleep. The haveli was looted by a mob pursuing Muslim Meo herdsmen in 1947 and all its books, presumably including the diary were burnt. The haveli, however survives after restoration as a tenanted building and perhaps still harbours its old secret. But the pack of cards was never found – and Sayeed Uddin Vakil (whom one used to meet at Faiyaz Manzil before his vendetta murder) regretted all his life not marrying the coy Afshan, who died a spinster.

Shaheed-e-Azam Bhagat Singh

WHENEVER Sardar Bhagat Singh's birth anniversary approaches (he was born on 7 September 1907) one's thoughts turn to the life of the man who has come to be known as *Shaheed-e-Azam* for laying down his life for his country.

One remembers anecdotes about the way Bhagat Singh outwitted the colonial police and spies who were trying their best to capture him alive. The revolutionary had sneaked into Agra and rented a room from an old disinherited Rani near Ghatia Bazaar. Throughout the day he stayed indoors but at night he and his companions (all sworn to rid the country of the British) came out and walked the streets covered up in blankets. They would generally go to the milk shop of Salga Ghosi and order *khular*s of milk, with a layer of *Rabri* on it, which they drank slowly as an after-dinner treat.

Dinner for them, however, was sparse, mostly vegetarian fare (dal-sabzi). Sometimes mutton from Barati butcher's shop was bought early in the morning by one of the non-veg comrades whose photo did not occupy the 'Rogues Gallery' in the *thana*. These men also bought vegetables from Taron-ka-Bazaar (so named as there were a lot of electric wires overhead) and dal-chawal from the shops of Moti and his uncle Antee while ghee was bought from Panna Lal, who sold the best desi variety. The stuff was cooked by them too but sometimes the landlady and her daughter-in-law helped to make it really delicious.

After living in Agra for several days the

revolutionary party moved to Delhi, according to old *Agrawallas* who are all dead now. In Delhi too the revolutionaries adopted the same life-style. They stayed atop a halwai's shop in Katra Neel, some with beards, though Bhagat Singh had shaved off his *darhi* and also cut his hair against the tenets of his religion. He, however, justified it by saying that the motherland demanded sacrifices and parting with *kesh* (hair) was among them.

It was by chance that Sarin Bhai, a revolutionary from Chillint Ghatia, who was staying incognito in Chandni Chowk, met Bhagat Singh in Parathewala Gali where he had come to drink milk. It was a winter night and wrapped in a blanket Sarin Bhai peered at the face of the man who was standing near him at the shop (now taken over by a zari sari trader) and suddenly it dawned on him that he was Bhagat Singh, the most wanted revolutionary. Sarin picked up a conversation with him and they walked out of Parathewala Gali towards the Town Hall and then Queen's Park, opposite Old Delhi Station. Here they discussed plans to make the British pay for their atrocities on Indians. Sarin Bhai was later arrested and jailed for some years but he was released fairly early as there were no heinous charges against him.

Sarin Bhai used to talk about those days after Independence. He related the story of how he, Bhagat Singh and two others went to meet Lala Hanwant Sahay who used to stay opposite Fort View Hotel in Chandni Chowk. Lalaji was one of the accused in the Hardinge Bomb case in which a bomb was thrown at the Viceroy while he was going in a royal procession to the Red Fort in 1912. Hardinge was wounded and his elephant mahout killed. Lalaji, his teacher Master Amir Chand, Master Awadh Behari, Bhai Balmukund and Basant Sanyal were arrested as conspirators. Lalaji was sentenced to life imprisonment (which was later reduced to seven years rigorous imprisonment) and the others to death. Bhagat Singh was just five years old then and on meeting Lalaji he was greatly enthused. 'We will eventually drive the British out', he told him and left after having some gajar-ka-halwa.

While Lala Hanwant Sahay was a religious-minded man, Bhagat Singh had declared himself an atheist. In a pamphlet, *Why I am an Atheist*, at a time when the noose was being prepared for his hanging, undaunted by the lurking death, when many fall on their knees to seek pardon from God, he states: 'God has become a useful myth and was useful to the society of the primitive age.'

Moreover, 'the idea of God is helpful to man in distress'. God and religion enabled the helpless individual to face life with courage. 'God was brought into imaginary existence to encourage man to face boldly all the trying circumstances, to meet all dangers manfully and to check and restrain his outbursts in prosperity and affluence.' 'Belief softens the hardships, even can make them pleasant. In God man can find very strong consolation and support. Thus to the distressed, the betrayed and the helpless, God serves as a father, mother, sister and brother, friend and helper.'

But, says Bhagat Singh, 'when science has grown and when the oppressed begin to struggle for their self-emancipation, when man tries to stand on his own legs and become a realist (Bhagat Singh uses this word in place of rationalist and materialist), the need for God, this artificial crutch, this imaginary saviour comes to an end. In his struggle for self-emancipation, it becomes necessary to fight against the narrow conception of religion as also against the belief in God.' 'Any man who stands for progress', says Bhagat Singh, 'has to criticise, disbelieve and challenge every item of the old faith. Item by item he has to reason out every nook and corner of the prevailing faith… A man who claims to be a realist has to challenge the whole of the ancient faith ...the first thing for him is to shatter the whole down and clear a space for the erection of a new philosophy.'

Bhagat Singh was born on 27 September 1907 (just four years after the writer George Orwell of Motihari fame) at Banga in Lyallpur district (now in Pakistan) to Kishan Singh and Vidyavati. From early childhood Bhagat Singh was imbued with the family's spirit of patriotism. At the time of his birth, his father Kishan Singh was in jail. His uncle, Sardar Ajit Singh, was a great freedom fighter and established the Indian Patriots' Association. He was well supported by his friend Syed Haidar Raza, in organising the peasants against the Chenab Canal Colony Bill. Ajit Singh had twenty-two cases against him and was forced to flee to Iran. Bhagat Singh was considered to be one of the most influential revolutionaries of India's Nationalist Movement. He became involved with numerous revolutionary organisations.

Kishan Singh enrolled Bhagat Singh in Dayanand Anglo-Vedic High School. At a very young age, Bhagat Singh started following the noncooperation movement called by Mahatma Gandhi. Bhagat Singh had openly defied the British and had followed Gandhi's wishes by burning the government-sponsored books. Following the violent incidents of 'Chauri Chaura', Gandhi called for the withdrawal of the noncooperation movement. Unhappy with the decision, Bhagat Singh, isolated himself from Gandhi's non-violent action and joined the Young Revolutionary Movement.

He was studing to take the B A examination when his parents planned to get him married. He vehemently rejected the suggestion and said, 'If this marriage is to take place in Slave India, my bride shall be only death.' He later joined the Hindustan Republican Association, a radical group, later known as the Hindustan Socialist Republican Association. He returned to his home in Lahore after assurances from his parents that he would not be compelled to get married. He established contact with the members of the Kirti Kishan Party and started contributing regularly to its magazine, the *Kirti*. In March 1926, the Naujawan Bharat Sabha was formed with Bhagat Singh as its secretary.

On 30 October 1928, an all-party procession, led by Lala Lajpat Rai, marched towards the Lahore railway station to protest against the arrival of the Simon Commission. Stopping the procession, police made a lathi-charge at the activists. The confrontation left Lala Lajpat Rai with severe injuries and also led to his death. To avenge the death of Lala Lajpat Rai, Bhagat Singh and his associates plotted the assassination of Scott, the Superintendent of Police, believed to have ordered the lathi-charge. The revolutionaries, mistaking J P Saunders, an Assistant Superintendent of Police, as Scott, killed him instead. Bhagat Singh quickly left Lahore to escape arrest. To avoid recognition, he shaved off his beard and cut his hair, a violation of the religious tenets of Sikhism.

In response to the Defence of India Act, the Hindustan Socialist Republican Association planned to explode a bomb inside the Assembly premises, where the ordinance was going to be passed. On 8 April 1929 Bhagat Singh and Batukeshwar Dutt threw a bomb into the corridors of the Assembly and shouted *Inquilab Zindabad.* Following the blasts both Bhagat Singh and Batukeshwar Dutt courted arrest.

The British authorities, while interrogating them, came to know about their involvement in the murder of Saunders. Bhagat Singh, Rajguru and Sukhdev were charged with the murder. Bhagat Singh admitted to the murder and made statements against the British rule during the trial. While in jail, Bhagat Singh found that the authorities were following a dual policy in treating the prisoners, who like him were badly tortured. The criminals of foreign origin were treated better than Indian political prisoners. As a protest, he, along with some fellow prisoners, decided to 'go on a hunger strike'. The strike continued for over a month and finally the British had to accept their conditions. Bhagat Singh, along with other revolutionaries, was found responsible for the Assembly bombing and murder of Saunders. On 23 March 1931, he was hanged in Lahore with his fellow-comrades Rajguru and Sukhdev and was cremated at Hussainiwala, on the banks of Sutlej River.

When we celebrate his birth anniversary we are reminded that such a man who gave his life for his country's freedom still inspires patriotism eighty-five years after his martyrdom. He was just twenty-three years old at the time he made the supreme sacrifice. Like the romantic poet John Keats, who also died at about the same age, he too could have achieved much more had he lived longer and seen the dawn of Independence in August 1947. We can only take our hats off in homage to such a patriot who had imbibed the worth of patriotism as enunciated by Sir Walter Scott in his famous poem, starting with the words: *Breathes there the man with soul so dead who never to himself hath said, 'This is my own, my native land'*. And if it be so, no sacrifice is too great to preserve its sanctity as proved by Bhagat Singh. All praise to him.

* Included here is information from the Creative Commons.

Royal Love For Gangajal

ROYALTY'S love for *Gangajal* is well known in the annals and mythologies of Hindu rulers since the time of Raja Shantanu, Bhishampitamah's father, and even earlier when sage Bhagirath brought the turbulent Ganga down from heaven in his hoary locks after a penance lasting an aeon. But few are aware that the Mughal emperors too loved Ganga water. Though Akbar's liking for it has been chronicled, what is overlooked is that Babar and Humayun too were convinced of its purity and thought it to be only next to *Aaab-e-Hayat*, the water of paradise. The cool streams of Kabul were the delight of Babar and he missed them when he conquered Hindustan in 1526. The alternative he found in India was Ganga water, which Humayun, his son too liked because of his father's preference for it. The Jamuna (not known to them as Yamuna then) was the second option as it flowed between Delhi and Agra. One reason for the liking of *Gangajal* was that it could be stored longer and also because of the belief that it did not get contaminated with bacteria at a time when the concept of germs was not known.

After the first Battle of Panipat, the wounds of the nobles and prominent generals like Bairam Khan were washed with Ganga water if Maulana Mobin-uz-Zaman, late royal hakim to the Prince of Berar (as the heir apparent of the Nizam of Hyderabad was known) is to be believed. The Maulana was no historian, of course, but was quite knowledgeable about the qualities of various river waters, having frequently traveled through the length and breadth of the country, particularly the Ganga-Jamuna belt. Ghalib too couldn't help mentioning the Ganga in one of his letters when he journeyed all the way from Delhi to Calcutta at a time when trains had not been introduced. The poet Alama Iqbal's famous lines were often quoted by the Maulana in this connection,

Aiya ab-rood-e-Ganga
Hai din woh yaad tujko
Utara-tere kinare
Jab karavan hamara

(Oh, hallowed water source Ganga do you remember the day when our caravan alighted on your banks?)

The *shayar* Nazir Banarasi, according to the Urdu litterateur Rakhshanda Jalil, also waxed eloquent on the Ganga, which flows past that city. And the poet Akbar Allahabadi, like the Hindi poetess Mahadevi Varma, too glorified the river's influence on Prayag where it forms the Sangam with the Yamuna and the invisible Saraswati. Incidentally, Akbar Shah Sani's son, Jawan Bakht, while in exile at Allahabad usually diluted his evening drink with Ganga water.

The historian, Dr Ram Nath, now leading a

retired life in Ajmer, states in his *Private Lives of the Mughals*: 'Whether at home or on travel he (Akbar) always drank Ganga water. Adequate arrangements were made for its regular supply. Some trustworthy persons (perhaps to prevent poisoning) were stationed on the banks of the river Ganga. They dispatched the water in sealed jars daily. When the court was at Agra or Fatehpur Sikri (1560-85), the water came from Soron, near Kasganj-Etah (Uttar Pradesh) in carts. When Akbar was residing in Lahore (1585-96) Ganga water was brought from Haridwar. Obviously he attached greater importance to the water of the Ganga than that of the Jamuna or Ravi, and this he did, not out of some superstitious belief, but because of the excellent quality of Ganga water from the health point of view.' For cooking (royal) food, rainwater or water from the Jamuna and the Chenab was mixed with a little Ganga water. On journeys and hunting parties Akbar, from his predilection for good water, appointed experienced men as 'water-tasters' to replenish his drinking supply.

Since Jahangir, his son, moved about the country a lot, including destinations like Kabul, Kashmir, Ajmer, Ahmedabad and Mandu, he could not continue to use Ganga water, 'which he always admired the most', the historian goes on to say. However Shah Jahan could not help but drink Jamuna water in Agra, though Ganga water was brought during special occasions.

When Aurangzeb besieged the Agra Fort in 1658, the emperor could not drink any other water available from tanks and *baoli*s, 'so accustomed was he to the molten snow (water) of the Jamuna'. In the burning heat of June he held out for three days against his rebellious son to whom he wrote this partly quoted letter: 'Only yesterday I was master of nine hundred thousand troopers and today I am in need of a pitcher of water. Praised be the Hindus in all cases as they even offer water to the dead.' It only brought the sarcastic remark from Aurangzeb, 'It is your own doing'.

If oral history is to be believed, Raja Mansingh during the Battle of Haldighati, boasted to Maharana Pratap that his adversary Akbar flourished on Gangajal, and not Pratap among the steep hills of Rajputana. This is to be taken with a pinch of salt but is nevertheless factually true. Now piped Ganga water is available on the other side of the Yamuna in Delhi and bottled Gangajal is being distributed by the Postal Department, something that even some of the Great Mughals could not get on the battlefield. But the quality of the water is not the same as in those times, for the Ganga, like the Yamuna, has been polluted so much that even claims by Uma Bharti, the Union Minister in charge of their cleaning up a few years ago, carry little conviction. Akbar the Great would surely have been horrified at this state of affairs were he, by some quirk of time-travel to reappear now. To make things worse the *Akash Ganga* (Milky Way) too has disappeared from Delhi's starless skies because of pollution.

Scene At The Adda

THERE are all sorts of *Addas* – like the ones in the *Para*s or localities of Bengal, besides those held by some newspapers for hi-fi discussions. But the real Addas are the ones where people, who cannot afford to go to bars in hotels, restaurants and clubs, sit down to drink local brew or *tharra*. Rajasthan, Haryana, Uttar Pradesh and Madhya Pradesh are well known for them. Few may be aware that they also existed in Delhi proper and now are found on the fringes of the Capital. The scene there is no different from the medieval taverns and opium dens. Omar Khayyam based quite a few of his *rubayat*s or couplets on the tavern, with impatient travellers banging on the doors, asking the tavern-keeper to open it as they had to begin their journey before the sun cast its first rays and 'caught the Sultan's turret in a noose of light'. Many must have heard actor Raj Kumar singing (or lipsyncing) those memorable lines:

Kis tarhe jeete hain yeh log bata do yaron
Zindagi jeene ka andaz bata do yaron
...Yah phir maikhanay ka rasta bata do yaron

(tell me the secret of how these people live or show me the way to the tavern).

The Adda is also known as the *Kalhari* or *Kalali*. A European padri who often went to it always asked for *tharra* even when he came to town from his church in Chandu-ka-Nagla. Talking of the kalhari, an acquaintance helped to enliven a bus journey to Faridabad with the following account: On an impulse on a dull day he had entered the kalhari where the colourless stuff was sold. Very few sat and drank slowly. The romance of the tavern was hardly felt in the kalhari as it was just a cheap watering hole. And yet one could weave a pattern of emotions there too. The kalhari-keeper was not around – only his contractor, sitting with big bulging eyes, his moustaches bristling like those of a hungry zoo lion. The acquaintance, Shamsher, did not relish the drink and decided to gulp it down. The stuff was crude. The *kabab*s being sold were not of halal meat and he did not like them, but the other stuff helped to dilute the effects of the drink.

Two men, who looked like *safai karamcharis*, were quite drunk, They probably had been there since the afternoon. *Mai us ko goli mar doonga*, said one. *Mai usey jabhi goli mar deta,* replied his companion. 'What *goli mar deta, goli mar deta*', chimed in the contractor. 'Do you have a bandookh (gun) to shoot with?' Apparently neither of them had one and they both looked baffled at this unwarranted intrusion. But soon they were indulging in the same sort of talk again. From the far corner a drunk was cursing some woman and her family too. His face showed that he couldn't hold his drink. He stared at Shamsher and then pointed out two lines on his palm which merged in a funny way. *Yeh chidya hai*, he said. Shamsher realised that the lines did form a sort of bird all right. *Sheila ki chidya*, said the man, who looked like a tailor. 'Who's Sheila?', asked Shamsher. 'My wife', replied the thin man with great emotion 'and she is very fond of her "chidya" and so are those who visit her', he added with a sigh. 'Another frustrated soul', thought Shamsher and moved two places away where he was nearly throttled by another drunkard.

Still in the kalhari after his fourth drink, Shamsher went philosophic with a cigratte struck in between his fingers like a hookah without even the benefit of a paan to compound the taste: 'What a place this kalhari is! People come here to shed their complexes', he thought. Those who popularised the tavern were not just out to cash in on the craze for booze. They were surely psychologists. The clubs took over much later. But they couldn't introduce characters like the tavern-keeper's maid at whom everyone could wink.

The *maikhana* was the mid-Eastern version. It was here that poetry like *Muddaton roya, karenge jam-o-paimana mujhe*, could be written, though Shamsher was not sure whether he had remembered

Jigar Moradabadi's observation correctly, and as he thought he dozed off because of the tharra he had drunk without cheers. By the time Shamsher finished recounting his reverie, the journey to Faridabad ended and also a tedious December evening when other boozers were probably already in their cups at the local kalhari. But Padri Daniel died long ago with no one bothering to turn down an empty glass on his grave – as old Khayyam wished some would do for him at the *kabristan* in Khorasan.

The Mystery Of Two Mazars

THERE'S a mystery of sorts at Turkman Gate where the saint after whom Shah Jahan named one of the fourteen gates of Shahjahanabad in 1648, lies buried. Researcher Surekha Narain, who led a heritage walk to the place, got confused as to which of the two graves in the area was the one in which Shams-ul-Arifin (sun of knowledge), Hazrat Turkman Bayabani was buried. According to Maulvi Zafar Hasan's famous compilation on Delhi monuments, quoted by INTACH (Indian National Trust for Art and Cultural Heritage), the saint is actually buried in Mohalla Qabristan, also known as Dada Pir Wali Dargah. Close by in Bulbuli Khana are buried Razia Sultan and her sister Sazia, both daughters of Sultan Iltutmish, the second ruler of the Slave dynasty. They were both devotees of Shah Turkman Bayabani. According to Sadia Dehlvi, author of *The Dargahs of Delhi*, the saint was a disciple of Sheikh Shahabuddin Suhrawardi of Multan and a contemporary of Hazrat Qutbuddin Bakhtiar Kaki, with whom he used to converse often.

While it is true that Shah Turkman Bayabani's grave is in Mohalla Qabristan, the grave near Turkman Gate marked 'Shah Bayabani' is puzzling. Was it of another person? Probably a devotee. There are some other graves close by too. Professor Aslam Parvez, an authority on Delhi's history, whose family has been living in the area for several centuries, says the grave pointed out to tourists by guides as that of the saint is not the real one.

'It is either that the tourist guides are ignorant or too lazy to go to Mohalla Qabristan that they do so', opines Khaliq Anjum, former head of the Anjuman Taraqqi Urdu (Hind), New Delhi. Dr Anjum says for that matter even the shrine known as Matkewala Pir on Mathura Road is regarded by some as a creation of the British for political reasons. It is said to have come up overnight, though it is true that the saint it is supposed to honour, Hazrat Azmat Sheikh, was a devout Pir from Tartus who had set up abode in medieval Delhi and was a contemporary of both Shah Bayabani and Hazrat Qutbuddin.

According to INTACH's account, Shah Bayabani's tomb is built of white marble and the entrance is 'through a cusped arch below street level'. On the south is a mosque and round about other graves too giving the locality its name, Mohalla Qabristan, where goats are tethered in the winter sunshine. Sadia Dehlvi says that the saint died on 19 February 1240 during the reign of Muiz ud-Din Bahram Shah, Razia's brother and also the one accused of being responsible for her death. Turkman Bayabani was a saint who did not mind interacting with people of all communities, especially those living on the outskirts of the capital of the Delhi Sultanate. He was fond of celebrating basant, or so it seems, as in earlier times a basant fair was held at Turkman Gate to herald spring. Among the later saints, Hazrat Nizamuddin Auliya and Amir Khusrow where also fond of celebrating basant – and so were the Mughal emperors, especially Muhammad Shah Rangila. People who migrated to Lahore after 1947 still celebrate basant as the festival of kites, even though the police try to ban the celebration every year.

Now to come back to the two-mazar controversy, even the Taj Mahal has two sets of graves, one in the cenotaph chamber and the other set below. There is a belief that actually there are six graves in the Taj. The real ones of Shah Jahan and Mumtaz Mahal being *kutcha* (mud) ones below the Jamuna level, so that the last resting place of the emperor and empress was never desecrated by invaders or others. Babar's real grave is in Kabul but the original one is at Charbagh in Agra. Bahadur Shah Zafar is buried in Yangon, though the tomb he had planned is in Mehrauli.

Yet another interesting example is that of Father Joseph Tieffenthaler, an Austrian priest who died at Lucknow on 5 June 1785 but was buried in Agra, where he had first come in 1744.

The historical researcher T S goes on to point out that surprisingly enough there are tombstones in Lucknow, Mathura and Ajmer also purporting to be the graves of the great mathematician and astronomer, who spoke German, Italian, Spanish, French and Latin and had also acquired a fair knowledge of Urdu, Persian, Arabic and Sanskrit. As a matter of fact, he compiled a Sanskrit-Persian dictionary too.

There are other examples also of people with more than one tombstone, like General David Ochterlony, who is buried in Meerut, but built his *maqbara* in Delhi. And do you know that Akbar's grave at Sikandra could also be having a twin, re-discovered some fifty years ago by T S? It's not at ground level but in a secluded top portion of the mausoleum. No wonder then that, in keeping with tradition, Shah Turkman Bayabani too should have an imitation grave or why would somebody be foolhardy enough to have 'Turkman Bayabani' inscribed on a mazar on the roadside, near the gate, under a tree?

Kishanganj's Claim To Fame

KISHANGANJ in Old Delhi lays claim to fame because of the historic D'Eremao cemetery which is now to be renovated and at least partly restored by the Archaeological Survey of India (ASI). The cemetery actually came under the charge of the ASI in 1919, according to Beverly Hallam (a descendant of the medieval Captain Manuel D'Eremao), who lives in England. Dr Rosie Llewellyn-Jones, editor of *Chowkidar Journal* of BACSA (British Association for Cemeteries in South Asia), quotes Ms Hallam as saying: 'The cemetery can be accurately dated back to at least the late eighteenth century, 1781 to be precise, when the Carmelite Padre Gregorio Della Presentatione came from Bombay to Delhi to take charge of the Delhi Mission, previously run by the Jesuits. There had been an earlier Christian burial ground in Delhi, to accommodate the numerous Armenians and Christians working for the Mughals. A Jesuit priest, Father Joseph Tieffenthaler had remarked on the cemetery in the 1760s, which was said, perhaps with some exaggeration, to have been destroyed by the Persian invader Nadir Shah in 1739. It does seem likely however that the D'Eremao cemetery forms part of that first European cemetery, and is contemporary with the earliest European burials at Agra in the 1600s.

'Manuel D'Eremao, after whom the cemetery was named, was born in Delhi about AD 1744 and was probably brought up by his maternal grandfather, Manuel Gascoine, though most of the wealth he inherited came from his paternal grandmother, Donna Juliana Diaz da Costa. The Captain served as an officer in Scindia's army, and was in charge of the Fort at Hansi until he surrendered it to Lord Lake in 1803, in return for a large pension and confirmation of his ancestral holdings in Delhi.'

The Persian inscription on his tomb reads 'Captain Manuel Deremao Bahadur, having passed eighty-six years of his borrowed life with a good report and a happy conclusion in munificence and charitableness, left this perishable inn four hours after sunset on Friday, the fifth of June 1829 AD corresponding to 2nd of Zilhijj, 1244 Hijri, and took his abode forever in Paradise after having acted up to the tenets of the Christian faith. His relatives were left helpless, and this sorrowful event caused them profound grief and sorrow. Sad is it that the Captain, who was a good natured kind-hearted and generous man went the way of the world all on a sudden.'

When I pondered over the year of his death I heard from the unknown *Wai Daregh* (it is sorrowful indeed) that Domingo Deremao, son of the Captain, erected this stone in memory of his father. The inscription has now disappeared.

The D'Eremao Cemetery had been squatted

since the 1950s, mainly by Indian Christians. 'Despite a modern stone that labels the site "Armenian Cemetry", recent research has found it is probably the first European cemetery of Old Delhi, and thus not exclusively Armenian. Captain Manuel D'Eremao's grandmother Donna Juliana Diaz da Costa was of Portuguese descent and born in Bengal in 1658, attached to the Mughal court. On her death in 1732, she left four villages and their income, which had been gifted to her by the Emperor Shah Alam-I (or Bahadur Shah I, eldest son of Aurangzeb). The cemetery was certainly in use before then for in it lie the remains of Judith Gascoin (died 1808), the wife of Captain Von Der Osten, chief of the Danish Factory at Patna. The earliest Armenian inscription in it dates back to 1787. There were six more Armenian tombstones according to the historian Mesrovb Seth.'

However to come back to the cemetery, when Brigadier Bullock visited it, in 1936, it was in excellent condition. But on a return visit in December 1947, when the Brigadier was conducting an audit of all European cemeteries in newly independent India, he found a terrible sight. 'During the disturbances in August and September 1947 it had suffered much deliberate damage. All marble tablets were stolen and wanton damage (though perhaps random) done to many graves and to the large D'Eremao mausoleum, which forms the principal feature of the cemetery. Beverly Hallam has found numerous letters from Brigadier Bullock to administrative bodies in Delhi, trying to submit a claim for compensation, then to have the cemetery cleared of squatters, and chowkidars installed. Very little help was offered.' 'The British High Commission, with responsibility for maintenance, was happy to hand it over to the Delhi authorities in 1952,' says Dr Jones Now that its history is better known, Captain D'Eremao's great-great-grandaughter has written to the ASI and INTACH , asking that the cemetery should be properly recognised and given the respect it is due, as a unique piece of Indo-European history. Hope the ASI makes this hope come true.

Metro Tunnelling Into History

TUNNELS do make sensational news in history, besides the ones on the Indo-Pak border and in Tihar and other jails. There is one in the Agra Fort which is believed to lead to the Red Fort in Delhi. How long it would have taken for those of the royal family using it to reach the twin-capital is anybody's guess. There must have been *roshandan*s or ventilators in it so that the users could come out and breathe the fresh air of the jungles through which the tunnel passed. Besides the fact that no such roshandans have been found, at least three incidents, including the Agra Fort siege by Aurangzeb imprisoning his father, the plight of Dara Shikoh after the battle of Samugarh and Jahandar Shah's flight following his rout by nephew Farrukhsiyar, also near Agra, in the struggle for the Mughal throne discount the possibility of such a 122-mile tunnel. Jahandar Shah had to escape to Delhi with his vivacious mistress, the ex-dancing girl Lal Kanwar, both disguised as *mirasi*s, or wandering minstrels. In the process Lal Kanwar was nearly gangraped by *badmashe*s festering the Agra-Delhi road. Although this is an unverified story, the possibility cannot be ruled out considering the unsafe conditions after the death of Bahadur Shah I.

One remembers peering into the tunnel in the Agra Fort years ago with noted tourist guide Ikram Uddin asserting its inter-city link as per his and late journalist Bishan Kapoor's initial findings. But the smell of bat droppings put off one from closer inspection of the *surang* or tunnel. In all probability it leads to some secure places as an escape route for the emperor and his family during a revolt or an invasion or as a shortcut on a summer's day to the Yamuna.

Then there's the likelihood of a tunnel leading from Shah Jahan's Persian vazir Ali Mardan Khan's palace in the Kashmere Gate area (which later housed the British Resident) to the Red Fort. The vazir is said to have visited the emperor secretly by making use of it during emergencies. Another tunnel is said to lead from Shalimar Bagh to the Red Fort. It was to be a direct link between the Sheesh Mahal (where Aurangzeb was crowned) to the Dewan-e-Am. One wonders why Muhammad Shah Rangila did not make use of it to escape the clutches of Nadir Shah in 1739. It is obvious that the tunnel did exist but did not link the bagh, laid by Shah Jahan's begum Bibi Akbarabadi, to the Fort. Even Colonel Ochterlony, who was so fond of camping at Shalimar Bagh, never thought of using it to reach his official residence as it did not lead to Shahjahanabad. Yet another tunnel was said to lead from the haveli of Hakim Ahsanullah Khan, in the heart of the city to the fort through which the chief Hakim and adviser to Bahadur Shah Zafar used to secretly go to meet the Last Emperor. The

Hakim is believed to have advised Zafar to leave the fort secretly to dodge the British looking for him but why didn't he use the tunnel to escape on the collapse of the Great Revolt? All he did was take refuge at Humayun's Tomb where he later surrendered to Lieutenant William Hodson. There are tunnels in Fatehpur Sikri, besides the *tehkhana* or basement chamber in Metcalfe House which was used as a torture chamber after the 'Mutiny'. The latest to make news is the Metro tunnel for the Heritage Line from Central Secretariat to the Kashmere Gate, with the underground Red Fort Metro Station as the showpiece.

However this heritage tunnel has disturbed the Skinner family in London. Patsy Sedwards (nee Skinner) who visited Delhi disclosed in an email that she was greatly concerned on learning that the tunnel would pass under St James Church, built by her ancestor, Colonel James Skinner in the first half of the nineteenth century. It is the oldest existing church in Delhi and Ms Sedwards worried how 'the building and the graves in the family cemetery would stand up to the initial excavation and the continual rumble of trains passing underneath'. The Reverend Hitter, the presbyter-in-charge of the church was requested by her to make a representation to the Metro authorities. It seems he did so, along with his chief adviser, Mr Baluja and Samuel Joseph, a social activist and formerly a director of the New Delhi YMCA. The Metro administration calmed their fears, saying enough precautions had been taken to safeguard the historic buildings, including the church, Qudsia Masjid and of course Red Fort and Jama Masjid to see that no damage was done to them. But Patsy Sedwards added a note of caution in her 5 March 2016 message to this scribe, with the remark, 'Only time will tell whether there will be any structural damage'.

Skinner's Church suffered terrible damage during the upheaval of 1857 when its top cross and bells were knocked down by cannon balls. The cemetery, besides the Skinner graves, also contains the tombs of William Fraser, Sir Thomas Metcalfe and the Beresfords. Beresford, incidentally, was the manager of the Delhi Bank in Chandni Chowk and he, his daughters and wife were all murdered by rebel sepoys. But Mrs Beresford put up a heroic fight and killed two of her assailants with a spear before being struck down. Historian Dr Rosie Llewellyn-Jones, an authority on the Raj days, was consulted by the Skinners in London and she too wondered if there was substance to the family's concerns. But now that most of the work on the Metro tunnel has been completed such fears should be laid to rest at least temporarily, though tunnels do sometimes suddenly collapse, causing great damage.

Shrine of Dada Pir

Sufi Shrines Of Delhi

THE World Sufi Forum's Delhi conclave focused attention on Sufi saints. There are twenty-two *khwajas* or saints who are highly venerated and buried in Delhi, which has come to be known as their threshold or courtyard. Sadia Dehlvi has compiled a book on Sufi shrines, the foremost among which are the *mazars* of Qutbuddin Bakhtiar Kaki, after whom the Qutub Minar was named by the first ruler of the Slave dynasty, Qutbuddin Aibak. After him the next in importance is Nizamuddin Auliya, his successor, Hazrat Nasiruddin Mahmud Roshan Chirag-Dehlavi, his favourite disciple, Khusrow, Hazrat Turkman Bayabani, after whom Turkman Gate is named, Bhure Mian, whose shrine is just outside the Red Fort and Kaleemullah Jehanabadi, buried across the main road from there. Below the steps of the Jama Masjid are the graves of Sarmad Shaheed, beheaded by Aurangzeb for alleged apostasy and his guru, Hare Bhare Sahib. While the tomb of the disciple is painted red as a sign of martyrdom, his mentor's is coloured green as a sign of immortality.

Among the hundreds of Sufi saints of Delhi listed by Sadia are Khwaja Rasool Numa, Hazrat Baqi Billa, Pir Ghaib, Matkay Shah, Bibi Noor, Bibi Zulekha, mother of Hazrat Nizamuddin, Inayat Khan and his son Vilayat Khan, Bibi Qarsum Khatoon, Patey Shah, Khwaja Makhdoom, Imam Zamin, Mazhar Jane Jana, Bibi Hambal Daiji, Bibi Noor, Mirza Bedil, Bibi Fatima Sam, Jamali and Kamali, Bibi Jannat, Junan Shah, builder of at least seven mosques, Badruddin Samarqandi, Hazrat Shah Alam. There are many more of note and fame, like Hazrat Mandir Marg Wale, Shah Mandi House Wale, the Pir Sahib after whom a mosque is named opposite Odeon Cinema, Hazrat Nurullah and Abdun Nabi.

Hazrat Qutbuddin Bakhtiar Kaki was the chief disciple of Moinuddin Chisti of Ajmer. Mahatma Gandhi visited his shrine in Mehrauli to pray for communal peace shortly before his assassination. Nizamuddin Auliya had among his followers Muhammad bin Tughlaq and Hasan Gangoo, who founded the Bahmani kingdom in the Deccan. He is the most honoured Sufi in Delhi. Pir Ghaib was a saint of Firoz Shah Tughlaq's time and just disappeared one day, hence the name. Amir Khusrow served seven kings and loved Nizamuddin so much that he died of a broken heart a few months after his mentor's death. Bhure Mian was tempted by Aurangzeb with a dish which contained dog's meat in order to test his all-knowing spiritual power. Hazrat Kaleemullah saved Delhi from a Jamuna flood in Jahangir's reign.

The miracles performed by Sufi saints are too many to be recounted. It is said that so long as their shrines exist, Delhi will survive. The saints are venerated on Thursday by both Muslims and Hindus as God's favoured friends who foster communal harmony. Bibi Fatima, who is known as Rabia-e-Delhi is the patron of girls seeking good husbands and Bibi Zulekha as the one who pleads with her son, Nizamuddin Auliya for the acceptance of his *mureeds* or devotees' wishes. *Sufiana* music binds all commuities not only with enthralling Qawwalis but also with the propagation of the message of human brotherhood.

Many of the Sufis came from the middle-East or Central Asia and Afghanistan and made India their home. That they died here and were buried mostly in Mehrauli shows their love for the country of their adoption. Here are amazing stories associated with some of them:

There is a mini-park in Mayfair Gardens' bungalow locality, touching the walls of Siri Fort, where is situated the fifteenth century tomb of Makhdum Sahib, visited by devotees throughout the year. Sheikh Makhdum Sabzwari came to Delhi from Sabzwar in Central Asia, at the end of the reign of Bahlul Lodi or the beginning of his son, Nizam Khan Sikandar Lodi's reign in 1488. He had been directed in a dream to go to India and preach his mission there. Makhdum Sahib's Sufi discourses were ardently heard by those who visited his jungle abode, where wild animals roamed about but did not harm anyone because of the influence of the saint, says a legend. Eventually the Lodi Sultan (father or son) heard of him and invited the *dervish* to the royal court. He went there reluctantly and came back dissatisfied with the sultan's conduct.

Perhaps realising that he had offended the Sheikh, the sultan, while out hunting one day, decided to visit his *khanqah* or hospice. What he saw there amazed him, for Makhdum Sahib was feeding a wild leopard with a bunch of grass as though it was a goat. The sultan immediately dismounted from his horse and after offering his salaam decided to sit in a corner. The leopard was ordered to leave by the saint, who then turned his attention to the sultan. The latter apologised for having been rude at the court and requested him not to leave his kingdom but continue to reside in it and bless its subjects.

Makhdum Sahib nodded and gave the sultan (Bahlul or Sikandar) a *tabiz* or amulet which he had brought from Mecca. He told him that so long as it was tied to his arm or that of his successors, the sultanate would continue to flourish otherwise it would be conquered by an invader who, followed by his descendants, would rule for long, undisturbed. The sultan took the tabiz, *salaam*ed the saint again, mounted his horse and rode away. As history shows, the third ruler of the dynasty, Ibrahim Lodi lost the kingdom in 1526 to Babar, with whom the Mughal dynasty started and continued to rule India until 1858, when Queen Victoria proclaimed herself empress and Bahadur Shah Zafar was exiled to Rangoon.

One tends to believe the story about the saint's prediction but at the same time wonders what happened to the amulet. Did Ibrahim Lodi forget to tie it around his biceps at the fateful first battle of Panipat or did the tabiz somehow get lost?

The reason for me to visit the mosque and mazar of Makhdum Sahib was a strange story related by Hafiz Manzoor Ahmed of Basti Nizamuddin during a winter evening in 1981. The Hafiz died not long after but what he said continued to feed one's curiosity for the past thirty-three years until the temptation to visit Makhdum Sahib's shrine could no longer be resisted. Now this is the story Manzoor Ahmed related:

There was a widow named Nadira whose husband Saddique had died without leaving an heir. Nadira was fifty-five years old, lonely and sad, when she came to the shrine one afternoon in the first decade of the twentieth century. She had either been told by somebody, or had the urge herself, to pray there. And the prayer was strange for a woman of her age. She sought the saint's blessing for a son who could continue his father's lineage. She prayed with tears in her eyes and all at once experienced a sensation which passed through her face, bosom and lower abdomen and then ceased to excite her. Nadira then had a great urge to go to the toilet but as there was no one near the shrine she squatted under a tree. When she got up she felt as though she had just conceived. The widow went home dazed and had a dream the same night in which she saw a bearded old man blessing her and confirming that her wish had been fulfilled.

Believe it or not, nine months later Nadira gave birth to a son who was strange in his behaviour at first and neither spoke nor walked properly.But after three years he began to improve and by the time he was five, he was able to attend school and turned out to be a brilliant student.

Incidentally, Makhdum Sahib's tomb is still in a fairly good condition on Khel Gaon Marg, its stone-domed roof (with four decorative minars) supported on twelve pillars. Both the tomb and the mosque on the north are protected monuments. The masjid has several prayer chambers and a fluted roof. However the huge gate near it, which was erected earlier in Tughlaq times, is not in a good state of preservation though it too is protected by the ASI.

When Firoz Shah Tughlaq built his *Kotla* or Fort in the fourteenth century, he did not have to look far for a site. The ruins of an earlier citadel were already there and these belonged to the time of the Slave Sultans. Some aver that they are actually a part of the ancient Indraprastha.

But when the Mughals took over, Kotla was a forsaken building and the haunt of Sufis and *Mast Qalandar*s. The latter were a sect of dervishes who wore camel skin shirts or just wrapped themselves up in blankets. They were generally big, sturdy men, neglectful of their hygiene, who went about beating themselves with iron chains or brandishing huge steel chimtas or fire-tongs. Ahmed Ali, the author of *Twilight in Delhi*, talks of a Mast Qalandar who hadn't brushed his teeth for years, with the result that pieces of meat kept sticking to them and emitting a bad odour. He like the others of his tribe came to the Jama Masjid area from the Kotla, especially during the time of the various *urs*.

Now you don't find Mast Qalandars in the Kotla, but the Sufis are still there. Go on a Thursday and you will find them in full sway. People do not flock to see them but seek the intervention of jinns in their daily lives. The jinns have been associated with the Kotla ever since it became a discarded citadel. It is believed that they were formed from fire, and not earth like man, during the time of creation. There are two kinds of jinns, the *tairan* and the *haiwan*. While the former are blessed beings that help mankind and even takes wives from it, the latter are destructive and hostile in their dealings because of their baser instincts. William Dalrymple mentions *Djinn*s in his famous book on Delhi. They are also found in Mehrauli around the Makan-e-Khizr. Hazrat Khizr is believed to be the grandson of Adam, the first man, who keeps travelling around the world. His journey will terminate only when the world ends. By the way jinns are fond of sweets and pretty women. They are dressed in white and, being invisible, cast no shadow.

Interestingly, people of all faiths throng the Kotla to seek the blessings of the jinns. So there is a regular *mela* there on Thursdays. Some will remember that many years ago the king of the jinns was supposed to get married on a certain day somewhere in Iran. Reports in newspapers quoted mystics as urging people to seek boons during the mythical event, with a stern warning to those who tried to scoff at the idea. The reverberations were felt in the Kotla too, where jinns were seen frolicking at night after consuming milk in mud kulhars. Several of these were recovered the next day and many wondered how they got there. You remember the tale of the midwife who was blindfolded and led away one night to a dilapidated house in Delhi. When she opened her eye she saw a woman in labour and after the delivery was escorted back safe and sound with a present of a handful of coals, which turned into gold coins when she reached home and threw them down in disgust. But don't expect the ones at the Kotla to repeat the act.

About 1.5 km north of Majnu-ka-Tila is the giant grave of a Naugaza Pir. Nobody seems to know what his name was but some claim that it was Abdullah Nasir Shah Tilawaley. Of late qawwalis are held near the nine-foot-long tomb of the saint (believed to have been a disciple of Majnu) who rebelled against his mentor when the latter became a follower of Guru Nanak. That would mean early sixteenth century. Another belief is that he was a disciple of Shah Alam, a venerated Pir of Firoz Shah Tughlaq's time (1351-88).

As is the trend these days, anonymous mosques and tombs are being increasingly adopted by those who have started calling themselves *Sajjada Nashin*s or hereditary caretakers. The offerings made every *Jumairat* (Thursday) amount to a lot and fill up their coffers. In course of time boundary walls come up around hitherto neglected graves which are renovated and dubbed old miraculous Sufi mazars. Such seems to be the case with the grave of the Naugaza Pir. Khaliq Anjum, who has written a history of Delhi's monuments in Urdu, is also of the opinion that the said mazar has begun to be venerated because of tall tales and gossip, exploited by opportunists. Naugaza Pirs, whose graves are found all over North India, right up to Kashmir, were not giants but their mazars are large as they were buried along with the green flag-bearing staff they carried. As time went by their stature, as measured by their last resting place, began to draw awe and wonder.

However for those interested in qawwals the mazar of the Naugaza Pir is a new attraction. On Thursdays a big crowd collects, making commutation that way difficult. But the zeal of those gathered is to be seen to be believed, with some going into a trance or *hal.* There are women too among them. Remember that Queen Victoria almost reached that state when a group of qawwals performed in nineteenth century England, courtesy her Urdu teacher, Munshi Abdul Karim. Others who heard the singers at Buckingham Palace also became ecstatic, without understanding a word of what was being sung. You may luckily see the same effect at the Pir's grave.

In this time of World War anniversaries few are aware that Noor Inayat Khan, super secret agent, had a close link with a Delhi shrine. And thereby hangs a tale that goes back to Tipu Sultan, who died fighting the British at Seringapatam during the Fourth Mysore War in 1799. Long after that one of his descendants founded a Sufi order in Delhi. Hazrat Inayat Khan, great-grandson of Tipu, was a man of many tastes who went abroad in 1920 to give music concerts, having become a musician of note early in life. He was initiated into Sufism by Sheikh Abu Hashim Madani but during a visit to the West wed an American woman, Ora Ray Baker (renamed Ameena) who gave birth to four children. According to Sadia Dehlvi, Inayat Khan died in 1927 and was buried in Delhi, though he had settled down with his wife in Suresne, a Parisian suburb. His son, Pir Vilayat Khan succeeded him.

His successor was Pir Zia Khan, head of the Sufi Order International.

'Inayat Khan's daughter, Noor Inayat Khan (just as famous as Mata Hari) was a British Special Operations Agent (Madeline) during World War II. She became the first female radio operator to be sent by the Allies into occupied France to aid the French Resistance (under General Charles de Gaulle). Captured by the Germans, Noor was executed in September 1944' when she was thirty and was posthumously given the highest civilian award (George Cross) by the British Government in 1949. Recently a special postage stamp was issued and a statue installed in her memory in Britain.

Probably the latest Sufi shrine to come up is in Hari Nagar, south west Delhi. This one honours Pir Naseer Uddin Sahib. In 1947, a neglected grave marked the site where Meo herdsmen sometimes burnt *diya*s or earthen lamps. In later years an enterprising sufi-lover built up the place and now a regular shrine greets the passers-by. Not only Muslims but also Hindus and Christians come to the dargah on Thursdays when a mini-market springs up on both sides of the road, selling joss-sticks, candles, diyas and flowers to those wishing to make offerings. Even nurses and doctors from the nearby Deen Dayal Upadhyay (DDU) Hospital are among the devotees. The nurses are mostly South Indians belonging to the Marthomite Church, which they still attend on Sundays. But they too seem to have developed great faith in the saint. That is how faith inspires people and draws them to Sufism, which does not interfere with one's hereditary beliefs.

The message Pir Vilayat Khan preached (like his father) was that one doesn't have to embrace Islam to become a Sufi. Hazrat Inayat Khan had defined Sufism as a religious philosophy of love, harmony and beauty for all. His dargah is not far from the one of Hazrat Nizamuddin. Situated in an 'elegant modern structure', it is quite unlike the usual conception of a dargah. Some call it the 'white man's dargah' as most of the visitors are foreigners, who stay in the rooms attached to it and attend cultural events hosted by Dr Fareeda of the West Indies.

Descent Of The Tiranga

FOR those who have watched the film *Tiranga*, starring the swashbuckling Raaj Kumar in the lead role, and the arch-villain Gendaswami, love for the national flag radiates always on the screen and elsewhere, especially during Independence

Day and Republic Day. Visit Sadar Bazaar and see for yourself the enthusiasm of those buying this national symbol or go to the Khadi bhandars, where the khadi-spun variety is sold in large numbers. No wonder when the Tiranga flutters in the morning breeze after the Prime Minister has unfurled it from the ramparts of the Red Fort (where once the Mughal flag and the Union Jack occupied pride of place) the heart of every Indian swells up with pride.

One remembers an Independence Day in the late 1960s when, after Indira Gandhi had performed the ceremony and the last of the three cheers of *Bharat Mata ki Jai* had been raised, an earthquake hit Delhi as though Nature too was joining in the celebrations, which had started when Jawaharlal Nehru had unfurled the tricolour on 15 August 1947 before a huge multitude, while 50,000 refugees were sheltered in the Purana Qila. Hence on this Independence Day too one's feelings are permeated with the same joy and one is inclined to trace the glorious history of the Tiranga.

What is it that makes a man sacrifice his life for a flag? A piece of cloth is hardly worth the most precious gift a person possesses. And yet he goes ahead without fear or remorse and loses it just to defend a flag. The answer may lie in the fact that a flag is much more than a cloth. A word of Teutonic origin, it represents patriotism, honour, loyalty, pride, belief, chivalry and what not. That is why when the standard bearer was killed in a battle another rushed in to take his place, even to the last man, whether commoner or king. So long as the flag was aloft victory was denied to the opposing force.

Flags have been around since time immemorial. The inhabitants of Mohenjo-daro used flags which bore, besides other images, those of a unicorn and an incense-burner. Even prior to the Indus Valley Civilisation, flags were regarded as totems of clan or tribal loyalty and strength, observes Lieutenant Comander K V Singh (Retd) in his book *Tiranga, our National Flag*, that was reviewed by me and of which this story forms a part. The *Rigveda* refers to totemism commemorating god, man, bird, beast, tree or plant, the sun, the moon, the stars, the sky, the clouds or any other natural or supernatural phenomena.

The practice of carrying flags to the battlefield during war and before kings and other members of the royalty during peacetime, says Commander Singh, was followed by the Indians, Chinese, Egyptians, Assyrians, Greeks, Romans and other ancient civilisations. It was as much a sacred symbol as a political and social insignia which was carried by even ships on the high seas.

In the Ramayana and Mahabharata too flags have been given due importance. During his 14-years exile with Rama, one day Lakshman sighted a huge army with the flag that had been adopted by Bharat, which bore the emblem of *kovidara* (a supernatural tree), and sought permission from his brother to destroy it. Fortunately he was pacified, for as it turned out, the army was not a hostile one. Rama's flag bore the figure of the sun, which was his dynastic deity. Ravana's flag had a *kapala* (human skull) inscribed on it as he was a devotee of Shiva. Some, however, say that it depicted the veena to denote wisdom. His son, Meghnad's flag bore the emblem of the lion, Prahasta's the snake and Kambanan's the Sheshanaga.

In the Mahabharata, the standard of Yudhistir bore a pair of thunder drums, Bhim's the *simha* (lion), and Arjun's *Kapi* (the divine monkey), Nakul's the *Sarbha*, the mythical two-headed animal with wings, Sahadev's flag had the swan, the symbol of the Ashwini or Gemini twins, engraved on it, Abhimanyu's the bird *saranga* and Krishna's the omnipotent *Garuda*. Bhishma's flag had the *tala* tree with a cluster of five stars. Duryodhana's a serpent to denote strength. Dronacharya's an altar covered with deerskin, while his brother-in-law Kripacharya's standard had a humped bull, Karna's an elephant chain. Ashwathama's a lion-tail, Jayadratha's a boar, the Pandavas' uncle Salya's flag had the image of the plough while that of Balram bore the *Tala-dhvaja*, like Bhimshmapitamaha's standard. Before killing Karna, Arjuna destroyed the latter's flag just as Rama had destroyed Ravana's pennant before slaying him.

The earliest standard of the Muslims was the Roman eagle, but the latter Caliphs adopted a black flag with the name of the Prophet superimposed on it. Mahmud of Ghazni's troops carried that sort of flag with a crescent on it. Muhammad Ghori's standard also had a crescent, but his successor Qutbuddin added a lion to it, while the Tughlaq insignia bore a fish, an old symbol signifying the triumph of faith – as in the Deluge. The Mughal standard, the moss green *Alam* displayed the rising sun partially hidden by a magnificent lion. The *Alam* was the flag of Hazrat Imam Hussain at the Battle of Karbala which was adopted by Taimur the Lame and hence was passed on to the Mughal who descended from him.

The Rajputs, who claimed descent from Bappa Rawal, had the sun as their emblem. Known as the *Changi* it was the banner under which Maharana Pratap fought Akbar's forces at the battle of Haldighati. However the Jodhpur flag, the *Panchranga*, as the name suggests had five colours, with a black kite, a bird which represents the goddess Durga. During the uprising of 1857, the sepoys fought under a green and gold banner which was hoisted by them on the Red Fort after Bahadur Shah Zafar was proclaimed as their supreme leader. The long story of the flags has been brought up-to-date by Commander Singh right up to the adoption of the Tiranga as the national flag after experiments with different designs by Madame Cama, Annie Besant, Sister Nivedita and others. This included the Calcutta flag of August 1906. One wonders whether our love for the national flag would have been any less had this or any other flag been adopted instead of the Tiranga!

Prince Philip's Tryst With The Taj

NOW that Prince Philip, the Duke of Edinburgh and consort of Queen Elizabeth II, has decided to retire from public life, one has to sift through hazy memories to recall his first visit to India in 1958. On landing at Delhi Airport (there was no Indira Gandhi International Airport then) he remarked that he was surprised on seeing fog in Delhi, probably because he thought it was warm and sultry throughout the year. And who could blame him for this misconception? After all, the closest he had come to India earlier was during World War II when he was in the Royal Navy and his ship had anchored in Sri Lanka (then Ceylon) with its all-year tropical climate. Nephew of Lord Mountbatten, last Viceroy and first Governor-General of liberated India, he had not had an opportunity to come during his uncle's tenure.

The prince's first outing after landing in Delhi (where he had to attend a conference and later another one in Bangalore) was to Agra to see the Taj. One remembers that quite a few British nationals in the city thought it worthwhile to greet him. Among them was the Reverend T D Sully, principal of St John's College, a *haft-zaban* padre (linguist) who was a mathematician, musician, English language expert, philosopher and, of course, theologian of note. Among those who also trooped in was the cynical Uncle Ceastan of Armenian descent (from Siestan), dressed in late nineteenth century clothes like Rudyard Kipling, who read newspapers in the Queen Mary Empress

Library in the Cantonments and discussed each item even with passers-by, Mother Joan, in charge of St Joseph's School, an Irish woman who hadn't stirred out of the convent for forty years, and Abid Bhai, as stated earlier given forced retirement after he went daft. Abid Bhai came in Kale Khan's tonga to meet whom he thought to be *Badshah Salamat*. Curiosity also brought the burqa-clad women from Tajganj who wanted to see *Unaan (*Greece) *ka Shehzada*, married to Malika Elizabeth – with pretty Begum Anwar 'Anardana' lifting up the *niqab* to wave to him with her bejewelled hand.

The Duke, wearing a fine Saville Row suit, was the cynosure of attraction of students, both boys and girls. The latter found him very handsome, but Mota Dixit was fascinated with his shoes and the laces he thought were tied to perfection. The Duke was taken around by the chief guide, Islamuddin but the Commissioner of Agra Division, John Stanley Lall, himself a history buff, also helped to explain the mysteries of the Taj. When the Duke heard the sonorous echo in the cenotaph chamber he wanted to know whether the same *khadim*s gave the *azaan* in the Taj masjid and also why there was a mosque facing east on the opposite side of the main one. He was told that the khadims were not *muezzins* but only the ones who demonstrated the echo of the azaan. The other mosque, it was pointed out, was known as the *Jawaab* and had been built just for the sake of imparting symmetry to the ambience of the monument.

On seeing the Yamuna and being told that it wended its way up to Allahabad, where it met the Ganga and the mythical Saraswati to form the Sangam, the Duke suggested that there should be a lot more water in the river so that besides regular boating the more adventurous could go all the way to the Sangam. He also opined that there should be a bridge connecting the Taj with Mehtab Bagh, where Shah Jahan wanted to build a black marble Taj.

There were no grand hotels in Agra then but the prince spent the night in the best one from where he could see the Taj. Desmond Doig, the noted journalist who covered his visit, wrote the next day: 'Thousands of parrots awake Agra every morning. They probably awoke the Duke for he was up early, sitting on a chair and admiring the rosy tainted hue that enveloped the monument before the sun rose over the Jamuna.' Doig accompanied the Duke on his extended tour and wrote endearingly about night falling on the royal visit: 'A policeman throws a stone at a dog, a *chakor* calls to its mate in the hills.'

When the Duke accompanied Queen Elizabeth on her first visit in 1961 he was able to explain better the nuances of the Taj to her but when Princess Diana came, unfortunately without Prince Charles, purportedly held up in Delhi for some official assignment, she had to sit alone on the Lotus Pond marble seat where the Duke and the Queen had been photographed in a memorable pose. However to make up for Diana's disappointment her son and daughter-in-law, Prince William and the Duchess of Cambridge, Kate Middleton posed on the famed seat years later and perhaps gladdened the hearts of the Queen and her consort, the nonagenarian Prince Philip.

Remembering Shah Jahan

THE 360th Urs or death anniversary of Shah Jahan was observed at the Taj Mahal, but there were ripples of it in Delhi too with a busload of people reaching there to pay homage to the emperor. Mohammad Saqib of Suiwalan was one of them. He has been attending the Urs for years as one of his ancestors was among the artisans who worked on the inlay work at the mausoleum, or so he claims. Another interested visitor was Shahnawaz Khan of Basti Nizamuddin who went for the first time to offer *fateha* in observance of a vow. Earlier Khan Abdul Haye Khan was a regular Delhiwallah who never missed the Urs. Abdul Haye was a Pathan who was very fond of fishing. One remembers that in 1966 during the monsoon he sat down on the rear side of Itimad-ud-Daulah to fish in the Yamuna, which was in flood and whose waters were beating against the mausoleum where rests the father of Nur Jahan and grandfather of Mumtaj Mahal. A *rohu* caught by Abdul Haye was so big that it sufficed for dinner for the whole family when cooked in Matia Mahal.

Shah Jahan like the unlucky Muhammad bin Tughlaq was fond of Yamuna fish and so also presumely Mumtaz Mahal, but he did not drink wine till the age of twenty-three when he was persuaded by his father, Jahangir, to do so. He however, never drank after the death of Mumtaz at Burhanpur on 16 June 1631. According to Ishwari Prasad, Shah Jahan died in January 1666, aged seventy-four. Why his Urs was celebrated in mid-May is not understandable unless the date is fixed according to its proximity to Mumtaz Mahal's death or some lumar calculation or as per the convenience of the khadims (caretakers). One remembers attending an Urs in 1958 when among those who prayed for the emperor's soul was Nawabzada Faroque Rehman Khan of Datoli. Earlier the Nawab of Chhatari, Chief Scout of India and Freemason Grandmaster, had offered his obeisance. The first Urs of Shah Jahan, a year after his death, was presided over by Prince Muezzim, eldest son of Aurangzeb, who came from Delhi partly on horseback and partly in a horse-driven carriage, past Akbar's Tomb at Sikandra, where he dismounted to offer fateha at the grave of his great-great grandfather. Aurangzeb came a month later. The same thing happened at the first Urs of Mumtaz Mahal at the Taj after Shah Jahan's death.

A special feature of the Urs of Shah Jahan, which was later merged with the Urs of Mumtaz Mahal, is the laying of a gigantic multi-coloured Hindustani *Chadar* at the grave. This was offered on Friday, 17 May with the Urs continuing on the subsequent Saturday and Sunday. Entry to the Taj was free from the afternoon of Friday (when the Taj is usually closed for visitors). The shehnai was played, along with the *naqqara* (drum), at the top of the main entrance to the monument and on the following days the big kettle drums were beaten to mark the occasion, as in Mughal times when Shah Jahan is believed to have once remarked to Mumtaz: *Naqqare tumhari amadh ka ailan karenge aur tum Manno Malika kehlaugi* (The drums will announce your arrival and you dear will be called Empress). Not much information is available of the first Urs of Shah Jahan but the one for Mumtaz Mahal is recorded as follows by father (Thomas Smith) in his 1977 memoirs:

> The celebrations traditionally begin with the washing of the tombs of the emperor and his wife with rose water and the lighting of *agarbattis*. Prayers are offered and flowers and cloth chadars, one of them on behalf of the Department of Archaeology, are placed on the graves. Occasionally a visitor whose prayers have been heard sends a chadar as a token of thanksgiving. Atop the gate facing the mausoleum sit shehnai players and as evening advances, qawwalis in praise of the dead couple attract a big audience from neighbouring Tajganj, where reside the descendants of the builders of the monument. In keeping with tradition, food is distributed to the poor. The entire cost of the Urs is borne by the khadims from offerings made at the tombs. The first

Urs of Mumtaz Mahal was performed by Shah Jahan himself in 1631. The Emperor wore a white dress and the nobles were in mourning habit. A covering with strings of pearls worth several lakhs of rupees was spread over the tomb. Prayers were offered for the soul of the queen and *fateha* was performed. Asif Khan, father of Mumtaz Mahal, was assigned a prominent place at the ceremony. A lakh of rupees was sanctioned for the ceremony; Rs 50,000 of it was given in alms to the poor.

A few years ago, the Urs followed the earthquake which did not have any significant effect on the monument, except Sahilion-ki-Burj. Believe it or not, Mufti Ehsan Sahib of Mehrauli thinks Shah Jahan and Mumtaz Mahal always protect those who come to offer homage to them.

Fort With Weird History

THE American Jesuit fathers came from Jaipur in 1960 and opened a branch of St Xavier's School in the erstwhile Cecil Hotel in the Civil Lines, but their love for Jaipur continued and after two years a picnic was organised to Nahargarh there. The fort was a gift in 1734 to the new capital of Rajputana by Sawai Jai Singh II, a great friend of Muhammad Shah Rangila (1719-1748), the Mughal emperor who allowed him to build his Jantar Mantar in Delhi. Sawai Jai Singh, besides being an astronomer was also a great builder who was attracted by the Red Fort and the older Agra Fort, one built by Shah Jahan and the other by Akbar. But he wanted his fort to be more impregnable and so he built it atop a steep hill.

The staff (staying in Ludlow Castle Road) and students of Delhi St Xavier's who went to see it fifty-five years ago were amazed to observe the fort's ambience at a time when there was no talk of Padmavati. They were told that it was actually named Sudarshangarh but the name was changed to Nahargarh to pacify the spirit of Nahar Singh Bhomia which created obstructions in its construction. A temple dedicated to him was also built in the fort. Yet Tiger Fort (because of the presence of tigers), as it translates into English, has been the scene of some strange events, the latest one being of the gem polisher Chetan Kumar Saini, whose body was found hanging there in a mystery that is yet to be solved. Whether it was suicide or murder, God knows. But it is not the only incident of this type that has occurred within the precincts of the old fort. Lieutenant Colonel Altaf David, who would have been a hundred years old now, once disclosed that his grandfather had told him two tales dating back to the times of Sawai Ram Singh II (1835-1880) and Sawai Madho Singh II (1880-1922), when also some weird incidents were reported from there.

Colonel David lived in retirement in the Civil Lines area of Delhi although he originally belonged to Ajmer, where his sibling, Professor Goodwin Iqbal David (Guddan Sahib) died some years ago, though he was active most of the time as a luminary of the English Department of St John's College, Agra.

To come back to Colonel David's tales, during Sawai Ram Singh's time a goldsmith who had become half-blind and was forsaken by his family, one day stumbled upon Nahargarh. Lost in thought, he sat alone on a boulder till night fell and he started feeling scared in the darkness. Hurriedly trying to retrace his steps, he saw a light in the gloom. On approaching it he found a group of fairies dancing in a circle. He was mesmerised at the sight and tried to sneak away when the fairies accosted him and asked him why he was loitering around in the desolate place all alone. The goldsmith told his tale of woe and the fairies, taking pity on him, taught him how to make gold leaf by blowing bubbles in the air. They also saw him safely down the fort early in the morning.

The goldsmith went back to his family and taught his sons the art of making gold leaves. As a result the family prospered again but a rival goldsmith heard the tale of how the old man had learnt the secret art and decided to venture into Nahargarh one night. Whether he met the fairies or not is not known but his badly mauled body was found on the ramparts of the fort. There are two flaws in the story: did fairies actually exist? And were gold leaves not made before early nineteenth century? But the sum and substance of it is that while one goldsmith prospered after a visit to Nahargarh the other lost his life because of his greed. You may believe it or not, but Colonel David was convinced that his grandfather's story was not unture, although he agreed that the greedy goldsmith might have been mauled by some wild animal.

The tale of Sawai Madho Singh's time is different. According to it, a Meena woman, who had been chased out of the house by her husband as she had given birth to only girls (five of them), climbed up to Nahargarh and was raped and killed by badmashes, who had found her asleep late at night and took advantage of the situation. The woman's body was discovered hanging from a tree and led to quite a sensation, with the Maharaja ordering the sentries of the place, from among the 1500 guarding the forts of Jaipur, to ensure that such incidents did not take place in future.

The latest incident in Nahargarh lends credence to the belief that it is not just an old fort but a medieval structure that is the focus of strange happenings from time to time. Something like what Major James Alexander had also once emphasised, citing an incident of his youth when he met a woman in tribal dress near Nahargarh while benighted during a shikar trip. It was a moonlit night and he was astounded when the mysterious woman asked him to marry her and no one else or he would regret it. But he did marry a girl from Agra, though he nearly died when as a Captain he led a regiment of Jaipur troops during the Third Afghan War at the time of Sawai Madho Singh II in 1919. The staff and students of St Xavier's School returned to Delhi quite bewildered by the trip.

Requiem For Masihi Shayari

THE era of *Masihi Shayari* or Christian Urdu poetry recitation will now virtually come to a halt because of the death of its patron, T David Lall, whose pseudonym was 'Ghayal'. Lall, a body builder and fitness expert, became an educationist under the influence of his late wife Aleline who started a chain of institutions and finally St Mary's Senior Secondary School in Ambika Vihar, past Paschim Vihar. His wife's demise resulted in Lall acquiring a religious bent of mind and he started holding Masihi Shayari sessions every year around the time of his birthday on 5 August.

Christians writing Urdu poetry were invited from all over North India to recite their poems at weeklong conventions during which he arranged for their boarding and lodging and rounded off the annual function with a grand party. This was something unique as there was no other forum in the country (nor even in Pakistan) which gave so much encouragement to a tradition begun in the nineteenth century when such shayars as the Italian Filoses and Portuguese De Sylvas, Fitrat and Maftoon, and the British Gardners of Etah – all writing impeccable Anglo-Indian Urdu poetry flourished. Among them was Ellan Christiana Gardner alias Raqia Sultan Begum who excelled in poignant verses at the expense of her lover: *Tujko qasam hai khuda ki jo zulm se baaz aiye* (you are abjured by God not to desist from your cruelty).

T D Lall, who passed away on 23 July 2017, aged eighty-three, was buried in the War Cemetery at Brar Square and will be remembered as one who revived the little-known saga of Indo-European Urdu poetry in Delhi with his wife who came from the distinguished Jacob family of the curled-up hair. One of her uncles, Solomon Sahib, was the Urdu tutor at St Peter's College, Agra, where the great revolutionary poet Josh Malihabadi also studied for some time. T D Lall's contribution has to be viewed in the light of the over 200-year-old history of Anglo-Indian Urdu poetry.

A paper written on the subject by father Thomas Smith fifty years ago, says:

> In the realm of Persian, Urdu and Hindi poetry and to a lesser degree in Sanskrit, the Europeans have made their contribution felt. It is to the painstaking research of Dr Ram Babu Saxena and some others, that we owe our knowledge today of the intimate interest and the assimilation of the domiciled European with Indian culture.'
>
> In his foreword to Dr Saxena's book, Sir Tej Bahadur Sapru said in October 1943, 'Judging by the test of classical writers of Urdu or poets of the front rank, the poetry of many of the Europeans and Anglo-Indian writers in Persian and Urdu cannot be described to be of the highest order and yet, it is remarkable that some of them at any rate should have written

graceful verse – In my youth I came across several members of the Indian Civil Service who knew Urdu remarkably well. I can recollect Dr Howard, who afterwards rose to be judical commissioner at Lucknow. Dr Hoey and Dr Fisher commanded very graceful and correct Urdu idioms. There was, however, one Irishman who, in my opinion, stood unrivalled forty years ago for his command of the Urdu language and that was Thomas Conlan, who for a whole generation was the leader of the Allahabad bar'. Dr William Hoey, was a scholar of great ability who occasionally also composed poems in Urdu. After retirement, he was a lecturer and reader in oriental languages at Trinity College, Dublin and at Oxford. An example of his Urdu verse is:

Hone ko hain is shehar men mashuq hazaron
Bechara Hoey ek hai kis kis ki khabar le

(There are many beloveds in this city, but only one poor Hoey, how can he take care of all of them).

Robert Paget Dewhurst ICS wrote ghazals in Urdu and his *takhulus* (pseudonym) was 'Saqib'.

Among the other notable European poets were Colonel John Baille, Sir John Shore (late Lord Teigmouth 'Shore'), General John Smith and Edward Henry Palmer, who was one of the very few distinguished orientalists who wrote fluently and flawlessly in Eastern Language. Besides English he knew Romany (gypsy tongue), Italian and French. His knowledge of Arabic, Persian and Hindustani was vast. He translated Moore's *Lalla Rookh* into Arabic verse and his *Paradise and Peri* into Persian verse.

Zara muskarakar chhidak do namak tum, Keh muh zakhm ka bemaza ho raha hai. (Smile and sprinkle some salt, the mouth of the wound is tasteless).

Shakishtah Khatri hai furqat saqi men kuch aisi, Bohat milti hai tute jam se soorat mere dil ki (I feel so broken in my longing that my heart greatly resembles a broken wine-cup).'

The number of Indo-British poets is perhaps the largest: Alexandar Heartherley 'Azad', General Joseph Benshey 'Fana', and Suleiman Shikoh Gardner 'Fana}, wrote copiously and are considered outstanding among them. Heatherley was one of the best exponents of the Urdu verse. He was the pupil of Nawab Zainul Abdin Khan 'Arif', (a pupil of Ghalib) and was descended from Baron Heatherley. He left a complete *diwan* of his poetry. The poetic work of Joseph Bensley 'Fana' in Urdu and Hindi is also considerable and he deserves to be ranked as one of the great Anglo-Indian poets. 'The poetic efforts of these European and Indo-European poets', says

Dr Saxena, 'demonstrate the great appeal and flexibility of the Urdu language. It gives one more proof, if proof is needed, of it being the lingua franca of India'. Tajamul David Lall was a latter-day keeper of this hallowed tradition till his death, 'Ghayal' (wounded) as he was by Cupid's arrow.'

Braving Delhi Summers Down The Ages

SUMMER is a harrowing time in Delhi but even it has certain natural safeguards which offset the effects of the blistering loo wind in the day and the sweaty nights. The loo may blow at its worst but there are sherbets and cool lassi as also juicy fruits like mangoes, melons, water melons, oranges and lemons, besides cool glasses of water that slake thirsty throats. The first sign of hot weather setting in is the call of the *koel.* Hidden in the leafy foliage of some tree, this little harbinger of the mango season coos the whole day long – pitching its voice high when children irritate it. From then until the first monsoon shower, the koel makes its presence felt all over in towns, villages and fields. Legend has it that the koel was once a proud beautiful princess who was punished for her pride. She sleeps in fairyland all through winter, and when the sun regains its scorching heat, in late April or early May, she hurries to earth. She wants to free herself from the curse and hopes that one day she will be rewarded for being able to lessen the weariness of summer – a chore she has been performing since time immemorial.

Closely following the koel to Delhi are the gypsy girls. They walk ever so gingerly in the lanes and bylanes, selling toys, curios and tribal bric-a-brac for a song. But the tribes are dwindling fast – and so are the girls. Perhaps it is modernisation that is driving the gypsies out of their nomadic existence or perhaps it is wanderlust which makes them give a wide berth to the fast-developing urban regions.

For a time they became puppeteers but television has spoilt the show. Now, their only forte is a fast-eroding tradition. Still they come in March, though in fewer numbers. There is Tara, coy beyond her years, and Malini, the flower gatherer and the best of them all, Bindia, who sings the prettiest songs and charms the children with her 'come-hither' look.

In two full months from March, the lambs born in the old quarter of Delhi have grown enough wool to require shearing. You can see them lying on the road with the shearer's knee on their throats looking as silly as only sheep can look. They do not know what is happening to them, but they seem to enjoy it and perhaps know that the fleecing will give them relief from the heat. The shearers are from Rajasthan, which has a sizable population of sheep. But after business is over there they move to neighbouring areas like Delhi and Agra in search of work. The ewes are mostly confined to houses in the thickly populated localities of Delhi. But the rams are trained in open spaces for fighting. They are taught to butt against the palm of their owner. And before their horns grow they would have tested their strength against tree trunks and walls to be ready for the Sunday evening bouts in the Red Fort grounds. Big bets are laid and garlanded rams, looking very self-conscious are taken in a procession through the streets to the arena with drums beating the call to battle. A lucky owner might make as much as Rs 10,000 on a bet.

Summer means good business for the *topee* sellers of Delhi, after the winter windfall. Gone are the days when *sola topees* were the fashion. Very few *Delhiwallahs* wear them now. And the newer *topees*, particularly the de Gaulle cap, are to adorn more shops than heads these past few years. But now the order seems to have changed. In April and May, there is a great demand for headgear, including the Robin Hood hat which rests more on the eyes then on the head. Scooterists seem to prefer it next to the white cricket cap which can be folded and carried in the pocket. Felt hats, of course, have long been out of fashion as also the *Turki topee* or fez with its dangling pigtail.

This is a busy season for Imamuddin, the water carrier, but not as busy as he would wish. He is one of the fast disappearing tribes frequenting the old quarter of the Capital. At sixty-five, Imamuddin is a lonely man who finds himself out of tune with modern times because of competition from the refrigerated water seller. He offers you a bowlful of water from his *mashak* (waterskin) with medieval grace, inquires about your welfare and exclaims *Alhamd-ul-Illah* (Praise be to God) with old world courtesy. He will accept anything provided you have enjoyed the drink. Imamuddin wistfully remembers the days gone by and relates the story of the 'Mir Sahib' who once left an expensive ring in his copper bowl. The romantic Mir had caught a glimpse of his beloved while drinking from the bowl.

Imamuddin claimed that, word of the day on which the 1857 uprising was to break out had been spread by water carriers in the bazaar to those awaiting the news. This expedient had been hit upon by Begum Zinat Mahal, Bahadur Shah Zafar's wife, to outwit British spies. His tale over, Imamuddin with a low *adab*, shuffles away to relate it, like the Ancient Mariner, to the next thirsty soul.

In May and June it is melon time again and the bazaars are laden with the musky fruit. Melons are grown in the sandy soil of the Jamuna by *Mali*s, *Kathchi*s, *Mallah*s *and Sheikh*s who migrate to Delhi every year from Shahjehanpur and Bareilly. They take the riverside fields on contract as early as March and prepare the soil for cultivation. First pits are dug in rows to a depth of three or four feet. Two seeds are sown in each of them, and the plants, which start coming up in about a fortnight, are protected by fences, usually made of grass. At night fires are lit to keep away predators like jackals and cattle that are very fond of the fruit and liable to damage whole fields in a few hours. Delhi melons are not as sweet as those grown in Lucknow and Agra but they are a delicacy all the same, especially the *Sarda*. The variety was imported to Delhi from Afghanistan some 400 years ago and like the *Mow kharbuza*s of Agra is sugar-sweet. Melons need heat and the scorching *loo* of May and June to sweeten them. The first monsoon showers end their season. Melons have been the subject of songs, poetry and legends. Babar was fond of them because they reminded him of the cool vales and streams of Kabul. The melon parties of Wajid Ali Shah, the colourful Nawab of Lucknow, have passed into legend. In Delhi the puppet Mughal Emperor, Jahandar Shah, bought all the melons on sale in the Capital on a summer's day after he had fallen in love with and married Lal Kanwar, a dancing girl who was inordinately fond of the fruit. Her friend, Zohra who was a melon seller by caste, was exalted to the high office of *kaneez* or maid of honour in the palace and it was 'melons, melons all the way' to the Red Fort.

With summer at its peak, the cry of the *attar-*

farrosh is heard again in the old city. You will find him in Chandni Chowk and in Jama Masjid, sitting on the roadside with bottles of perfume. They are antique bottles of odd shapes and sizes, reminiscent of the flasks and jars one sees in illustrations of Omar Khayyam. There is an indolent charm about him, and the perfumes he sells breathe of the enchanted woods, fairy castles and haunted streams of the Arabian Nights. The *attar*s are mostly made in Kannauj (UttarPradesh), where it is a cottage industry. Khas and Rat-ki-Rani are the attars which are in great demand in summer as they are supposed to be very cooling. Then there are the more modern ones like Mehboob and Firdaus and the all-time favourite Gul. Last night as one walked through the narrow Matia Mahal one heard the perfume seller cry, *Attar le lo*. The cry seemed to find an echo in the blind beggar boy who roams the street and he started singing with great emotion:

Gul mehboob ko pyara hai,
Mehboob ashiq ko pyara hai,
Magar Tujhe toh murjhai phool
Chaman se zyada pyare hain.

Translated into English, the song means: The rose is dear to the beloved, the beloved to the lover; but to the perfume seller the crushed petals of the rose of yesterday are dearer then the whole smiling garden.

The Mughal emperors, especially Bahadur Shah Zafar and his friend Ghalib were fond of melons and mangoes cooled in buckets of iced water. They ate them in the Sawan-Bhadon pavilion of the Red Fort before taking shelter from the hot sun in the Rang Mahal through which and the Dewan-e-Khas flowed water in an aqueduct. The princes spent the afternoons sending paper boats with messages of love to their beloveds in the *zenana.* Some of them cooled themselves in the *baoli*s or step-wells or bathed in the *Shahi Hammam*s with their fountains of cold and hot water and the fountain of perfume in between. At night boats were tied in the Jamuna so that the royals could sleep in the cool breeze flowing over the water. The practice started in Akbar's time in mid sixteenth century and continued till the reign of Muhammad Shah Rangila (1719-1748).

That was also the time when melodious songs were sung by the maids of honour for heat-stricken princesses who spread out their tresses to cool in the east wind known as the *purva.* The film song lip-synched by Sharmila Tagore harks back to those times, with the romantic lines: *Jaron ki naram dhoop aur garmiyon ki raat... Purvaian Chalen* (the mellow sunshine of winter and summer nights when the *Purvaiah* blows). It comes from as far away as the Bay of Bengal and is so soothing that besides gladdening love-sick hearts also revives snakes gasping for life. The British, who followed the Mughals, either escaped to the hill stations or tried to beat the heat with the help of *khas tatti*es and cloth *pankha*s pulled by servants or their women and children.

So who says summer doesn't have its delights in Delhi? There are no princes and princesses now and no boats are tied in the Jamuna at night for the sleep-weary. But still the populace faces the travails of the hot weather with the help of cool drinks, juicy fruits and, of course, the comfort of electric fans, desert coolers and air-conditioners (which sometimes are rendered useless by power-cuts). Those denied the luxury of air cooling gadgets pass the afternoons under shady trees and the nights under the open skies, despite the annoying mosquitoes, which however are blown away by the early morning breeze (*Naseem*) that gently lulls the common folks to sleep till dawn, when summer loses its sting and the rising sun casts its soft rays on one and all before another sizzling day. Summer woes end with the onset of the monsoon when the *papiha* (pied-crested cuckoo) calls and the rain beats down from dark clouds lit by lightning on the thirsty earth, making it smell sweet while the *Malhar raga* is sung in homes and music halls to welcome the advent of the rainy months of *sawan* with its widespread mirth and merriment – women swinging from trees, swaying in balmy breezes that infuse new life into the heat-ravaged souls and the withering grass in fields and gardens.

The Drums Of Durga

THE Drums of Durga have fallen silent after Dusshera 2018 even as her idols sink in the Yamuna and the dhakis prepare to return to their distant homes. But last week they beat loud and fast at the neighbourhood pandal, reminding one of

E M Forster's *The Hill of Devi* which he wrote while having an intense relationship with the gardener of his bungalow, assigned by Maharaja Tukoji Rao III of Dewas, whose private secretary he was in the early decades of the twentieth century. There's a 'Hill of Devi' also in Delhi, while one climbs up the steep road from Karol Bagh sloping into Jhandewalan, with its temple of Vaishnodevi at the incline but Forster missed seeing it.

However the drums of Durga are not beaten there but further up in Aram Bagh and in the reverse direction in the Puja Park next to the Christian Colony bordering D B Gupta Road. Here the talk is of the ones heard near the Mayapuri Government Press Colony. The drum-beaters Kanti Das and Shankar Haldar had come all the way from Kolkata to earn a pretty penny in Delhi, along with the idol makers of Kumartoli.

When the *Kash Phool* blooms, along with the Kans grass it's time for Durga's arrival with Lakshmi, Saraswati and her other sons Ganesh and Kartikeya. But before that the drum-beaters leave their semi-rural localities and head northwards, leaving the field clear for local dhakis to reap their windfall. Kanti and Shankar are actually farmers but at Puja time they turn dhakis. 'It is the call from *Ma* that makes us do so every year. She starts appearing in dreams while the summer is still instense and the only relief is the purabia wind that blows from the Bay of Bengal and brings in its wake seasonal songs of the still to come *sawan*, when the east wind helps the majhis to row their boats with greater vigour, for instead of trying to test its strength they glide along with the purbia powering the sails.' Well the dreams of the dhakis goad them to prepare for long journeys up country, by train, of course.

They treat them as yearly service to Durga Mai for without the drums being beaten how can the Pujas be completed? The pundit, waits for the drum beats to cease before he begins his prayer ritual and after it is over, the girls take over the scene as they dance with the dhunchis or incense containers in ecstasy, the drum beats egging them on to dance more vigorously. The roll of the drums always has a message conveyed by the dhakis. While the Pujas are still some days away the message is *Ma jaldi, jaldi aa* (come fast dear mother). And when the Pujas are underway the drums beat the welcoming tune of *Agman*, interspersed with the plea that Durga should stay on longer. At *Vijaydashmi*, after the women have finished with the revelry of *Sindur-Khela* or dabbing each other with vermillion as a farewell to the departing goddess, (just like the tearful one to a daughter going back to her in-laws place) the dhakis go with the processions in which the image or *pratima* is carried to the river banks for immersion. The drumbeats on the waterfront have a mournful note of parting, after which the drummers pick up the refrain of *Ma phir jaldi aana* as a bluejay or nilkanth flies heavenward. All these drummed messages are of course in Bangla and only the dhakis know how to make them vocal.

After the *bisarjan* the drummers stay on in Delhi for a few more days, tending to the big kettle drums they have brought with them, after which men like Das and Haldar catch the train back to Kolkata and thence to their villages, where eager families await them. From the money earned the dhakis take gifts for each family member, starting with the oldest to the youngest and a surprise one for the good wives who waited patiently for the return of their husbands, missing from home at festival time.

Shantanu Sen, former IG and Joint Director of CBI (relaxing in his Delhi home), remembers erstwhile days when Durga puja was a novelty in Jaipur, started by his great grandfather, Sansar Chandra Sen, brother of the famous doctor,

Hem Chandra Sen, who died in 1906, plunging Chandni Chowk into mourning, with all the shops closed as a mark of respect to the man who not only brought the gift of healing with him from Bengal but also started the first Durga Puja in the Capital, along with other pioneers starting with Sawai Jai Singh II.

The dhakis were persuaded to come to Jaipur and arrangements made for their stay in the palatial Sansar Villa which was home to Sansar Chandra Sen, Prime Minister of the princely State. That was the only place where the Puja was held.

The dhakis accompanied the procession on the arduous trek, beating the drums till the image sank in the water to cries of *Durga Mai ki Jai* (after which it was time for Kali worship in Amber). The sounds of the drums reverberated in the surrounding hills unlike in Delhi, where they reverberate on the banks of the Yamuna in a memorable tattoo, and then the 'Drums of Durga' are not heard till the next year, with the ritual going into hibernation.

Durga Puja In Jaipur

DURGA Puja in Jaipur has an interesting history which goes back to the time of Maharaja Man Singh who had brought an idol of Kali after his conquest of Bengal as Chief General of Akbar's forces in the late sixteenth century. He first installed it in Agra and then brought it to Amber where he initiated both Durga Puja and Kali Puja after the royal *purohit* told him that Durga had to be worshipped first and then Kali. In the early eighteenth century after Sawai Jai Singh II moved the State capital to newly-built Jaipur, the Durga Puja participants were only members of his family.

In late nineteenth century, Sansar Chandra Sen started holding Durga Puja for his relations and friends in the palatial house he occupied, known as Sansar Villa at the cross-section of Ajmer Road, MI Road, Station Road and Church Road in Jaipur. After his death his cousin and, later his son Avinash Chandra Sen, continued the family tradition. It was known as Barwari Puja. Then Durga Bari was built by the family on an open piece of land near where Jaipur Station is now located, thanks to Dr P C Roy. Purana Chandra Sen was the one who made Durga Puja popular for the Bengalis who had come as doctors, teachers, lawyers to the city. In the early 1940s and 1950s, Durga Bari Puja became a famous event due to the initiative of Hathi Babu (Kanti Mukherjee). Now there are five or six venues of Durga Puja, including those in C-Scheme, Jai Club near St Xavier's School and of course Durga Bari.

One remembers a Durga Puja when the pandal was flooded after unexpected rain and Mrs Banerjee, who trained boys and girls for the cultural show, had a difficult time in holding it. But then late in the night the rain and wind ceased, the half-moon came out smiling and the performance could be held on *Ashtami* – the day when *Astra* (weapons) *Puja* also takes place. Now theatre artistes from Delhi and Kolkata are specially invited for the cultural shows and on *Navami* night the strains of the music are nostalgic indeed because *Ma* would be leaving for her heavenly abode after a brief sojourn on earth with Lakshmi, Saraswati, Ganesh, Kartikeya who had all come with her to their maternal grandfather and grandmother's place from the snowy heights of Kailash.

It is worth noting that the Durga images are made by the artisans of Kumartoli of Kolkata, who come accompanied by the dhakis or drum-beaters all the way to Jaipur by train with a break at Delhi or Agra. The soil of Rajasthan is desert sand which is not very suitable for making the images and has to be mixed with soil brought from nearby non-desert States.

There is also a belief that the idol of Durga is not complete unless the clay is mixed with soil from a courtesan's *kotha.* Courtesans too are after all dear to Durga Maa whose love does not discriminate between people of various shades of society.

When the Alexanders of Ghat Gate and the Daribawallah De Sylvas were Sirdars of the Jaipur State court they were prominent among those present for *Astra Puja*. Major James Alexander was the head of the Am Khas Fauj which distinguished itself in the Afghan War of 1919 after the assassination of Amir Habibullah in Kabul. The Am Khas regiment was a part of the Jaipur State forces sent by the Maharaja to aid the British troops to quell the Afghan rebellion. Major Alexander distinguished himself with exemplary bravery, even though he was injured in the fighting.

The De Sylvas were Portuguese whose ancestor Don de Sylva was invited by Sawai Jai Singh II to help in the building of the Jantar Mantars and other astronomical projects of the enterprising Maharaja who was a close friend of the Mughal emperor Muhammad Shah Rangila. The Daribawallahs produced two noted poets of Urdu, Hakim Don Eltis De Sylva Fitrat and Hakim Don Augustine Maftoon who had merged themselves completely with the local populace and whose family women observed purdah even in church.

So the history of Durga Puja in Jaipur is a chequered one that links the Pink City to Portugal, Kolkata, Agra and Delhi and with the Mughal emperors too. Now, as a retired octogenarian, Shantanu Sen looks back nostalgically and, of course, with some pride – at the Durga Puja tradition started by his ancestors – pioneers in various fields, including medicine and administration, whom people still remember with great admiration.

Durga Pujas have begun to be held in other parts of the State too but the ones in this city are still special – with an aura of their own, thanks to the endeavours of the Sen Family. Meanwhile as the *Kash Phool* blooms, the dhakis beat the tune of *Ma jaldi, jaldi aa* and when she departs strike up the tune of *Ma phir jaldi aana* while the women play *Sindur-khela* in farewell to the eternal bride, Durga's departure enthuse many, including the girls dancing their hearts out with dhunchis (incense containers). And as the smoke curls up heavenwards the assembled devotees send up their prayers to the almond-eyed goddess with it. Thus does Jaipur celebrate *Pujo* from *Panchmi* to *Vijayadashmi*.

Owls For Slaughter

WHEN John Keats wrote about the Nightingale: 'Thou wast not born for death, immortal Bird/ No hungry generations tread thee down', he didn't mention the owl which too is spared by meat eaters because it is considered a bird of omen, whose hooting at night spells misfortune (sic). After Mahmud of Ghazni's ruthless invasions, his wise minister thought of instilling some sense into him. He took him out for a ride in the wilderness one night and pointed to two owls sitting on a withered tree under a waning moon. 'What are they doing?' asked the Sultan. The minister said 'one of them wants to marry off his female offspring to the male birdie of the other, who desires to know how many deserted villages the mother owl would give in dowry'.

The Sultan asked, 'What's the reply'? The minister said that as he knew the language of birds, he understood that the mother of the 'bride-to-be' responded that there was no dearth of deserted villages so long as Sultan Mahmud was alive. The revelation had its effect and Mahmud decided to sheath his sword after that.

Those fond of bird flesh can never think of making the owl (considered to be both wise and idiotic) part of the menu. But come Diwali and, believe it or not, the slaughter of owls begins for Kali Puja. They are highly priced at over Rs 30,000 a bird. But there are people in Delhi prepared to shell out even Rs 50,000. The reason being that the superstitious believe that sacrificing an owl on the night of Lakshmi Puja brings untold wealth as the goddess is compelled to stay in that house till next Diwali.

The trade is most widespread in Uttar Pradesh where owls are caught by Kalandars residing mostly in the Fatehpur Sikri area. The village of Korai-Karavili is notorious for clandestine trade in owls. Nearer to Delhi, Kosi Kalan is just as infamous for it. The tribals catch owlets and breed them for the festival of lights. A fully grown bird is by then ready for sale. Each of its body parts is a money-earner. The beak, the claws, the skull, the eyes and even the meat are all used in tantric puja on *Amavasya* night, preceding the new moon.

The one performing the puja is guided by a tantric well-versed in black magic. He has to avoid sexual intercourse, shave all unwanted hair, bathe at midnight, wrap a white dhoti around his waist, keeping the top portion of the body bare. After that he has to sit with closed eyes while the tantric recites the mantras in which the sanitary pad of a girl who has just attained puberty is burnt around the captive owl, which has been intoxicated with a strong drink. The stool of a new-born infant is smeared on the bird, covered by the petticoat of a bride worn on the wedding night. After that more rituals are performed taking care that no woman or child is around. The curse is that if a woman even peeps in out of curiosity she would become barren for life and if a child does so he or she would die an early death.

According to Ibrahim Bhai, who was born in Ibrahim Patti and died some years ago, there was a lot of mumbo-jumbo associated with the sacrifice of the owl (*vahan* of Lakshmi) and people greedy for instant wealth did anything ordered by the tantric. An old resident of Fatehpur Sikri, he claimed that owls were sacrificed at Diwali even during the decadent years of the Mughals. He mentioned that Muhammad Shah Rangila and before him Muizzuddin Jahandar Shah and his successor Muhammad Farrukhsiyar were some of them. Lal Kanwar, the concubine who was elevated to the exalted title of Begum Imtiaz Mahal by Jahandar Shah was the one whose menstrual cloth was used, he said. Ibrahim Bhai was no historian and semi-literate as he was, had heard such fanciful tales from his elders and their ancestors made weirder by years of repetition.

If history is to be relied upon, Muhammad Shah was crowned at Fathepur Sikri alright but spent Diwali in the Red Fort. After his defeat by

Farrukhsiyar near Agra, Jahandar Shah and Lal Kanwar escaped to Delhi where the ousted ruler met his end at the hands of the victorious nephew whose only association with Agra was the Delhi Gate he built there, twenty-six miles from Fatehpur Sikri.

A man called Kanje, because of his blue eyes inherited after an American soilder's affair with his mother, a kanjar woman, during World War II, used to breed owlets the year long and sell them at Diwali. He was warned that he would meet a bad end. Kanje, his wife and four children all died of tuberculosis within a short time. Was it the curse of the slaughtered owls? Owls are predators and help to clean up the environment. To invest them with magical powers is mere superstition which made even Shakespeare mention that among the weird stuff brewed by the Three Witches in *Macbeth* were parts of an owl, lizard and toad too. But to tolerate the wanton massacre of owls in our times is sheer madness. As for the wealth the ritual is supposed to bring, the less said the better or Fatehpur Sikri and Kosi would be teeming with *crorepaties*!

Armenian X'mas Link

CHRISTMAS is much the same everywhere but the medieval Armenian one was different. Even the Cross (that proclaims Christ's crucifixion) had its own peculiar shape, hardly seen in other Catholic or Protestant churches, except in old cemeteries, like the one in Agra which was once a Mughal orchard gifted to an Armenian lady by Akbar in the 16th century. In Armenian celebrations cakes were there, of course, but the emphasis was on animal sacrifices. The cakes and sweet breads were embellished with raisins (kishmish). No wonder non-Christians started calling Christmas *Kishmish*.

The visit of the former Armenian President, Levon Der Petrossian during Indira Gandhi's time was a reminder of the age-old ties between India and Armenia, two countries where the Aryan influence predominated. The visit of Vice-President Hamid Ansari in early 2018 was a follow-up to the one by Mrs Gandhi's to Yeravan.

Armenia is an ancient country which has been regarded as 'the doorway between East and West'. Mount Ararat, where Noah's Ark rested after the Deluge, was in the present Turkish part of Armenia and it was there that those who were saved from the great flood along with the patriarch settled down to create a new world. It was, therefore, natural for Christianity to take root there in its initial days. It is worth mentioning, however, that the old beliefs of the Armenians were incorporated into the Church for quite a long time. Animals were sacrificed in the church porch before the celebration of the Eucharist, especially at X'mas and Easter. The Armenians had started coming to the Mughal Empire some years before the invasion of their country by Turkey. They found the hospitality that they needed and built churches in Delhi, which however do not exit now. At Agra also they built a chapel and the son of a nobleman, Mirza Zulquarnain was brought up by Akbar. He was later to become the head of the salt works at Sambar. The Mirza is known as the Father of Christianity in North India because it was during his time that the cross and the crescent met in the Mughal capital.

Mirza Zulquarnain's palace occupied the land where the British later built the Agra Central Prison, which in recent times has made way for the ambitious shopping project known as Sanjay Place. It was on this piece of land that a cathedral was erected by the Capuchins 200 years later. The Armenians planted olive trees, one of which still survives near Akbar's church. The mystical cross was used as an emblem on even residential buildings. It is said that during Akbar's time after Christmas Mass the sick members of the congregation drank the water in which earlier a crucifix had been bathed. It was supposed to cure patients, or so the belief went. In the Martyrs' Cemetery at Agra are the graves of many Armenians which look like Muslim graves with Persian inscriptions. One of the graves, that of the saintly Armenian merchant, Khwaja Mortiniphas is still venerated, along with that of Father Santus. Some say he was related to the Bishop of Tabriz and became a hermit in later life after giving all his wealth to the poor. In Delhi the most famous Armenian tomb is that of Sarmad Shaheed at the foot of the Jama Masjid. Kishanganj, between old Delhi and Sarai Rohilla stations also has some Armenian graves, besides those of Dutch nationals some connected to the Mughal Court like Bibi Juliana. Incidentally, the Chief Justice in Akbar's reign was Abdul Hayee, an Armenian Christian.

There were two Armenian churches in Delhi, one near the slaughter house, beyond the old Sabzi Mandi, another in Sarai Rohilla; though accounts of their exact location differ. According to Sir Edward Maclagan, there were 120 Catholics in Delhi during Shah Jahan's reign in 1650. Their number went up to 300 by 1686, when Aurangzeb was on the throne. Two priests looked after them. A Catholic cemetery was also in existence from 1656. Father Desideri, who came to the city from Tibet, found the churches in ruins in 1732 (Muhammad

Shah's reign). He stayed on for three years and built a new Armenian church dedicated to the Virgin Mary and blessed on All Souls' Day, 2 November 1723. In 1739, this church and another Armenian one were destroyed by the Persian invader, Nadir Shah during the massacre of Delhi. One of the churches was rebuilt in 1746, and blessed on Christmas Eve. Later another Armenian church came up, but both seem to have been razed in the early nineteenth century.

When the Armenians held X'mas celebrations boys and girls dressed as angels greeted Akbar and later Jahangir at their church in Agra which still exists. After that the two emperors watched the Christmas play and later sent the ladies of the harem to see the crib depicting Christ's birth in a manger. Armenian X'mas is now a nostalgic memory but when the church bells peal for Midnight Mass at Christmas in the Cathedral near Akbar's church, the Armenian spirit is revived as the local Padritolians pull the ropes of the five huge bells imported from Belgium by the Italian Capuchin fathers. This tradition dates back to Armenian times, when one of the bells broke and was lifted with great difficulty by two elephants, who deposited it in the Mughal Kotwali till Jahangir had it repaired and restored to the old church.

Christmastide In The 1890s

JUST imagine Christmas of the 1890s. Rudyard Kipling was still writing on themes he had imbibed during his years in India while working for the *Civil & Military Gazette*, Lahore and the *Pioneer*, then published from Allahabad, whose editor later was the legendary Desmond Young and contributor Winston Churchill.

The 1890s was the time when Mahatma Gandhi was still in South Africa and Jawaharlal Nehru was just a few years old. But *Twinkle Twinkle Little Star,* the nursery rhyme, had already been written twenty years earlier by Ann Taylor and was being recited by children of the Anglo-Indian families in Alwar.

Besides it, as December came around, the festive spirit gripped the sahibs, memsahibs and *babalog*s. There was no boarding school for European and Anglo-Indian students in the Princely State so most of them were sent to study at Mount Abu or to St Peter's College, Agra, that was established in 1846, and St Patrick's School for girls that came up near it about the same time in the bungalow of a retired British General. The boys' school was under the Italian Capuchin fathers and the girls' one was supervised by the sisters of the Jesus & Mary congregation.

It was in this school ninety-three years later that the daughters of Harry Alexander of Jaipur, studied as boarders. They came home only for the summer and winter vacations, for which Harry Sahib went to Agra twice a year to escort them and their schoolmate Martha Francis back by the night train.

But let's talk of things earlier. Alwar State Forces, like Jaipur and many other States in Rajputana and elsewhere in India, were headed by European officers who missed 'White Christmas' back home and so celebrated a brown one, lit up by the cold stars of the year-end. While singing *I'm dreaming of a White Christmas/Just like the ones I used to know/When tree-tops glistened and children listened to sleigh-bells in the snow*, they revelled in nostalgia.

The children in Alwar listened (instead of the sleigh-bells) to the long-drawn-out wail of steam engines that drew the trains to Rajputana from distant destinations. Their drivers were Anglo-Indians and the jacks or firemen who shovelled the coal into the burning furnace of the engines, were boys from the same community who had dropped out of school with the ambition of becoming Mail and Express train drivers themselves some day. Among these boys was Raymond Wilson who used to come home for Christmas. He was a good singer who led the local choir and enticed the girls with his handsome looks and bulging muscles, not to talk of the puff that crowned his hair long before Dev Anand took to sporting one as his trade mark of attraction in filmdom. But he had copied Gregory Peck and not

Wilson who was some fifty years their senior.

On the cold Christmas week nights Wilson and the boys and girls of the choir went from house to house singing carols, *Silent Night, Oh, Come All Ye Faithful* and *Three Kings,* the most popular among them. On one such night when the choir had made its rounds, Wilson had to drop a girl called Holly home, who lived in the railway quarters far away. A freezing breeze was blowing and the two clung to each other. They clung so often that by the time they reached the railway quarters they had fallen in love and Wilson planted a sizzling X'mas kiss on her chaffed lips. They got married two years later after Holly had given birth to a bonny boy as a token of their night together one bleak X'mas Eve.

But beyond these youthful ventures Alwar also had a vibrant literary environment in those days in which Anglo-Indian families participated in plays, skits and musical competitions. Talking about English plays there is a memorable piece by Thomas Smith, written with the heading, *Mystery of an X'mas Play* that appeared in *The Statesman* long before his death in the 1995 Easter season:

> There is a peculiar building in Bagh Muzaffar Khan, Agra, known as 'East Lynne'. It was once owned by Helen Morton Plough, a widow, who

usually lived at the palace of the Raja of Alwar. But whenever she came to Agra, she resided at 'East Lynne'. Helen Plough was the daughter of Edward Emmanuel Plough and Mary Nicholas; Edward was the son of John and Marie Plough and the latter was the daughter of Colonel Francisco Meil of the Alwar State Forces. Helen had married Thomas Morton, a barrister, who died in 1917; she herself died, after losing her eyesight, some years later in England. They had no children.

People often wondered, as I did, why Morton's house was named 'East Lynne'. Today after some seventy years, it brings back nostalgic memories of my mother and her parents, who also hailed from Alwar, with whom I sometimes visited Helen Plough. The subsequent discovery in my quest that at Christmas 1893, William Burvett of Lucknow had staged a drama based on the novel *East Lynne*, the parts in which were acted by members of his family, added to my curiosity. The drama was staged at Agra, which was then an important centre of the European and Anglo-Indian community.

My own efforts to find the novel, *East Lynee* were not successful, but luckily for me, about this time, the well-known Urdu writer, L Ahmed Akbarabadi returned to Agra after a long absence. I decided to renew my acquaintance with him, hoping to hear more of his old days. We made conversation over a cup of tea and I was pleasantly surprised to learn that he was after all not as unfamiliar with English literature as people would generally think. He knew English to the extent that he had translated some of the fifteen best works in that language into Urdu.

For me, however, the more interesting point was that the first English novel L Ahmad read in 1911-12 was none other than the famous *East Lynne* by Ellen Wood and it was this work that had impelled him to delve deeper into English literature and translate into Urdu some of the works of Thomas Moore, Oscar Wilde, Anatole France and Leo Tolstoy.

Ellen Wood (1814-1887) was a prolific writer; she produced a number of novels, some of them running into several volumes and published in several editions. *East Lynne* was the craze of the time. It unfolded against the backdrop of two mansions in the English countryside, 'East Lynne' and 'West Lynne', the former figuring more prominently and hence the title of the book.

Now the question before me was that if Morton's house in Agra was named after the 'East Lynne' of England, was it not likely that a 'West Lynne' also existed somewhere in India? But how to find that out?

Inquiries addressed to the Raja of Alwar

elicited no reply. Mrs Helen Morton Plough did live somewhere about the palace but none knew if there was any building in existence that was once occupied by Anglo-Indians in the State Service and known as 'West Lynne'. After all efforts seemed to have failed, news dropped in from an unexpected quarter that there existed at Alwar a house called 'West Lynne' and that it was part of the Raja's property.

To this extent the mystery was solved, but the point whether there is more to it or not remains. Why were these people of French descent so much enamoured of the English novel to produce from it a Christmas drama and call their homes in India after two mansions in England? Was Helen Plough the heroine of 'East Lynne' (India), as Lady Isobel Vane was the heroine of 'East Lynne' (England)? To this extent then 'East Lynne' is still shrouded in mystery.

Incidentally, in later years Dr Yashpal Singh, the eye-surgeon, and his family resided at East Lynne. He was the eldest son of the famous surgeon Dr C B Singh whose second wife Winifred was an Anglo-Indian lady related to the famous Skinner family of Delhi. Winifred Singh's daughter Pamela married a noted Jaipur boy, Julian Francis while he was the Chief Manager of an Andrew Yule tea garden in Assam.

After Yashpal Singh's death his wife and grown-up children continued to reside in East Lynne, just opposite the house of the Kashmiri Thakurs, who ran the first news agency in Agra. Now East Lynne has fallen on bad days and the descendants of the Thakurs have sold their house at the crossroads after closing the news agency. So East Lynne is now more or less a forgotten legend which is however revived in the memories of old timers at Christmas time.

New Year's Eve 1857

WHENEVER the year draws to a close, one's mind goes back to New Year's Eve 1857 when the (British) Government Agency Committee was established in Delhi to investigate the actions of the Prize Agents, running almost lawless. That very evening the congregation gathered to pray for wellbeing in the coming year at the still-damaged St James Church while the Tommies danced at nearby Ludlow Castle and the others let their emotions merge with the strains of Auld Lang Syne.

Writing in her publication, *The Great Uprising: Untold Stories, Indian and British* (Supernova Press), Rosie Llewellyn-Jones observes: 'The (Prize) Agents, sanctioned by the British Army in India and the (East India) Company army, were licensed looters, whose job it was to raid houses and properties and seize anything of value to punish "the rebels."' She says, 'the misery caused by the Prize Agents… after the fall of Delhi and subsequent capitulation, cannot be underestimated. It led to disputes between the military officers, who began to regard property seized by their agents as belonging to the Army and not the Government. Civilian administrators like Sir John Lawrence complained bitterly but without effect to the Governor General that confidence among the Indian merchants could not be restored until the Prize Agents were reined in.'

James Gibbon, an army officer, wrote to his mother (in England): 'The people are all coming back to the city and the shops are being opened so that we shall have many things that we want. There has been a great deal of plundering, or as it is called here "looting"... We have to get some prize money but nothing has been ordered on that subject yet.' This was as much true of Lucknow as of Delhi.

The Prize Agents had been active since the autumn of 1857 and by December they had plundered as many houses, havelis, palaces and other properties as they could. It is pertinent to conclude that the royalty of Delhi was pauperised overnight. Begums surprised by white men in the zenana, who not only ogled at them but also manhandled them to make a mockery of the sacrosanct purdah system, screamed their hearts out, while *Baniya* merchants terrified by agents who threatened them at gunpoint revealed the hidden treasure that had been part of their family heritage. Nawabs, nawabzadas, Mirs, Mirzas and munshis – all found themselves in a similar predicament. The Red Fort gate had earlier been blown open by a 250-pound charge of gunpowder 'and though the king of Delhi was not as rich as the Nawabs of Awadh anything of value that was found was taken away. Charles Saunders, Commissioner of Delhi was among those who resented the actions of the Prize Agents.'

Rosie L Jones goes on to say that 'those troops

who were not plundering were drunk and incapable of action for several days.'

'It is tempting to imagine what would have happened if the sepoys, who had held Delhi for four months, had been directed by an inspired leader. A determined attack on the city... would have found little resistance. But the sepoys had moved on.' It is well known that the Prize Agents and their Indian informers tore up house floors, broke down bathroom walls and dug up courtyards to gain access to the riches hidden there. But even among the Agents surely there were men who halted in their tracks out of pity for an old man or woman or a pretty girl bereft of parental protection, who had captured their heart or an orphaned child. That was the scene that had continued until 31 December but before the sun set the government of the day constituted the high-profile committee to control the unbridled actions of the Prize Agents. So when New Year's Day 1858 dawned, many in Delhi, including Sahibs and Memsahibs picnicking on the Ridge, must have heaved a big sigh of relief.

Two miles away, the sweetmeat sellers and wine merchants of Chandni Chowk probably did their best business since the city was stormed on 20 September, thanks to the Firangi revelers. The lucidly written stories of the Mutiny, 'dedicated to all the victims' provide ample scope for the reader to imagine more than meets the eye in cold print.

New Year's At Ludlow Castle

LUDLOW Castle was demolished in the late 1960s. It owed its inception to Dr Samuel George Ludlow, surgeon of the East India Company days, at a time when the likes of William Fraser and Colonel Skinner, along with the Maratha nobleman, Hindu Rao were among the cream of Delhi society. At the castle, built in the second decade of the nineteenth century in imitation of a large castellated house in Dr Ludlow's village in England, a motley group of Firangi men and women collected to celebrate Christmas and the New Year.

It was the exclusive sahibs' Delhi Club and much later admitted a few Indian businessmen, educationalists and other bigwigs. Also joining in the celebrations were Tommies (English soldiers) stationed in the Red Fort after the revolt of 1857 as a safeguard against another uprising in sympathy with Bahadur Shah Zafar who had been sent into exile, and the Mughals decimated. The Last Emperor's *Samadhi*, Mirza Illahi Bux, whose daughter had married a son of Zafar and who used to stay at Chandi Mahal was however among the survivors.

Two of his sons, Mirza Suleiman Shah and Prince Soraya Jah also enjoyed a high status in society but they were not among those who took part in the activities at Ludlow Castle. After the death of Fraser and Skinner and also Sir Thomas Metcalfe, the latter's heir, Sir Theophilus Metcalfe was still around and visited the club sometimes by driving in his carriage from Metcalfe House (known to Delhiwallahs as *Matka Kothi*). Would you believe that Hindu Rao, brother-in-law of Maharaja Daulatrao Scindia of Gwalior, played Santa Claus and distributed gifts to the ladies who had attracted his attention, bohemian as he was?

New Year's Eve at Ludlow Castle was a grand affair with a forenoon picnic at the Ridge, a lip-smacking lunch (of rabbit pie and vindaloo) and a sumptuous dinner which followed drinks and a ballroom dance at which many a couple tied the bond of love. Theodore Jones and Dorothy Smith were one such pair who swore eternal friendship. Douglas Hynes and Victoria Marian also decided to get hitched, but Norah Nicholson and James Brown had a misunderstanding as Norah felt that the tipsy James was ogling another girl, Dolly who came and sipped from his glass, and then sang *Auld lang syne*, holding his hand. Sadly enough, they broke up the next morning, when New Year's Day was only a few hours old, if old Mrs Violet Maguire's yarns be true.

She used to live in a bungalow on Ludlow Castle Road and when one met her in the 1950s the Anglo-Indian matriarch was eighty-six years old and a great repository of the gossip of the days when Rudyard Kipling was writing for *The Pioneer*, along with Winston Churchill. 'But his stories were avidly read in Delhi', asserted Mrs Maguire.

She was a near-nonagenarian when Bombay House in Ludlow Castle Road was converted into residential quarters for teachers of the newly-opened St Xavier's School. Quite a contrast to the New Year festivities at Ludlow Castle were the celebrations at Bombay House (more than sixty years later) where stayed the Beckwiths, the Halges, the Dawsons, the lively young couple of Maxie and Ann and hockey wizard George Marthins, who scored the winning goal for India in the 1928 Amsterdam Olympics.

Old Mr Beckwith had been a police officer in Bihar but had become an invalid after retirement He was being looked after by his wife who had passed some of her younger days in the Agra Fort, where the families of the British and Anglo-Indian members of the armed forces stayed in the pre-war years. The Gardners were the descendants of Lord Gardner after whom Gardner's House was named. They belonged to Kasganj in Uttar Pradesh where the family had settled down on the vast estate of their illustrious ancestor. Alan Gardner was the head of the family in the 1960s and for the villagers and his relatives still very much the Lat Sahib in-charge of the *haveli* and *bibikhana* of the first

Lord Gardner, who had married a princess of Cambay.

Mr Dawson had been in the erstwhile Ceylonese Navy, and though a physical instructor then, could enliven an afternoon with tales of his encounters with smugglers in Palk Strait. Mr Halge was a big-built man with lantern jaws who sometimes related family yarns like the one about his grandfather, who once spent his entire salary wiping himself during a bout of dysentery on a train. Ironically they were all crisp notes which in the dark bathroom he mistook for the roll of tissue paper he was carrying in the other pocket. Eric Gardner recounted a tale about a headless ghost at the Kasganj bibikhana.

The Honourable Gardner swore that the tale was true and dated back to 1867 when the first train steamed into Delhi with a piercing whistle on the midnight of New Year's Eve. Few remember Ludlow Castle now whose site is occupied by a model school, while the old Delhi Club is beyond the ken of living memory. Probably the spectre still haunts the bibikhana. Meanwhile far away from Bombay House Ann fights for life in distant Melbourne, with Maxie at her side, while the bedroom stereo plays the perennial ditty, *Can auld acquaintance be forgot and days of auld lang syne*!

Bygone New Year's In Jaipur

NEW Year's Eve at the Dariba was a grand affair but the one at the Alexanders' thatched-roofed bungalow was no less memorable. The land on which it was situated originally belonged to the Jaipur Raj but Sawai Madho Singh II gifted it to Major Alexander one X'mas for his heroic role in the 1919 Afghan war. There was a *gharial* (old-time ghanta clock) in one corner from which a gong was sounded every day but also at midnight on 24 December for Christmas and on 31 December to herald New Year. Around the gharial *patuas* for X'mas jelly were grown by Alvina Bua and troughs of water were placed on top of it for pigeons to drink water from. Not far from the gharial was a well from which the Am Khas troops of the Major got their drinking water supply in the absence of piped water. The well was also used to water the garden on the west, which was supposed to be haunted throughout the year, except in the Christmas season 'when holiness pervaded the place' – or so it was believed. Even the chameleons (the big *girgits*) disappeared from sight during this period, said the khansamas who served the Alexanders during Yuletide.

The outhouses in the vast compound were leased or given gratis to two Indian Christian families, the Francis' and the Montrose', who claimed Scottish descent, like the poet Benjamin Montrose 'Muztar', who was a pupil of Ustad Daagh Dehlvi and who wrote some excellent ghazals for Christmas but is best remembered for the couplet he composed on the death of his Ustad: *Ek Daagh tha, so woh bhi toh, Muztar guzar gaya / Baqi bacha hai kaun Abh Hindostan mein* (There was a Poet Daagh who is no more. Now there is no other great poet left in Hindustan).

The two local Christian families earlier lived elsewhere but moved to the new location on New Year's Day 1888 to be nearer the Sacred Heart Church outside Ghat Gate where they could attend Sunday and festive season Mass. The church was built in the 1860s after the site chosen for it earlier had to be abandoned as digging revealed that there was a dried up reservoir underneath of Sawai Ram Singh I's days which once supplied water to the Walled City. The first Mass in the then only Catholic Church was held on New Year's Eve, 1865 and was attended by sisters from the nearby convent and a few Christian families. Prominent among them were the Alexanders and the De Sylvas of Portuguese descent, whose astronomer ancestor, Don de Sylva was invited to Jaipur by Sawai Jai Singh II for help in building his Jantar Mantars. Incidentally, there are now five Catholic Churches in Jaipur, besides Protestant ones, which are all gaily lit for the year-end Christmas and New Year services.

Christmas was a big celebration but New Year's

Eve was no less spectacular for Jaipur Christians. Naney Joseph had a large family with sons, grandsons and great-grandsons – all of whom were married and together with their wives and kids, filled up the church. The old man was eighty in 1947 but still active enough to take charge on festive occasions. His ancestors had been Tyagi Brahmins from Mewat who had migrated to Jaipur in mid-nineteenth century after facing a tough time during the revolt of 1857 as they were converts. For this they were attacked by those who considered them as stooges of the British. But though some perished, the rest managed to survive by declaring their allegiance to the Mughal emperor. Their dhoti-kurta dress and dehati lingo lent credibility to their claim that they had changed their religion but not customs, celebrating Diwali and Holi too besides Christmas and the New Year.

When the British retook Delhi and Bahadur Shah Zafar was sent into exile in Rangoon, they thought it was time to bid goodbye to those who had spared their lives by proclaiming their innocence. After that the Tyagi Christians began to be regarded as friends by the local population, particularly by the inhabitants of Ghat Gate. In the changed circumstances they were greatly sought after by non-Christian families seeking favours from the new dispensation in Delhi.

Well the Tyagi Christians now coming into their own celebrated church festivities with greater fervour. At Christmas they sang bhajans of *Nanna Balak Yesu* and at New Year's *Naye sal-ke-geet*. It was in the evening that the whole community congregated to bring the sun down with singing and dancing. There was typical rural *naach-gana* and also some ballroom dances learnt by the girls from English lady teachers.

According to the late Rehmat Masih, New Year's Eve 1947 became a glamorous event as it was the first time that it was being celebrated after Independence. Refugees from Punjab and Sindh did not quite understand what all the gaiety was about as they were not familiar with such celebrations. But those were times when even old women danced at Dariba House, which was gaily illuminated with diyas and bunting on 31 December.

Andrew and his brother Philip, who were children then used to talk about the post-azadi *Naya Sal*. Bannu Chacha, who had finished off half a bottle, decided that after the young people had enjoyed themselves, no woman would cook *khana* at home and stuff brought from the non-veg dhabas could be eaten. The pulao-zarda arrived, along with tandoori rotis, korma and kababs. Some ate to their heart's content while others were still on 'liquid diet'. Their wives and mothers, following the old custom of eating after the males, passed the time singing to the beat of the *dholak* and the tunes of the harmonium. Perpetua Bua, Kali Mumani and Ganno Bhabi clapped as they were too old to sing because of cracked voices, but Allo Bua and Sanno Ba's wife added to the fun by showing off their dance *thumka*s in imitation of the bais of the bazaar. Then William Sahib, who had had one too many, took hold of the dholak and beckoning the others staged a qawwali until he swooned away mid-way and Keti Ba, taking off his turban, crowed like a cock, to make the others realise that it was past midnight and New Year 1910 had begun. Everybody then sang in unison, *Naya sal phir se aya hai/mubarak ho mubarak ho,* and the assembly broke up to sleep till dawn, when it was time to go to church for the New Year mass. But before that Chhinga Bhayyia kissed his new bride and made her blush. They had been married just before Christmas by the saintly Father Polycarp, who subsisted on the leaves of the Ardo tree, after giving away his dinner to the Muslim khansama who prepared it so that he could feed his large, impoverished family and whose matriarch, Zarina Bibi always remembered the priest while offering namaz.

As stated earlier, for the Daribawallahs and the Alexanders' Christmastide and New Year's were occasions, besides Easter, when they could really let their hair down and celebrate with gusto. However the Dariba women restricted their activities to the Zenana but the Alexanders had no such inhibitions. As for the Francis family, Joey Sahib (his father died in 1909) who had been adopted as a son before the Kaptani (as Major Alexander's wife was known) had conceived several years after marriage, preferred to have a quiet Christmas and New Year's with readings from the Bible and constant prayers. But his wife Alvina and her friend, Agnes of the Montrose family along with daughter Vicky, who was still to give birth to pretty Alice, joined in the celebrations of the Anderwallahs (as the Alexanders were called by those living in their outhouses) to add the Desi touch to Anglo-Indian customs.

In those days the festive season of X'mas began on 1 December, as if to abide by what Shakespeare wrote – that the month of Christ's birth brings joy both in heaven and on earth. No ghosts, spectres or spirits haunted the land and the cock bird crowed throughout the night to proclaim the fact.

After shopping for new clothes, the maida, atta, mewa, ghee, butter and eggs began to be collected from the first week of December for the making of cakes which were baked three days before Christmas by Abdul Sattar, the old baker. The first cakes were eaten on 23 December and the last ones on 6 January, Epiphany Day or Twelfth Night, marking the feast of the Three Kings or Wise Men who came to worship Christ and after whom the Weizeman family of Jaipur was erroneously believed to be named.

This feast marks the end of the New Year celebrations. Now things have changed and only Adrian of the Alexander family survives after the death of his parents and brothers, Andrew and Allen. The Daribawallah family is also now disintegrating. No wonder X'mas and New Year festivities are not as lively as they used to be. Even the Major Sahib's thatched bungalow no longer exists and the whole compound has changed complexion with new structures coming up. The old times have become just a memory. As New Year 2018 approached one looked up at the moon from above a flat in Jawahar Nagar and recited Omar Khayyam's rubaiya:

Now the New Year reviving old Desires
The thoughtful Soul to Solitude retires
Where the White Hand of Moses on the Bough
Puts out and Jesus from the ground Suspires.

Patriarch Moses had a white hand and Jesus rose again from the dead.

But Lord Tennyson took a different view when he exclaimed, 'Ring out the old, ring in the new'. The Victorian poet was inspired by the ringing of church bells on New Year's Eve to bid goodbye to the old year and welcome the new one. The Sisters of St Angela Sophia School, Jaipur ring the bells though they used to be helped once by a girl, Laura George, who died in childbirth on 10 December, 1935 at the age of 21, and on whose demise the poet Maikash Akbarbadi wrote the pensive lines,

Na aye raas – e chaman ko woh naubahar hoon mein
Kisi ke aish do-roza ki yadgar hoon mein

(I am the blossom that did not bloom – a reminder of someone's two days of happiness.)

Well how long happiness lasts is a moot point. But even so we all hope to be happy in the New Year after the trials and tribulations of the old one.

Holi Through Vivid Colours

HOLI has its own nostalgia which lingers throughout the year, what with film scenes and songs extolling the festival, day in and day out. But long before Rajesh Khanna's *Hum toh khelenge Holi* and a similar number featuring Amitabh Bachchan, a bus full of students gatecrashed into Nandgaon, with enterprising girls of BA (Part II) among the lot. One of them was dressed as 'Radha', the boy Krishna's sweetheart – and Radhika Das indeed enjoyed the role she was persuaded to play.

Named after Baba Nandalal, the village is not far from other religious sites in Mathura district and Radha's own village, Barsana. The villagers greeted the party with some apprehension, wondering what they were up to. That was in 1958 when few tourists, foreign and Indian visited the place for *lathmar Holi*. Radhika was presented as the betrothed of Kishan Lal to justify her closeness to the boy.

In the battle of colours that followed the students were at the receiving end as the aggressive rural folk made them feel like lightweights. Doused with a thick coat of gulal, mixed with green, blue and yellow paste, they were a sight to behold, especially the girls and 'Radha' in their midst. The bus journey back saw many of the boys still reeling under the stupor of *bhang* and the girls 'mothering' them. The reception at home was severe because of the sad state in which the boys were – soiled clothes, hair stained with myriad colours and the bizarre look that bhang gives to the countenance.

The girls, however, got off lightly as they did not look so dishevelled.

Another memory that lingers is of Joseph Sebastian Paul, whose parents reprimanded him even more severely for playing Holi in the fasting month of Lent in which smearing with colour was not permitted in the community. Here is a recollected version of Joseph's account, with some variations that forgetfulness obviously brings over the years:

> To make up for that loss, many families in Delhi and the neighbouring cities played Holi before they began the period of fasting. General Ochterlony and his thirteen Bibis revelled in Kashmere Gate, and then William Fraser daubed his countryside companions (with whom he had fathered blue-eyed children) with the colours of Fagun in the area that now forms part of Haryana and so did his friend, Colonel Skinner.

In this context memory brings to mind the Indo-Armenian Albina Francis Bua who used to come from Ghat Gate, Jaipur just to play Holi with her near and dear ones, especially her daughters-in-law. She would arrive at the ancestral house, acquired by her grandfather in 1869, in a tonga, from the station and even while climbing the stairs would make her intentions clear, calling out loudly to her eldest daughter-in-law, 'Bahu I've come to play Holi'. It was only then that many in the family realised that Lent was approaching. To get the red powder, *gulal*, days before the festival of Holi was a problem that the youngsters in the house had to encounter. The boys used to run up and down the Ghattia Bazaar looking for gulal. Moti, the grocer used to be at his wits' end wondering why on earth somebody wanted the red powder long before the arrival of Holi. He would rummage among his tins and eventually produce some left over from the previoius year. If the gulal available was not much, charcoal paste was prepared discreetly in the house. If that too was not enough, *potamitti* (Fuller's earth) paste was also made. Then suddenly on Shrove Tuesday morning, the house echoed to cries of shock and surprise as unsuspecting members were liberally painted with the gulal, charcoal paste and potamitti. The children fast asleep would get up crying, wondering what was happening in the family with the elders smearing each other and running after those trying to escape.

Round and portly and looking like Queen Victoria, in whose reign she was born, Albina Bua would be in her element, laughing away and coaxing her younger companions to enhance the fun. Her elder sister-in-law, Sussana Bua was not as amused but nevertheless allowed herself to be daubed with colour. Ellias Sahib, who also hosted a Holi gathering at his house, was known to have courted his future wife at one such event. No wonder she came to be known as 'Holi Bua'.

All this fun and frolic ceased after Independence. Albina Bua died long ago. Ruby Bhabi, her husband Tim, sister-in-law Natalia, and brothers-in-law James and Peter and Aunty Sybil too are no more. Dead also are the Jailor Sahib, his wife and daughters. The youngsters of those days are old people and do not play Holi on Shrove Tuesday (the day on which people are shriven of their sins) while their children are not even aware that such a festival was observed in their family.

Incidentally, Radhika got married to the engineer who had been chosen by her family but he died in an accident, leaving her childless. She then wed Kishan Lal who had been in touch with her even after college. She bore him two sons who must themselves be married men now, though their parents are dead. Whenever Holi comes around one is reminded of the couple and the long-ago outing to Nandgaon with Radhika's portrayal of Radha which by a quirk of fate turned into reality. Joseph and his Australian wife, however, live in Melbourne with vivid memories of Christian Holi.

The Mithaiwali selling sweets

The Historic Taste Of Festive Sweets

SWEETS become more mouth-watering during festivals especially at the time when *Vrat*s or fasts are observed. There is no religion in which sweets, of which there are a thousand kind, do not take prominence in celebrations. X'mas, New Year's,

Id and Bakrid all cater to the sweet-tooth, but during Holi, Diwali, Dussehra mithai is in greater demand, probably more than in any other religion. Now that we are approaching the Dussehra-Diwali season, it will be sweets, sweets and more sweets even during the Navratras. Legend says it was a laddoo given by Shiva to Parvati that made her conceive. The history of sweets goes back at least five thousand years if not more. They were there in the Ramayana and Mahabharata days in India. Egypt, Greece and Rome had them too – and earlier still the Phoenicians. Some assert that their traders came to buy not only jewellery, cloth and spices but also basketfuls of sweets made from ghee, milk, khoya, dahi and sugar.

Rama's wedding to Sita was significant because of the large number of sweets served, some say nine kinds. The saying goes, *Baman uchle nau, nau haath*. The Brahmins were so happy that they jumped up to nine arms' length. When the *shradh* of Raja Dasarath was held after Rama's return to Ayodhya, thousands of *thaal*s full of mithai were served and among the uninvited guests were the sun and moon gods, Surya and Soma or Chandrama, dressed as Brahmins. They ate so much that the food got exhausted and the sweets too. Rama's brothers asked for more *halwa-puri, sabzi, kheer, pedas, laddoos* and other sweets to be made. When Rama heard this he went up to the two voracious eaters and discovered their real identity. The two gods folded their hands in greeting and disappeared.

When Draupadi was brought home by the Pandavas, their mother is said to have offered *kheer* to her as there was no other sweet to welcome the new bride. During the exile of the Pandavas, Draupadi is said to have offered half a stale laddoo to Lord Krishna (very fond of sweets). But as soon as it came into his hands it turned fresh and wholesome again. In contrast Rajas and Maharajas had huge laddoos made at festivals and marriages inside which were hidden *asharfis* (gold coins). Helen of Troy probably ate Trojan sweets, after her abduction by Prince Paris, when she came into the presence of her lover's father, 100-year-old King Priam and his consort Hecuba. Perhaps she found them tasting different than the ones she had in Greece at the home of her husband Menelaus whose merchants brought cloth and *mithai* from India. Cleopatra, Queen of Upper and Lower Egypt, must have been offered Roman sweets by her besotted lover Antony, quite unlike the ones she had tasted in her Pharaonic palace. She had maids from Malabar who made both food and their desi sweets for her.

It was a Jewish sweet that won over Rebecca's heart when she met her distant cousin Jacob (Israel) the grandson of Abraham. The Prophet Muhammad is believed to have told a woman (who had rashly vowed to eat her refuse if her wish was granted) that she should sit down below the house of a moneylender (*soodkhor* who charged interest on loans) and whatever rubbish she ate would taste like sweets. Well these are stories, like King David eating the loaves of presentation to God as he was hungry, whose veracity by and large may be doubted but they show the special place of sweets in the life of all nations and communities. Even in ancient times Indian mithai was exported and was a craze in many countries.

When the English took over Delhi after winning the Battle of Dilli under Lord Lake, they settled down in Chandni Chowk. When Christmas came they could not eat the Western confectionery they had ordered from Calcutta, as it had got delayed. So they ate sweets from the shop of Ghantewala, established about a decade earlier and liked them so much that even their Resident at the Mughal Court, General Ochterlony had mithai every evening along with his thirteen *bibi*s. Same was the case with his successor William Fraser.

The shop of Ghantewala, which ceased to exist a few years ago, was patronised since 1893 by Shah Alam who used to send for sweets from it on festive occasions – both Muslim and Hindu. *Parmal-ki-mithai* was among his favourites. Even on other days he would send his servants on elephant-back to buy sweets. The story goes that the elephant used to ring the bell hanging in front of the shop to alert the shopowner who would first give sweets to the jumbo before taking the royal order. How much sweets were bought is difficult to guess but the whole royal harem ate them, princes, princesses, queens and, of course, the Mughal ruler.

Before that the *Dastarkhwan* of Shah Jahan had a sumptuous spread of dishes and also sweets which were eaten as dessert. The emperor did not like eating with the English merchants at his court as they ate with unwashed hands and drank water during the meal, when etiquette demanded that they did so either at the beginning or end of the meal. The Firangis preferred to eat the sweets offered by putting them in toilet paper so that their hands did not get soiled. This was highly displeasing to Shah Jahan as they used the same kind of paper in the bathroom.

A story is told of Aurangzeb that Hazrat Bhure Shah, a saint of his time whose abode was just below the walls of the Red Fort, had displeased the emperor. Aurangzeb one day sent a whole thali of sweetmeats to him. He wanted to test the powers of the saint – whether he could distinguish the stuff sent. Bhure Mian told Aurangzeb that what he had sent may be *bhala* or *haram* but left it to the emperor's conscience to decide. This meant he had guessed what really lay in the dish under the sweets – dog-meat. The same emperor offered wine and mithai to his brother Murad whom he had imprisoned in the Red Fort, after slaying his elder sibling Dara Shikoh. When Murad was dead drunk he was murdered.

His mother Mumtaz Mahal's fondness for sweets was well known and after each of the fourteen deliveries she had, several *thal*s (dishes) full of sweets and fruits were presented to her and her maids of honour. Shah Jahan, who fulfilled his beloved wife's every wish, incidentally, was the one who is said to have created the sweet *petha*, not only as dessert for the 20,000 odd workers building the Taj but also as nourishment for them. Even to this day the city of the Taj is famous worldwide for its petha. As a matter of fact, it was believed that basketfuls of petha were bought by the jinns from the Mithai-ka-Pul every night for their human sweethearts. Mithai-ka-Pul or bridge of sweets was not confined to Agra alone. Delhi also has a Mithai-ka-Pul in the Pul Bangash area but whether jinns visited it too is not known.

In Parathewala Gali of Chandni Chowk people who eat different kinds of paranthas end the meal by eating the sweet put on their *pattal* (plate made from sal leaf). A favourite is *rabri*, though some prefer *rasmalai. Jalebis* and *imarti* of Chandni Chowk are also famous as is the *kulfi* cooled in ice. While Odisha, Bihar and Bengal vie for the honour of having introduced *rasogolla,* it is Delhi which not only savours this sweet but also its twin, the gulab jamun that makes the mouth of everybody water. *Halwa-sone* also takes pride of place, more so as it is not as sweet as *gulab jamun* and even people who don't have a sweet-tooth can enjoy it.

Besides Chandni Chowk, Ajmal Khan Market and Bengali Market are also famous for chaat and sweets. Nathu's is a famous sweet shop and so also Haji Kallan's joint in Matia Mahal. Not far from it is Shreen or the palace of sweets. It is here that people congregate on festivals to enjoy mithai.

All in all, the amount of sweets made and consumed in Delhi during the festive season is anybody's guess. One conservative estimate puts it as 300 maunds per day. This, despite the fact that doctors keep advising people to avoid sweets at Holi-Diwali-Dussehra because of the risk of diabetes. But who listens? As an added zest the bhang laddoos of Holi are relished by some not so much for sweetness as for the kick they give because of the intoxicant in them. Talking of laddoos, *besan* ones are said to be medicinal in their effect. *Moong-ki-dal* laddoos are also for those not with a sweet-tooth. *Peda*s, both brown and white are just as delicious as *khoya barfi* – plain and the one embellished with condiments like pistas. *Khurma* and *balushahi* are also less sweet than other mithai but *kalakand* is a hot favourite, along with *gajar halwa. Boondi* and laddoo on Tuesdays are offered to Lord Ganesha and Hanuman. During Dussehra these are dedicated to the Devi-Durga Mata. But sweets at Diwali are an offering to Lakshmi, the goddess of wealth, along with *kheer-batasha. Khurchan* is cream scraped from the milk cauldron and sweetened. According to a Turkish doctor who visited the court of Aurangzeb, Indian sweets contained the pleasures of heaven and hell combined. Heaven when they were eaten at ease and hell if someone ate as a glutton.

Barfi may be the most expensive sweet but its variant made of *besan* is the delight of the villagers who cannot afford the high-priced white burfi, covered with silverfoil. To the wide array of mithai have been added cakes, pasteries, chocolates, toffees and puddings of late. However there is a difference between North Indian, South Indian, East Indian and west Indian sweets. They are made differently and also have different tastes. In the North sweetness is more than in the other varieties except *sandesh* and this goes for Lahore sweets too because the culture of Delhi and Lahore, along with that of Agra, has been the same for centuries. After Partition, Karachi, where most of the refugees from North India settled down, also boasts of the same assortment of sweets and, believe it or not, also has a Chandni Chowk street as a reminder of the good old days spent by the *mohajir*s in Delhi at a time when the sweet shops of their forefathers were situated in Fatehpuri. But the best *petha-dalmot* came from the shop of Bhimsen Baijnath. Now Panchhi has taken over and its shops abound everwhere. So sweet festival days to one and all, for as Shakespeare said, the last taste of sweet like music, lingers on – one in the mouth and the other in the mind. No wonder the *Purabia halwais* of Delhi are so famous.

Begum Of The Road & The Nawab's Wife

WHY are vintage cars left to rust? With proper maintenance it should be possible to use them for short distance trips. I knew of a man who had an old Austin of 1930 vintage which he kept in a good condition and used for marketing, sightseeing and dropping his grandchildren to school. Rao Bhavani Singh belonged to Jaipur where his ancestors once graced the durbar of the Maharaja. Independence came and with it the merger of the old princely States into the Indian Union, followed by the abolition of *zamindari*. The Raos lost their special privileges and many of them found it difficult to live a life of luxury.

But Rao Bhavani Singh's family was different. They invested whatever they had into business and soon were just as well off as in the good old days when elephants and horses were among their possessions. Later it was cars and they had at least six different models, including Marutis. But those were for the younger lot, who drove them at break-neck speed. The Rao's pleasure trips, however, were always in the old Austin which he drove slowly through the congested roads of Jaipur and into those open spaces which gave him the thrill of being close to nature. I accompanied him on one of his excursions. We went past Amber, and then parking the car climbed a hill from which we could see the city of Jaipur spread before us like a map. The fortress of Nahargarh loomed in the distance. It did look like a tiger crouched for its prey. The Rao waxed eloquent on the history of this citadel which once contained the princely treasure.

'The Minas guarded it', said the Rao, 'for they were the oldest inhabitants of Rajputana as it was once known. They were here even before we Rajputs came from Ayodhya. Blindfolded they led the ruler into the treasure vaults so that he could feast his eyes on the priceless family jewels, gold and silver' after the blindfold was removed.

We descended the hill and got into the Austin again. 'How did you acquire this vehicle, Rao Sahib?' I asked. 'That's a long story', he said. 'My father was interested in the latest cars, and at that time the Austin was among them. He bought it in Bombay and presented it to me on my birthday, a gift which I have kept all these years. For me it is still a present and something which I will retain till I die. After I am gone I am sure my grandsons will not part with it for I have made them love it. Every day when I take them to school I tell them a story in which the Austin played some part.'

'During the Partition I saved a family from a mob in Bharatpur thanks to my Austin. I happened to be there on some business and while returning to Jaipur saw a man, his wife, grown-up daughter and two young sons running as fast as they could. I stopped and inquired what the matter was. They told me about the mob, and though it was a problem accommodating them in the car I did so. On the way we were held up at Alwar. But I had relatives there and was able to keep the family with me.'

'Being young myself I was instinctively drawn towards the tall girl I had helped to save. I won't tell you her name. She must be in Pakistan now, perhaps a grandmother. But she did fall for me and by the time we reached Jaipur her father and mother were aware of the little romance that had cropped up on the way.'

'Marriage would have created problems both for them and for me. And in any case stolen kisses are sweeter, aren't they? Well, I saw them safely off across the border and got this postcard.' The old man took out his purse and from it very gently pulled out an old faded postcard with the head of George VI embossed on it. It was in Urdu, just a few sentences, and a name at the bottom, which I couldn't read.

'Well, it says that she misses me. There were three other postcards during the next fifteen years, one of them just before her marriage. Then from 1962 there was no word from her. But years ago I did receive a message saying she had been widowed. I cannot meet her but this Austin is a link between us – a romantic link. I sometimes think it is her, in the form of a car. It's a silly thought but good enough to humour an old man. How can I sell the car then? So I keep running it with the best of maintenance.'

We were now back at the Rao's house and that afternoon when I left for the station in the Austin to catch the train to Delhi I couldn't help patting the old vehicle all the way. There was a twinkle in the Rao's eyes when he wished me good-bye, wagging his finger and ending up with the remark: 'You made me feel jealous young man – the way you fondled the old Begum'.

I know what he felt, for that old Austin meant a romance of long ago to him. Surely the Ruby vintage of the years, with the 'R' in ruby a flourishing red letter both in the memory of man and vehicle. That is if vehicles could think, but I suppose they do or how else would they serve so well? But sadly enough the Rao Sahib is no more and I don't know if the Austin is still with his family, but here is another Vintage tale:

A Phantom beauty for vintage car lovers is a dream proposition. How one wishes that it could make the rounds like the Phantom rickshaw of Kipling or the Phantom bus that people say once used to be seen in a town where it had met with an accident. But our Phantom beauty is a stalled vehicle that ceased to run years ago and now stands in a courtyard that once belonged to a Nawab. The Nawab is dead and the car has no takers, for it is just a heap of junk, having had the worst of the elements buffett it for many a year. And yet there was a time when it was one of the first Fords that ran on sprightly wheels with real begums in purdah hidden in it from the public eye.

But to come to the story, the Ford in its heyday was the repository of many a scandal, one of which concerned the Nawab's wife. Ever fond of good company and good food, she used to wonder what exactly the quaint bottles of imported whisky that her husband hid from her really contained. She could not contain her curiosity and one day opened a bottle and sipped a little of the beverage. It made her head swoon but soon she learnt to control that for it was akin to the kick she got from her favourite Lucknow brand of tobacco.

Slowly the bottle was consumed and the next day the Begum Sahiba started on another. Practice made her perfect and soon she was able to consume half a bottle without anybody being the wiser for it. So one day the dear lady decided to finish off a whole bottle. She knew it had a big potential for making her merry and that pleased her all the more. After consuming it she ordered the driver to take her to Galta – a good three-mile drive from her haveli – and there her head really started swimming so she lay down on the velvet lawn and just freaked out. The driver was at his wits end and did not know what to do. There were few telephones then and the nawab did not have one. But he just couldn't take the liberty of bodily carrying the Begum Sahiba to the car and driving her back home. So he retired to his vehicle parked outside and having to wait long for his mistress to return, he had a look all around and found an unconsumed bottle, a spare one that the Begum had left behind. So he thought it best to pass the time gulping down the contents and by the time he had finished, the Begum Sahiba was standing near him for she was now sober enough to be driven back home. But despite his best efforts the driver crashed the car and both he and the Begum died, leading the Nawab to conclude that they were having an affair. He sold the Ford, married a girl from Tonk and bought a new car which he always drove himself to avoid another tragic scandal.

Alauddin Khilji In Limelight

THOSE going to Mehrauli Archaeological Park now don't make a beeline for the Qutub Minar but for Alauddin Khilji's tomb, thanks to the Padmavati controversy and the portrayal of the Sultan by flamboyant actor Ranveer Singh (Ranveerwala

Khilji) infatuated by a glamorous Padmini aka Deepika Padukone of the 'ghoomar' dance.

Malik Muhammad Jayasi, who wrote the *Padmavat* nearly two and half centuries after the death of Khilji and had conjured up a story about the Sultan's fascination for Rani Padmini of Chittor, was not a historian but a poet and dramatist who was just giving free play to his imagination during the Mughal era. A resident of Jayas, now in Uttar Pradesh, he had probably not even travelled to Delhi to see Khilji's tomb, and far removed as he was from the scene and Chittor too, he could just think like a romantic poet without contradiction in an age when communal passions were not ignited as now, though the Sultan is on record as having said that one word from him and his Hindu subjects just scurried away like rats.

In Alauddin's reign even members of the royal family could be put to death at the slightest hint of treason, then why talk of ordinary mortals. In domestic life however, he was more of a troubled husband, trying to play the arbitrator between his two wives. Once when he was relaxing in the Siri garden with second wife Mehru the first one came and started beating her up with slippers. Alauddin watched for some time and then drew his sword to threaten the aggressor and chased her away. But frequent quarrels between his wives so disturbed him that he couldn't even sleep in peace. He seems to have had enough of the so-called joys of conjugal life and any idea of courting Padmini Devi may have not even entered his mind, when two females were already making existence miserable for him. Further evidence of this can be gauged from the fact that during his Gujarat conquest Raja Karan Bugela, after his defeat, fled and sought shelter with Raja Ramchandra of Devagiri, leaving his wife to be captured by the invaders. But there is no evidence that Alauddin coveted the rani.

Instead of being a lecherous man, he was more of a conqueror whose kingdom extended from Lahore to Madurai in the south and from Bengal in the east to the coast of Sindh and Gujarat in the west. His general, the Hazardinari eunuch Malik Kafur had crossed the Mahakantara forest that separated North India from the South and brought several rajas under the yoke of the Sultan. Some of them fled but Alauddin never brought their wives into his harem. He was not a sex-crazed despot but an astute ruler who controlled market prices and punished errant traders without any distinction between Muslims and Hindus, according to historian Ishwari Prasad. However he did destroy some temples in the South, like in Madurai where a mandir was demolished to build a mosque.

Joining the visitors at the grave of Alauddin Khilji (actually Khalji), which lay neglected and forgotten hitherto, one noticed that there's no dome over it and neither an inscription to proclaim the greatness (or notoriety) of the ruler who, despite the advice of his fat Kotwal, styled himself as the 'Second Alexander'. A mongoose now stays in a hole in the wall. It probably makes its forages when nobody is around. The Sultan could not have dreamt that nearly 700 years after his death his monument would be so forlorn as that, confined to a few square yards enclosed by solid masonry. And yet at one time he was the most dreaded man in the country. Even the fierce Mongols, who invaded his realm, had come to recognise that. He not only defeated their hordes but had the heads of the captured Mongols cut off and displayed. As if that was not enough, he built a hall of thousand pillars over their bones.

What a fall for the despotic Alauddin over the centuries! At least this is the feeling one gets after visiting his tomb. Where is the Rajput princess who allegedly captivated his heart and whose reflection he saw in a mirror (when mirrors didn't exist)? Where are his great generals Ulugh Khan and Nusrat Khan, who captured for him the Deccan and Gujarat – and Malik Kafur, the thousand dinar slave who fell into the Sultan's hands after the storming of Cambay? The deliriously perceived charm of Padmini has vanished and so have all these medieval warlords.

Alauddin died a sad man. His excesses did it for him and his jealous and suspicious nature antagonised even his wives and children. He ruled for twenty years but when his end came in 1316 nobody lamented for him. However one trait – love of learning is his only saving grace. Though illiterate, the Sultan helped to spread education by setting up a madarsa for theologians. The walls of the madarsa still bear eloquent testimony to the fact and stand as sentinels before the tomb of the emperor, whom now even a mongoose defies. Malik Muhammad Jayasi, however, lies buried far away in his native village with a madarsa around his tomb. Boys learning the Quran there by rote play cricket in the courtyard in the afternoon without any trace of even a shade of a Sultan or Rani lurking in the shadows to cheer them on!

Such A Man Once Walked On Earth

THE day Gandhiji was assassinated (30 January, 1948) the bazaars closed immediately and groups of people collected at street corners discussing the shocking news. Picking up a knife from the kitchen elder brother rushed to the main door of our house. Mother caught his hand and asked him where he was going. He said to kill the man who shot Gandhiji. Just then father entered and restrained him. Later it was learnt that Godse had used the Italian Beretta revolver owned by Sir Augustine Filose which had been stolen from a gun repair shop in Gwalior, where Sir Augustine was a Sirdar in the court of Maharaja Jivajirao Scindia. Shaken by the incident Sir Augustine afterwards left for Italy, the place his ancestors had come from in early nineteenth century, leaving all his assets to the Maharaja. The revolver was probably used by his ancestor for the first time at the Battle of Maharajpur in 1843 against the British troops.

At the Mahatma's funeral trains to Delhi from every direction ran full with people travelling even on their roofs. One saw a sea of humanity behind the Red Fort where Gandhiji was cremated at Rajghat after Jawaharlal Nehru had famously said in an AIR (All India Radio) broadcast that 'the light has gone out'. It later emerged that Godse had been staying in a room in Marina Hotel of Connaught Place and going for target practice to prepare for his heinous act on the Ridge behind Mandir Marg (then known as Reading Road after Lord Reading the Viceroy).

Once on a visit Gandhiji met a young student from Shantiniketan. They had a discourse on 'beauty'. 'The moon shining among the stars at night is beautiful', said Gandhiji. 'So is a pretty woman', replied the boy. 'Even if she is not morally upright?' asked Gandhiji. 'Then her face would not be beautiful', was the reply he got. 'You are begging the question', said Gandhiji with a laugh. The student looked nonplussed but joined in the laughter. When he grew up he became a Congress leader but remembered that Bapu had asked him to read *The Hound of Heaven* by Francis Thompson for spiritual enlightenment.

Some years ago one visited the Sweepers Colony in Mandir Marg and saw the place where the Mahatma used to sit and deliver his sermon to those assembled after cleaning the colony latrines. He had once admonished Kasturba that he was willing to separate from her if she did not do the same. Pandit Nehru was often among them when he came to consult Gandhiji on important matters. The caretaker of the attached museum led one to the door on the southern side which opened towards the Mandir Marg St Thomas' Church built in 1931-32 and inaugurated by the Viceroy's wife, Lady Willingdon. The caretaker said that through this door Gandhiji would sometimes go to the church and meet the priest in-charge for lengthy discussions on religious and other matters. The priest then, incidentally, was an Englishman and the church was built for poor Christians with Urdu inscriptions, one of which said, 'The meek shall possess the earth'. On seeing it the Mahatma remarked: 'Doesn't that justify Ahmisa?'

At St Stephen's College Gandhiji used to go with his friend C F Andrews to meet Principal Rudra. At one of the meetings he was introduced to the great Christian mystic Sadhu Sunder Singh, who later disappeared on the last of his many secret visits to the then forbidden land of Tibet, causing much grief to the Mahatma, despite Sarojini Naidu's attempt to console him by reciting Shelley's *Adonais* on the death of Keats.

Gandhiji was no theoretical moralist. When news came from South Africa that the Mahatma's eldest son had been harassing his own elder daughter, he wrote a long letter to him, both advising and criticising him for his immoral conduct and ordering him to send the girl Manu immediately to him in India, where Kasturba would help the granddaughter in erasing the bitter scars left by her ordeal.

Another son, Devdas Gandhi was the editor of *The Hindustan Times*. The sub-editors working there used to be in a hurry to finish off their midnight tea and snacks at the shop below the old Bombay Life Insurance Corporation building, which kept open the whole night. The reason was that Devdas would get up from sleep and walk downstairs from the apartment he occupied in the building to the newsroom to keep track of events and make corrections in the page proofs as per Gandhiji's advice based on his own *Young India* newspaper days. These memories come to mind whenever Gandhi Jayanti approaches. Someone once tried to call Gandhiji's spirit during a seance in Agra but the medium replied it was not possible as he happened to be on the highest plane of the Blessed. No wonder Einstein said in a memorable tribute that 'generations to come would find it hard to believe that such a man once walked on the earth'.

Chowkidars, Glow-Worms And A Lantern

THE night chowkidar walks. And as he walks he thinks of his home up in the hills and wraps up a Jaipur colony in reverie. The flats he guards after the last car has zoomed in are so bare and sans character that anyone keeping an eye on them is bound to think of his own abode far away. Here the wild creatures that come out are the cats and dogs and an occasional bird that chirps to its midnight mate in some dark foliage of a tree in silhouette. Only the moon and stars are real and they too are not as bright as in places where pollution is still a distant evil.

There are four watches of the day and five of the night. At least that's how the Ancients divided the twenty-four hours, with the perennial question: 'Watchman what of the night?' and the watchman replying 'Morning comes and also the night'. That's what's written in the Old Testament of the Bible too. No wonder the chowkidar carries the mystery of the night with him and if you look at him hard you will know what I mean. Chowkidars are mostly *Meena*s, *Garhwali*s or *Poorabiya*s from East Uttar Pradesh and Bihar. In this writer's colony Thapa used to be an institution in himself, though his wife was more dominating. Both are dead and their son, who used to go about with a felt hat and a cigarette in his mouth, has disappeared somewhere.

However, others are there like Dulha, Babban and Ram Singh. Once I asked Babban if he had seen anything unusual during his nightly rounds. He scratched his head, trying to recollect. 'The peepul tree', he said, 'emits strange noises and flashes as though somebody was lighting diyas after midnight. In the adjoining park, two women, one old and the other young, are seen on some nights. They disappear after reaching the dust patch, where stray cows and calves rest at night'. 'Who are they?'

He hazarded a guess: 'Some years ago a girl committed suicide in one of the colony flats. Two days later her grieving mother also ended her life by hanging from a ceiling fan. Maybe their spirits haunt the park.' This may not be true but it lends an air of mystery to a dull and drab colony alright. Next time if your late evening walk gets tiring, befriend the chowkidar and he may well send you home with your ears buzzing with excitement.

Banshee wails of a woman in agony are said to emerge from another peepul tree in the wee hours when the city is asleep and only the night watchmen are astir on the road. But during the day the tree does not look so mysterious as buses swerve past it; nor for that matter does it seem to be 110 years old. It would be easy to demolish the myth on several counts, just as one would the legend of the headless man who is believed to patrol the road in front of the Galta road, or the *churail* who, gossip says, loiters near the Ghat Gate. But at night things do assume strange shapes and the senses are lulled into a credibility that defies rationality.

Be that as it may, few indeed remember the significance of the Walled City peepul tree in an age when even the grandmothers of nearby Ramganj have stopped amusing their grandchildren with uncanny tales. But the tree luckily stands until such time as man and nature connive to bring it down. Until then the peepul leaves murmur in the breeze and share their secret with the city gate – or so one would like to think; for it takes many generations to perpetuate a myth and just one to lay bare the facts and smother the charm that lingers around mundane things long after the deed is done.

Take the case of an officer who stayed at a Bandiqui Dak Bungalow for a night in the first decade of the twentieth century and this is what he had to relate: 'Salam Sahib', said the khansama. I nodded 'Myself Jumma Khan and this Ram Singh', he added. Then without another word Jumma Khan led me to my quarters. I remarked that they were dusty, but by the time I returned after seeing to the comforts of the horse they had been cleaned by the boy.

At long last, the khansama announced dinner. I responded immediately, walking with hasty steps to the middle room where I noticed that the table had been laid for three. But the khansama served me right away without waiting for the other two to make their appearance. I retired early and slept fitfully because of the strong perfume of flowers coming from the half-open window. Then, feeling thirsty and itchy (because of bugs, perhaps) I got up, drank from the glass on the side table and peered out of the window. Someone was walking below the trees with a lantern and from the dress it seemed it was a woman.

But what was strange was the fact that she was walking about in circles. I watched her for some time and then putting on my night coat ventured to see what she was up to, while the chowkidar was dozing somewhere. When I got up next morning, it was early and the Sun had not come up. After a quick wash I dressed up to find that the khansama had already laid the breakfast. After breakfast, I walked back to my room and was soon ready to leave for my next destination.

Before mounting my horse I told the old chowkidar about my experience of the night before. He shook his head and whispered: 'Memsahib here walking. She lost necklace week ago. *Eye half-bandh night round karta hai.*' And he chuckled.

That solved the mystery. The woman I saw was not a lost spirit. She was just a sleepwalker staying with her husband at the Dak Bungalow. No wonder the khansama had laid the dinner table for three.

Ask the neighbourhood chowkidar if you want to savour some tale like this one, though initially he will deny seeing anything unusual but then reluctantly come out with a yarn that may make your hair stand on end and bring the sweat to the brow, despite the chilly winter night.

The lights that blaze on the road are not like those dim ones that twinkle from mountain huts and beckon the lost traveller or remind him of the Will-o-the wisp and other such illusions of Jack-o-lantern and his song. The names are different in Garhawali but the fears they evoke are the same the world over – a confirmation of the tale of Babel one might say with diverse tongues uttering the same beliefs in diverse ways.

Glow-worms are different though. One hardly finds them in the Rajasthan Capital's colonies these days, except a rare one in late July or August. There was a time when children caught them after dinner only to discover that all that glimmers is not beautiful and the glow-worm is no exception, for it is a crude moth at which no butterfly would look twice. And yet the belief is that it lights the way of the lost ones and sees them home. Did Anne Taylor get the hint from this tale when she wrote the nursery rhyme *Twinkle Twinkle Little Star* and despite what Salim Ali had to say many still believe that the weaver bird (baya) keeps a glow-worm in its nest. But remember that only the females are luminous.

These tales apart, the chowkidar's thoughts are not of learned people or what they had to say. He has not read Aristotle but knows that one learns from the things one sees for things cannot err. He walks on the road and thinks of the pathways at home that are more like goat tracks that cling like a child to the hills. He sees the dusty pavements and thinks of the stream where he met the girl who became his wife. You talk to him and he will tell you all, provided you join him on his rounds when everybody else is asleep.

See your colony through others' eyes and it will transform the scenario from a dull humdrum place to a wonderous surrounding with its own myths and forms that hover in the darkness. That's the quality of night. And the watchman knows that – as did Boondan, the lantern seller who used to appear in the streets at dusk. He walked with a slow, swinging gait making the dozen-odd lanterns hanging on his shoulder flicker merrily. The urchins heralded his approach with shouts of *batiyonwala budha aa gaya*. And they had reason to be glad for the bearded old man brought the warm glow of lights to ill-lit galis where the wicker lamp was very much in use.

In the day Boondan collected discarded lanterns, mended and polished them. And when the evening star shone high in the sky he was out on his beat. He walked from house to house, crying *lalten laylo* and patiently waited for the housewife's response. He used to ply the second-hand trade with relish after retiring as a street lamplighter. Selling a lantern here or releasing a wick there, he moved about in the alleys, finally getting lost until the next evening. That was years ago.

Boondan is long dead and nearly all the houses even in the dimmest of galis, of Ghat Gate have electricity now. But frequent power-cuts keep the trade in lanterns going. The seller now is a younger man who prefers to sit near a kerosene oil dealer. He is a factory hand, who tries to make some extra money in his free time and buyers are not wanting. However one has to be choosy with old lanterns for they might leak or just fail to stay alight.

The dealer in old lamps is called *kabari* now – a junk buyer for sure because the art of turning old lamps to 'new' ones is fast vanishing. And when the evening star is up the children of yesteryear miss Boondan's flickering lanterns. You may light a candle or curse the darkness but the old man is still remembered whenever there is a power failure.

Ghalib in a palanquin

Ghalib At Home In Agra And Delhi

MIRZA Ghalib's death anniversary on 15 February (except for the Urdu literary festival in Connaught Place) did not evoke the same interest as his birth anniversary two months earlier, though the 210th one drew greater public attention than probably that of any other Urdu (or Hindi) poet. The haveli he lived in and the Town Hall were the main venues of the functions then, along with the Sabz Burj Park in Nizamuddin, now named after him. But nobody thought of holding a function at Kala Mahal in Agra, where Mirza Nausha was born on 27 December 1797 and of which he was so nostalgic because of childhood memories. Just goes to show how possessive *Delhiwallah*s have become of Ghalib and of Mir Taqi Mir, who was not only born in Agra but also had an affair with his cousin in the vicinity of the Taj. An enraged family then shunted off the Mir to Delhi where he attained great heights before moving to Lucknow at the invitation of the Nawabi Court of Awadh, where his outdated attire provoked him to recite his famous introduction:

Dilli jo ek Shahr tha alam mein intikhab…
Jisko falak ne loot ke bezar kar diya
Hum rehane wale hain usi ujre dayar ke

(I'm a resident of the same looted garden, Delhi, that was devastated by heaven).

Incidentally, it was the Mir Sahib who had predicted that the boy Ghalib (whose early recitals he had heard) would one day become a big *shayar*. But Yours Truly spent a whole afternoon in and around Ghalib's haveli and wondered at the sudden twist of destiny that has brought it into the limelight again. The area of Ballimaran, of which Gali Qasim Jan is a part, got its name (there are other versions too) from the boatmen who once inhabited it. Thereafter it saw a sea-change with the high and mighty deciding to build their havelis there. It is after Nawab Mir Qasim Jan, an Iranian nobleman, that the gali is named. Qasim Jan at first lived in Lahore, where he was attached to the court of the Governor, Moin-ul-Mulk, in the 1750s. That was the time when Ghalib's grandfather also migrated to India from Turkey.

Qasim Jan was an influential man and a great friend of the Governor. But when the latter fell, fighting Ahmad Shah Abdali who had invaded the Punjab, Qasim Jan helped Moin-ul-Mulk's widow, Mughlai Begum, to rule the province in the name of her infant son. He seems to have been particularly close to the begum, who admired his sagacity. But the admiration was mutual for Qasim Jan could not have been immune to the charm of the begum who continued to defy Abdali despite losing her husband.

It was during the reign of Shah Alam that Qasim Jan joined the court at Delhi. He was conferred the title of Nawab, and in order to be close to the Red Fort built his haveli in Ballimaran. After the death of Qasim Jan, his son Nawab Faizullah Beg resided in the haveli. Ghalib also lived in Ahata Kale Sahib for some time after his release from debtors' prison and that is the time he is said to have remarked that after being an inmate in the *Gora* (white man's) jail he had moved to *Kale*'s (black man's) jail.

Ghalib subsequently moved to the haveli in Qasim Jan Street. But during the 'Mutiny' of 1857 he lived for some time in Sharif Manzil, where Hakim Ajmal Khan's father used to reside. The reason was that Sharif Manzil was a protected place in those days because its owner was the personal physician of the Maharaja of Patiala, who was on good terms with the British. After the upheaval Ghalib went back to his house, where his wife Umrao Begum held sway and made it into a virtual mosque.

However, there is still a mosque next to Ghalib's house. An old bearded man, wearing a brand new sherwani and with a stick in hand, was standing next to it. Asked if Ghalib ever visited the masjid, he shook his head and declared, 'I don't think so, unless when he became old'. What else can you expect from a man who wrote: *Masjid ke zer say ek ghar bana liya hai/ Ek banda-e-qamina hamsaye khuda hai* (I have set up abode in the vicinity of a masjid so a wretch is now God's neighbour). As one walked away after hearing him, the first *degh* of biryani was being opened by the roadside seller and the smell was too appetising to resist the temptation of tasting it. Ghalib too must have eaten like this sometimes or sent his faithful servant Kallu to buy the stuff.

Before settling down in Gali Mir Qasim Jan, Ghalib lived in the house of his in-laws, where several *mushairas* were held. Why they were discontinued at the haveli is not known but one reason may have been the opposition of his puritanical wife. So the mushairas the poet attended were generally the ones held at the Red Fort and Haveli Sadr Sadur in Matia Mahal. In Agra, of course, he was too young to take part in poetry recitation and instead flew kites with the son of Raja Chet Singh at Kala Mahal, where some claim that his spectre is still seen on moonlit nights. He, no doubt, missed Kala Mahal and the Redstone Horse at Sikandra, Agra, to which he always sent greetings through his friend Mirza Tafta Secundrabadi. The Ballimaran haveli somehow did not evoke the same nostalgia in him, probably because most of his children died in it in infancy. Wonder if he would have approved of the museum set up there! But at Kala Mahal *fateha* is still offered for his repose.

Ghalib's Wife Deserves An Epitaph

THE grave of Mirza Ghalib's wife, Umrao Begum, in Basti Nizamuddin, just at the side of her husband's tomb, lacks an epitaph, probably because nobody tried to inscribe one on it in 1955 (when the poet's memorial was built) or because she preferred anonymity as per the strictest tenets of Islam. Even so she deserves one for posterity's sake. Umrao Begum was a pre-teenager when she married Ghalib, who himself was just thirteen at that time, and the two shared conjugal bliss for nearly fifty-seven years.

Umrao Begum was a kinswoman of the Nawab of Loharu, an erstwhile State now merged with Rajasthan, and her cousin was Bunyadi Begum, Ghalib's sister-in-law. The begum, who was the Nawab's sister, gave her haveli in Gali Mir Qasim Jan to Ghalib when he was in need of accommodation. Umrao Begum bore seven children, all of whom died in infancy, leaving her and the poet heart-broken all their lives. Even the nephew, Nawab Zainul-abadin Khan Arif, whom they adopted, died young at the age of eighteen, though he had made his mark in Urdu poetry by then.

Umrao Begum was a strict Muslim lady, whereas Ghalib was not at all orthodox. After the 'Mutiny' of 1857, the poet was accosted by an English officer who asked him if he was a Muslim (as most members of the community were suspects in the eyes of the British). Ghalib replied 'Half'. The officer sought an explanation to which Ghalib said that though he drank, he did not eat pork. The amused officer, marvelling at his wit, left him in peace.

Once Ghalib came home with a man, carrying a basket full of wine bottles, bought with his first pay. Umrao Begum asked him why he had spent all the money on liquor, to which his reply was that God had promised to feed everyone but had not made any provision for drink, for which one had to make one's own arrangements. At another time he entered the courtyard of the house with his shoes on his head. To the Begum's query, he replied that as she had made the whole haveli a masjid by her piety he had no other option. Umrao Begum died in 1870, a year after Ghalib, when Mahatma Gandhi was only a few months old and was buried according to her wish next to the poet. Unfortunately the Ghalib memorial built eighty-five years later became a barrier between the two graves, both of which should have come within its ambit. But it's never too late to make amends for an oversight – if need be with government help.

Her love for Ghalib was intense or he wouldn't have been able to lead the carefree life he did. She was the one who took care of the house despite the poet's love for gambling and dance girls, one of whom took undue advantage of him. Despite mischievous gossip by mohalla women,

Umrao Begum was unruffled because she was convinced of her husband's goodness of heart. Even when there was paucity of funds, she managed to see to it that Ghalib and nephew Arif got three square meals a day. After the death of her children she was the one who comforted her *Mian* Nausha so that the misfortune did not affect his mental equilibrium, without which his wit would not have continued to flow like the sparkling Thames.

Ghalib spent most of his time outside the haveli, except when he was writing poetry, having his meals or resting. So it was Umrao Begum who faced the creditors as she was the one who responded to the knock on the door in the absence of a regular maid. When the Fat Kotwal of Delhi tried to bully Ghalib, as he disliked the poet because of their love for the same *tawwaif* and considered him a potential rival (as he always stole the limelight at the kotha), his wife was the one who confronted the Kotwal's importunate minions at the haveli's entrance and sent them away with the proverbial flea in the ear.

When Arif was grooming Alexander Heatherley 'Azad' as a *shayar,* despite his Anglo-Indian antecedents, Umrao Begum took it upon herself to see to it that they were not disturbed and had some refreshments too during the long hours of coaching. Ghalib who had earlier imbibed the love for *shairi* in Arif, also fawned on him and when he died an untimely death, poured out his grief in a heartfelt elegy (quoted from memory) that is among his best poems:

Jatey huey kehtey ho Qayamat pe milenge
Kya khoob Qayamat ka bahana hai koi din aur!

(while departing you say, we will meet on the Day of Judgment – what an excuse this is, as though the Day of Judgement is just another vague day in Eternity).

Reading the elegy Umrao Begum burst into tears and told Ghalib not to rub salt into her raw wounds, according to Arif's pupil, Alexander Heatherley's descendant, George Heatherley who died in Perth a few years ago. Umrao Begum's grave close to Ghalib's is testimony enough, if one were needed indeed, of the emotional link between the two. Then why deny her the courtesy of an epitaph to seal the bond for the benefit of future generations? No matter how distant may be Arif's final place of repose.

The Ranas Of Mewar & The Bourbons

'FEW countries can claim that all their inhabitants are descended from one stock or that they are of one blood; India certainly is not one of those few', said father Thomas Smith in a history paper from which this extract is taken:

India, has in her long history, experienced a series of invasions from land and sea. Most of the invaders either stayed back for long periods or were wholly assimilated, thus not only mingling their blood with that of native inhabitants thereby producing a hybrid race, but also influencing in no little measure our religion and culture. It would, therefore, be idle for any section of the present Indian population – except, perhaps some aboriginal tribes – to lay claim to purity of blood. The hordes that swept into the plains of Hindustan from the north were not only Aryans (also a mixed breed) but people of different kinds; each of them contributed something to the history and culture of India.

Colonel James Tod's interesting thesis that the Ranas of Mewar are descended from the early Persians has been examined by Indian historians from time to time and the consensus of opinion has been in support of it. Some have tried to disprove the thesis, but their effort is unconvincing and confusing. Tod, as if anticipating the issue, has very aptly prefaced his analysis by saying:

'Historic truth has, in all countries been sacrificed to national vanity; to its gratification every obstacle is made to give way; fictions become facts, and even religious prejudices vanish in this mirage of imagination.'

Now that attempts are being made to rewrite Indian history so as to eliminate from it the dross of foreign historians, it should be even more necessary to guard against a chauvinistic sacrificing of historical truth to national vanity. It should also be admitted that nobody's version of history is ever wholly true. We may sift the major facts and, by wading through all that has been written in a certain period, draw our conclusions.

Akbar's famous historian, Abul Fazl, says that the Rana's family claimed they were descended from the Persian emperor, Naushirwan-e-Adil. They came to Berar (Berat) and became chiefs of Pernalla, 'which city being plundered eight hundred years prior to the writing of this book Ain-i-Akbari, his mother fled to Mewar, and was protected by Mandalica Bhil, whom the infant Bappa slew, and seized his territory'.

Tod has relied mainly on *Maaser-al-Omra* for his theory.

Noshizad was the son of Naushirwan, born of the daughter of Kesar of Rum who abandoned the ancient worship of fire and embraced Christianity and, with his numerous retinue, entered Hindustan. Then he marched a great army towards Iran, against his father Naushirwan, who dispatched his general Rambarzeen, with troops to oppose his son.

Noshizad was slain in the battle, but his line remained in Hindustan 'from whom are descended the Ranas of Oodipur'.

According to Tod, Yezd or Yedegird was the son of Shariar, the son of Khoosrti Purves, the son of Hormuz, the son of Naushirwan. Yezd's third daughter, Maha Nano, came to India, and from her is descended the tribe Sesodia. Khoosru Purves, grandson of Naushirwan the Great of Persia, married Marian, daughter of Maurice, the Greek philosopher and Emperor of Byzantium. Whichever proposition we adopt at the command of the author of the *Annals of Princes*, namely that the Sesodia race is of the seed of Noshizad, son of Naushirwan, or that of Maha Bano, daughter of Yezdegird, we arrive at a singular and startling conclusion, viz. that the Hindu Suraj, descendant of a hundred kings, the undisputed possessor of the honours of Rama, the patriarch of an Iranian princess; that the chief prince among the nations of Hind can claim affinity with the empress of 'the mistress of the world', though at a time when her glory had waned, and her crown had been transferred from the Tiber to the Bosphorus.

Tod's authority as a historian is acknowledged by all. He has founded his thesis on indigenous evidence and his conclusions regarding the descent of the Ranas of Mewar are accepted by historians among them

V A Smith, D R Dhandarkar and William Crooke. Smith observes: 'Foreign immigrants into Rajputana and the upper Gangetic provinces were not utterly destroyed in the course of their wars with the native powers. Many of course perished but many more survived, and were merged in the general population of which no inconsiderable part is now formed by their descendants. The foreigners, like their forerunners, the Sakas and Yue-chi, universally yielded to the wonderful assimilative power of Hinduism and rapidly became Hinduised. Clans or families which succeeded in winning chieftainship were admitted readily into the frame of Hindu polity as Kshatriyas or Rajputs, and there is no doubt that the Parihars and many other famous Rajput clans of the North were developed out of the hordes which poured into India during the fifth and sixth centuries.

Tod's theory has been criticized by some later Indian historians like C V Vaidya and G H Ojha. R C Jauhri formerly of the Department of History and Political Science, Agra College, who did research on the subject, had however, evolved a compromise-formula. While expressing the opinion that the foreign descent of the Rajputs 'does not rest on solid incontrovertible facts', he concedes that 'one cannot ignore the epigraphic evidence which shows how the Greeks, Scythians, Sakas and Huns, etc. had after a few generations of their settlement in this land been completely Hinduised in name, speech, manners, religion, dress and ideas. It is but natural that the blood of these foreigners intermingled with the native population, particularly with the ruling class, Kshatriyas or Rajputs and gotras and pravaras as those laid down in the Vedic Sutras. Though V C Vaidya regarded them as the purest portions of Vedic Kshatriyas, the fact remains that there is hardly a class or caste which has not a strain of foreign blood in it, the Rajputs included as 'they inter-married with the Mughals and both Jahangir and Shah Jahan were half-Rajput – and for that matter even Aurangzeb'.

Now take the case of the French descendants of Prince Jean Phillip de Bourbon who came as a refugee to Akbar's Court. The emperor found him to be a fascinating personality and married him off to the Portuguese head of his harem, Bibi Juliana. Their children and grandchildren multiplied and became a full clan. However, more than 100 years later the Indian Bourbons left Delhi and Agra during the reign of Muhammad Shah Rangila (1719-1748) as the dandy emperor preyed on their womenfolk and took refuge with the Raja of Narwar. Here however many of them were massacred by the Raja's men because of some misapprehension. The remainder fled to Bhopal where they were welcomed by the nawab and their leader, Balthazar Bourbon became the State's Prime Minister up to 1829. His wife was known as Madame Dulhan. The Bourbons intermarried with Rajputs and Anglo-Indians and the last of them still in India, Balthazar Napoleon Bourbon III stays in his house-cum-school with wife Elisha. To meet them, King Juan Carlos de Bourbon of Spain went all the way to Bhopal and opined that he could possibly be a successor to the throne in France if monarchy returned to that country. So you see how intermingling takes place and the Rajputs of Rajasthan have not been immune to it. Joseph Emmanuel Bourbon was a queer character, quite unlike the other Bourbons who find mention in C A Kincaid's *The Tale of the Tulsi Plant and Other Stories*. He fought during the Mutiny of 1857 and died at Allahabad in 1873.

Kasganj's Colourful Past

KASGANJ was in the news after a century of hibernation albeit for dubious reasons because of the rioting there and as such it's worth repeating the history of the town. Kasganj, in Etah district of Uttar Pradesh, was at one time an important tehsil.

A prominent building of it is the palace of former Raja of Kasganj, Dilsukh Rai, built by his son, Shankar Singh, a fortlike structure with a temple, courtyard, stables and an elephant house. Kasganj is said to have been founded by Yakut Khan or Khan Bahadur Khan, founder of Aliganj, who happened to be a eunuch of Mohammad Khan of Farrukhabad in the eighteenth century.

How Kasganj got its name is not known, though some think it's a corrupted form of Khasganj or main market and others believe that the kas grass that grows there (and is used for curing carbuncles) lent its name to the town. On the death of Yakut Khan the town passed into the hands of Khuda Baksh Khan and then to Mohammad Baksh Khan. The latter sold it to Colonel James Gardner. The Colonel's son, Sulaiman Shikoh Gardner in turn sold the town in 1859 to a former agent of his family, Dilsukh Rai, who was later made a Raja. After Jaswant Rao Holkar raided the Doab, the cantonment town, built by the British, was burnt down. This was replaced by a cantonment built for the English cavalry at Kunwarpur, two miles away by Colonel Gardner in 1809.

And that brings us once again to the most famous family associated with Kasganj, the

Gardners. According to E R Neave, ICS, the largest landlords in Etah were the Gardners. Their ancestor was Colonel (later Lord) Gardner, who belonged to a noble family but 'ran away from home to greatly distinguish and enrich himself.'

During the Nepal war of 1815, Colonel Gardner was given command of the force at Kumaon, after the failure of the regular British generals, and he and his brother, the Honourable E Gardner, were able to capture Almora and end Nepalese resistance. 'Col Gardner married a daughter of the royal family of Cutch', related to the Mughals and known as the Princess of Cambay, after which he settled down in Etah Chhaoni, where he lived in great splendour like a prince.

Neave goes on to say: 'By gift, purchase, or as farmer, Colonel Gardner held a large portion of Etah. He was succeeded by his son James Valentine Gardner, who ran away with Malika Kamarchera Banu Begum, granddaughter of Shah Alam, Emperor of Delhi, whom he subsequently married. He died at Chhaoni on 14 June 1845 and was buried there beside his father. He left five sons – Sulaiman Shikoh commonly known as Muna Sahib, James, alias Hinga Sahib, William Linnacus Sikandar Shikoh, and Jahangir Samuel.

E F Gardner, son of Sulaiman Shikoh, is still alive at Chhaoni, where the only relics of a splendid patrimony are a few acres immediately surrounding the house and mausoleum'.

That was in 1910. Now few of the Gardners remain in Kasganj, most members having moved to other places in the country and some settling down abroad. The last claimant to the baronetcy, Alan Legge, who styled himself as the Lat Sahib of Manota, died blind and helpless after crossings the age of eighty several years ago. Those of the Gardners who took Muslim names are almost lost to the family, which continues with its Anglo-Indian traditions even now in Uttar Pradesh, Dehradun, Mumbai, Australia and, of course, Kasganj, where Julian Gardner is now the head of the family.

Among the old buildings, the Bibi Khana of Lord Gardner survives as a dilapidated structure. The Chhaoni or Cantonment is still associated with his medieval clan which once played a leading role in the affairs of North India but the legendary charm of the Princess of Cambay has become a faint memory. It however recently found an echo in William Dalrymple's neo-classic, *White Mughals.* Kasganj itself became a neglected town after its Pathan zamindars lost their lands and ceased to play any worthwhile role, save for the few who entered local politics and sometimes managed to occupy a post or two in the *Nagar Mahapalika* or Muncipal Corporation. But people like Amanullah Khan, the carbuncle healer, who went about armed with a pistol, have disappeared from the scene. The Sherwanis, however, still hold some clout in Kasganj, which had become their fiefdom after the colourful Gardners faded away from the banks of the Kali Nadi.

One fondly remembers a Panditji from Kasganj, who used to sit in a ramshackle kiosk in Subhash Nagar, west Delhi. A huge neem tree shaded it and Panditji kept his stringed cot tied to its trunk lest somebody steal it. He was a slim man with a majestic face and moustache but polio had given him deformed legs so he walked with great difficulty swaying from side to side like a drunken man. His grey hair notwithstanding, he was a man with a bright outlook on life despite his age and handicap.

Panditji sold cigarettes, bidis and paan. But in the evening he closed his shop by 8 pm and spreading his cot sat on it cross-legged. All around him rickshaw-pullers and other daily wage earners would sit down to see him make chappatis and dal on a makeshift chulha. While the pot was bubbling with dal and the rotis were being baked red hot on the log fire, Panditji kept telling tales of his village in Kasganj.

The most popular one was about the kas grass that is an antidote to carbuncle infection. Amanullah Khan, a landlord, was a famous carbuncle healer. Once when the wife of the British Magistrate of Etah was almost on her deathbed because of the carbuncle on her back, he cured her and refused a reward from the Burra Sahib, saying if he took anything for his service he would lose the gift of healing.

Panditji suddenly disappeared in the early 1990s. His kiosk was demolished and the ground where the dal and chappatis were made is now the front yard of a house. But whenever one passes that way to Subhash Nagar market, one is reminded of Panditji and Kasganj.

Now some more details about the wife of the British Magistrate cured by Amanullah Khan. She lost her heart to a Rolls-Royce she had seen in Delhi. Blanche Memsahib used to dream about it and pestered her husband at the breakfast table to get her one as it would make up for the absence of children (since they had none). Robert, the Burra

Sahib, knew that it would be impossible for him to fulfil his wife's wish but he went on reassuring her that one day he would help her acquire the object of her desire.

Many months passed and Blanche kept hoping against hope that the car would land at her doorstep as if by magic and then fate condescended to smile at them. One fine day a young Raja of a princely State came to see the magistrate regarding a large piece of land that once belonged to his family but had been acquired by the government for some project that had not been implemented for twenty long years. Robert promised to help him and later, on going through the papers, learnt that the project had been shelved. He passed on this piece of information to the Raja along with his recommendation that the land be returned to his family.

The recommendation was finally accepted and the grateful Raja came personally to thank him and ask the Burra Sahib what present he could make in return for the kind turn that he had done him. Robert just shrugged his shoulders but Blanche reminded him about the car. The Raja knew little English and keenly inquired what the memsahib wanted. When her wish was disclosed to him, the Raja smiled and said, 'That shouldn't be difficult'.

He did have an old Rolls-Royce which he would gladly pass on to her as he hardly used it on the bumpy roads of his principality and was looking for a smaller and sturdier vehicle. Robert accepted the offer gratefully and a week later the Rolls-Royce was at his door, much to the delight of Blanche.

But soon after, she fell ill because of the carbuncle that had suddenly erupted on her back. It was a painful illness and one which the best of medicine could not cure until Amanullah Khan came to know of her plight. He took a handful of the kas grass and applied it for three days on the memsahib's back. The fourth day the carbuncle had dried up and on the sixth day she was back on her feet. Amanullah Khan (as already stated) refused all offers of a reward for his services. 'I don't want anything even the Rolls-Royce', he said. And so Robert and Blanche had to be content with giving Amanullah Khan a lift in their car right up to the tehsil, where he stayed. Amanullah Khan did not regret his decision to refuse the offer of a fabulous car and went on to heal many other people till his death in 1980.

Having told his tale Panditji was ready for his meal. One misses him now for he moved back to his village from Subhash Nagar and died there in anonymity while the Rolls-Royce was probably sold off as junk long after the British magistrate left Kasganj after Independence in 1947. But the kothi of Nawab Faiyaz Khan Sherwani, Faiyaz Manzil in Agra, where Amanullah Khan often came and stayed as an honoured guest is still there. The Nawab Sahib is dead and his family, which migrated to Karachi, also ended up there. One, however, wonders whether any more carbuncle healers are left in Kasganj, which up to fairly recent times had a cherished history of communal harmony.

Delhi's Lost Ambience

DELHI has lost much of its cherished ambience because of the changes brought about by time. Many of the melas, pastimes and odd professions have gone out of vogue. Up to the 1960s the streets of Old Delhi still had remnants of this vanished culture. There used to be a *hookahwala*, Khadim Mukhtar Ahmad, who used to walk up and down Matia Mahal Street, offering a smoke to passers-by, who tipped him at will. There was also a *pankhawallah*, Rais Mian, who carried a huge embroidered cloth fan fixed to a wooden frame which he waved over a person in summer and got *baksheesh*. Then there was a man (Alemo Qadamprasth) who carried a big broom with which he would sweep the ground in front of someone, *salaam*ed him and, more often than not, got a tip.

Another character who has disappeared was the *Singiwallahs*, Chandan Gujar. He appeared in the afternoon with the cry, *singhi lagowa lo. Singhi* was actually the aquatic leech found in ponds and lakes and other waterbodies and used to extract 'bad blood' from a person's veins in the leg or arm. Letting out blood was an old medical practice based on the theory of the humours or four fluids in the body (blood, phlegm, bile and choler) which determined one's mental and physical make-up. After drawing out the bad blood the leech bloated up and fell off the limb to which it was attached as though exhausted. Yet another character who has vanished was Masoom Albela, wearing a torn shirt, with red colour applied to his body (indicating blood marks). He had a rag tied to his forehead and with this haggard appearance enacted the part of the celebrated Majnu, who suffered physical attacks from those opposed to his affair with Laila, the rival tribe Arabian beauty. In the *tamasha* Majnu would recite parts of the epic by Nizami and cry and moan for his beloved Laila. A crowd always collected to watch him at his antics and left after throwing coins in the begging bowl of the performer, who then moved to another locality.

In this category also came the custom of *ghori chadna*, in which a boy dressed as a bridegroom was taken on horseback up to the steps of the Jama Masjid and back home after recovery from an illness. The horse owner got a hefty amount for the ceremony.

Another practice now discontinued was the blessing by the bhisti or water-carrier, who poured out water from his mashak on a laddoo brought by a child's mother after his recovery from typhoid, malaria, measles or some other disease. The bhisti also sprinkled some water on the child as part of his blessing and then collected the alms offered to him. One other custom that has almost ceased to be observed was the offering of the pankha.

People trying to fall asleep on the terrace on a

summer night would strain their ears in curiosity as the sound of music came faintly at first and then in a cadence. Some rushed downstairs, others leaned on the parapet. A pankha was being taken to the distant shrine and the music makers were the qawwals. Many are aware of the pankhas offered at Mehrauli during the annual Phool Walon ki Sair. But the offering of pankhas at the dargah of Shah Abul Ullah at Agra is peculiar to that city.

The offering is in perpetuation of a vow – a marriage, the birth of a child, recovery from illness, employment and various other reasons. The pankha is hardly a fan. It is more in the shape of a small *doolie*, decorated with curtains and a vase in the centre with joss-sticks burning. The one who is offering the pankha is among the procession of friends, relatives, acquaintances and others who join in out of fellow feeling, devotion to ritual or just for the fun of it.

The pankha is carried by a man who treats such occasions as a side business. When the qawwali singers stop, he stops but keeps the load on his head. Crossings and central places in the bazaar are the usual stopping points – or maybe the house of a friend or relative. Women peep from behind curtains, chicks or half-closed doors. The indiscreet stare at the unveiled faces, trying to catch a resemblance of someone they had seen at the Id fair or a Muharram gathering or at a wedding. But that's beside the point. We all love a pretty face, don't we?

Meanwhile the pankha procession reaches the shrine. Gone are the unveiled faces and gone too is the hustle-bustle of the bazaar. In their place is a serene setting of faith as the pankha is solemnly offered – only the trappings, for the doolie is returned to the man from whom it was hired. The processionists walk back home in small groups and the night begins to settle down to its long hours of solitude until it's time to offer the next pankha. This observance unfortunately is not witnessed in Delhi anymore.

Mystery Of A Grave

WHOSE is the mystery grave next to the one of Razia Sultan? Various conjectures have been made by historians and visitors. According to Gaynor Barton who, along with another Engliswoman, Laurraine Malone, wrote a book, *Old Delhi – Ten*

Easy Walks, Razia was murdered by robbers while resting under a tree in presumably present-day Haryana. Ishwari Prasad, the noted historian, however states that it was not robbers but some villagers who killed her and her lover, Altunia, probably to find favour with her jealous siblings. How did she then come to be buried behind the tomb of Hazrat Turkman Bayabani? Who brought her body there and what happened to the body of Altunia?

She should actually have been buried in Mehrauli near the grave of her father, Iltutmish. But Gaynor suggests that the reason was that her opponents, who included her brothers, didn't want her to share the limelight of the dynasty even in death and draw the sympathy of the high and mighty and of the common people who had taken her to heart. But then what about the other grave, which is believed to be that of her sister, Sazia? How did her body end up there and how did she die?

The conjecture is that Razia and Sazia shared a close relationship – as was natural for siblings. Since her sympathies lay with her elder sister, she probably willed that her last resting place should be beside her. Another reason could have been that her surviving brother, Muiz ud din Bahram Shah who later became Sultan, wanted her also to be away from the limelight so that the hoi polloi was not reminded of the tragedy of Razia.

In those days when there was no Turkman Gate and no Shahjahanabad either, the only known place of importance in the wilderness was the abode of Hazrat Bayabani, who also died the same year as Razia (AD 1240). Her father was a *mureed* (devotee) of the saint and hence the location of Razia's grave there and also of Sazia. But why aren't there any inscriptions on them? Probably because of the hostility of Bahram, who ousted her, or due to the Islamic injunction of burial in anonymity.

Some who are more imaginative think that the second grave is not of Sazia but of a faithful maid who sacrificed her life for her mistress. Yet another conjecture is that it is probably of her lover Altunia. Since they died together, they were buried side by side anonymously. But none of these suggestions seems plausible. Tradition is strong on the point that the grave is of her sibling whose name also rhymes with hers.

The Ambience Of Shiva

MAHASHIVRATRI is one festival that brings with it an ecstatic fervour not found in other festivals. Devotion to Shiva is a perennial observance. Shivbhakti precedes other observances as is evident from the Ramayana, Mahabharata and the Puarnas too. 'The third god of the Hindu Trinity is not only a destroyer but also a protector who, easily swayed by devotion to him, showers gifts on his devotees with abundance', the old pandit of Hari Nagar's Mohan temple told me.

The princely rulers venerated him as he was the one who bestowed power which they venerated more than anything else because of their Kshatriya ancestry which marked them out as the warrior caste and the protectors of their ancient domain, where pigeons were not killed, as they were sacred to Shiva, and who learnt the story of creation from him while he told it to goddess Parvati. 'Bhole Nath', as he is fondly called, gives an idea of the innocent benevolence of Shiva. No wonder even on vans, trucks and other vehicles you will find the slogan, *Bhole ki fauj karege mauj* boldy displayed.

'When Shivratri comes and people worship the bel leaves, they are harking back to the time when a hunter taking shelter on a bel tree kept plucking its leaves the whole night and throwing them down without being aware that in doing so he was unconsciously paying homage to Shiva on whose image below they fell', added the fasting panditji.

Bolo bhai bam/Ke bolo bhayi bam/Ke bam Bhole is the chant of the devotees who travel on Shivratri to distant shivalayas to offer water to Shambo Nath, whose seat is in the snowy Himalayas. Armed with *lathis* and wearing vests and *kaccha*s (underwear) they go about even in the dark to fulfil their mission without any fear, amid the cry of *Jai, Jai Shiv Shankar/Kanta lage na kankar*.

Delhi has several *shivalayas*, not counting the ones in Mehrauli where the Tomar and Chauhan rajas offered worship for power, strength and fortitude, as did Prithviraj Chauhan before the First Battle of Tarain against Muhammad Ghori, which he won – though he lost the second one because of treachery. A foreign tourist, David Sharpe visiting Delhi was fascinated by the small Shiv temples on the roadsides, under trees with flickering diyas, and beneath the old city wall, where a lone sadhu sat in meditation for the whole night, quite unmindful of the wordly happenings, lost in thoughts of Shiva.

David Sharpe had come from Australia and what he saw amazed him. His interest was not in the new colonies but in the old ones – the mohallas of the Walled City where a white ladoo or a kulhar of *dahi* or milk was left by someone as a humble offering to Shivji. A Christian, he at first used to make the Sign of the Cross thinking that what he was seeing was a manifestation of devil worship but slowly light dawned on him and he came to realise that it was God who was being honoured thus in the quaint ambience of Shiv devotion. The photographs David took back home were not only a record of his rambles but a discovery he wanted to share with his folks about strange worship and practices of which his countrymen were naturally ignorant. Here is a note left behind by him with this scribe in 1973:

> A sadhu sits trishul in hand at the gate of the Udaseen Ashram near the Kamla Market. His matted locks match his mien. Behind him on the cool ashram floor several inmates are either asleep or lying with an air of resignation that is peculiar to ascetics who drink Bhang of Lord Shiva, whose *bhagts* they are. Hardly any sunlight seems to penetrate the place. Perhaps long ago when Delhi was still partly inhabited with a Pathar Ghati in the centre, this ashram was just a mound below a tree where wandering sadhus set up abode for a while and went their way, like the Gauri Shankar Mandir which also came up on one such site.
>
> Now the place has an identity. Some of the sadhus are resident here and willy-nilly affected by the modernity of the Capital. There are among them those who go about with briefcases and bifocals. Perhaps it helps to strike

postures – a certain turn of speech, a gentle gaze, a fierce look, quick turning of the head, a gesture or a frown – all have a psychological effect on devotees.

Among the ashramites are the sadhus who sing bhajans morning and evening. They move in a group, six saffron robed men who wake up the residents with the popular *Uth jag musafir bhor bhai* (awake, oh traveller, for morning has come). In the evening the song is of a different kind with its emphasis on the introspection that comes when the day ends.

But to see these men at the ashram is a different experience. Here they move about as individuals both old and young, the fierce looking and the gentle ones. The ones who sit at the gate look like the sentries of Shiva. These sanyasis do have an air of mystery. What secrets of life and death do they harbour?

David Sharpe of course doesn't rattle the Damru of Shiva in far-away Melbourne at Mahashivratri or intone, *Aarti karo Shanker ki,* but says he still relishes an evening spent at a Chandni Chowk shivalaya long ago while munching *rabris* given as prasad.

Pir Of Bachchon Ka Ghar

THERE are many places in Delhi that attract one with their history or quaintness. Among them are old buildings, shops and tombs. One such is the grave that divides the road behind Bachchon ka Ghar in Daryaganj, which surprisingly enough was not disturbed by the British in the nineteenth century when they quartered their soldiers in the then newly-built locality. Next to it is the shrine of Pir Sabri and people believe that the grave is of someone related to the saint, who has come to be known as the Pir of Bachchon ka Ghar. When the road was being constructed the municipal engineer thought of demolishing it but was dissuaded from doing so out of respect for local sentiment.

Another factor that weighted in favour of the grave was the story that when the railway line was being laid for the Delhi station, a tomb had to be levelled up. This is said to have led to curious happenings, like the railway line being uprooted every morning. Whether it was the work of vandals or those opposed to the destruction of the grave is not known. But many started believing that it was the revenge of the Sayyid Baba himself who was displeased at his abode being disturbed. So the Daryaganj grave was spared the axe.

The Sayyid tomb in Narela, to which Delhi Transport Corporation (DTC) runs regular services, may also have an interesting history. Incidentally, it was in this locality that Shah Abul Ullah of Mashhad had come and settled down along with his parents during the reign of Akbar.

Later Abul Ullah joined Jahangir's court and served in Bengal. But on an impulse he forsook the life of a grandee and became a mendicant. Among his votaries was the Narela Sayyid. Abul Ullah's shrine is situated near the Delhi-Agra national highway where the annual urs is held, with people from far and near, including foreigners, coming to attend it.

Another disciple of Shah Abul Ullah is buried a short distance away in the Ghatia locality. There used to be an old *imli* tree above the grave. But few dared to climb it because such an action was resented (sic) by the saint and the climber invariably fell down. Soon after Partition a refugee boy attracted by the juicy tamarinds climbed up the tree. But agile though he was, he soon came tumbling down. Luckily he fell from a lower branch but even so lay dazed on the tomb until he was revived by a neighbour. An accident, perhaps as boys do fall off trees.

However, there were other incidents before this one which stretch the limits of credulity. A boy playing with a companion called Mushtaq thought it would be fun if he reeled out the name of the Sayyid Baba as he was being swung to and fro. Mushtaq's playfulness suddenly ceased and he threw the boy on the ground, dislocating his arm.

A childish prank or another accident, perhaps?

But here is yet another one. There was a wedding in the locality in a baker's house and when the bride was being taken away, the car stalled as it came near the grave. All efforts to restart it failed. Somebody suggested an offering at the grave and surprisingly enough the engine came back to life. Probably it had got heated up and started working again after having cooled down. This was followed by a more seious incident. A little girl who had come from Jhansi to visit her relations eased herself near the grave. The same evening she fell ill and died the next day. A mysterious viral infection, maybe.

Some forty years ago the people who had rented the *takia* or ground where the grave is situated decided to cut the imli tree. A few days later the person who had rented the place was shot dead. Two months after another son was held on a charge of murder. Was it the revenge of the Sayyid, nemesis taking its course or a mere string of coincidences? Say what you may there are few takers for the rational explanation.

But the grave in the middle of the road in Daryaganj has been singularly free of such incidents. People take it as an inevitable symbol of the past and shrug off talk of doing away with it to facilitate better traffic movement. Could be superstition but prudence surely seems to be the best course for many. The revenge motive is only an afterthought.

However the children of Bachchon ka Ghar continue to regard him as their patron saint. Orphans they may be but their faith in the Sayyid Baba is intense as succeeding generations of inmates have left behind a rich legacy of devotion. Every Thursday some of them sneak out of the orphanage to light incense sticks at the grave and seek favours for their welfare. The story goes that one of them grew up to become a Munsif Magistrate in Mathura but his one regret was that his wife was childless. After endless visits to the Daryaganj grave she bore him twins – a son and daughter, both of whom lived to a grand old age but did not get married as the Sayyid had told them in a dream that they were his spiritual progeny and celibacy was the best course for them to show their gratitude to him. Make what you like of it but the late Sajjadanashin of the shrine of Pir Sabri, Shah Shariff Husain who died in Medina, said that it was a made-up tale as both the children went away to Karachi after Partition, where they settled down after a fruitful marriage. Their descendants may still be – as a living testament of faith working miracles.

Royal Cuisine & Jinns

DOES the aroma of food and jasmine flowers intoxicate jinns too? Sadia Dehlvi draws some such comparisons in her *Jasmine & Jinns* treatise on Indian cuisine.

In the fourteenth century Amir Khusrow wrote that the mealspread (Dastarkhan) of Sultan Muhammad bin Tughlaq consisted of about 200 dishes. The royal kitchen fed 20,000 people daily. In his famous epic poem that later came to be known as *Mathnavi dar Sifat-e-Delhi* on Delhi culture, Khusrow wrote, 'The royal feast included sherbet *labgir, naan-e-tanduri, sambusak, pulao* and *halwa*'. They drank wine and ate *tambul* after dinner. Khusrow also mentions delicious dishes such as sparrow and quail curry.

The Mooirsh traveller Ibn Battuta describes a royal meal at the table of Muhammad's father, Sultan Ghiyasuddin at Tughlaqabad as a lavish spread comprising thin round bread cakes; large slabs of sheep mutton; round dough cakes made with ghee and stuffed with almond paste and honey; meat cooked with onions and ginger; sambusak that were triangular pastries made of hashed meat with almonds, walnuts, pistachios, onions, and spices placed inside a piece of thin bread fried in ghee, much like the samosa of today; rice with chicken topping; sweet cakes and sweetmeat for dessert. The meal ended with paan.

Sadia says earlier for the twelfth century Sultans, who belonged to warrior clans of Central Asia, food was more about survival than sophistication. 'The refinement in their cuisine came through interaction with Indian communities and the abundance of fruits, vegetables and spices available here. The tables of Qutbuddin Aibak, Iltutmish and Razia Sultan consisted of meat dishes, dairy products, fresh fruits and local vegetables.' It was only late that Firoz Shah's Kotla began to be haunted by jinns.

The arrival of the Mughals in the sixteenth century added more aroma and colour to Delhi's culinary range. However the founder of the dynasty, Babar complained about the lack of muskmelons, grapes and other fruits plentiful in his Afghan homeland. His son Humayun is credited with bringing refined Persian influence to Delhi's cuisine after years spent in exile in Persia following his defeat by Sher Shah Suri. 'The fusion of Indian and Persian styles of cooking came to be known as "Mughal cuisine."'

In Ain-i-Akbari, Abul Fazl, Emperor Akbar's courtier, mentions that cooks from Persia and various parts of India would serve in the royal kitchen. This led to the merging of Turkish, Afghan, Indian and Persian styles of cooking. Abul Fazl states that more than 400 cooks from Persia formed the large kitchen establishment that had head cooks, official tasters and numerous other staff. He mentions rice from different regions, duck and waterfowl from Kashmir and special breeds of chicken raised for banquets, handfed with pellets flavoured with saffron and rosewater. Beef was rarely eaten, and pork was forbidden.

During the rule of Shah Jahan, exquisite architecture, extravagance and luxury came to define Delhi's royal court. The cooks continued to be trained in Persian, Indian and Afghan cuisine. Despite political decline in later centuries, the Mughals maintained their lavish lifestyle. 'The indulgent tables of the last Mughal emperor Bahadur Shah Zafar are legendary. The Mughals faded away, but left Delhi with a cuisine that remains an integral part of the city's cultural heritage.'

In Sadia's ancestral home wafted the fragrance of *chameli* or jasmine flowers. Each evening the terrace was handsprayed with water. Small bunches of jasmine were put on the cots of the elders. But were taboo for young girls. 'The jinns are attracted to the fragrance of jasmine and if they smelled it on an unmarried girl they could become her *ashiq*, possessive lover. This would ruin their chances of getting married to a human being.'

Everyone in the author's Shama Kothi believed that jinns also inhabited it after midnight, when strange sounds would be heard. 'These resembled the creaking noise made when heavy furniture is moved. God created jinns from fire and human beings from clay. Jinns belong to different faiths with both good and bad among them. They love sweets and bought them from Agra's Mithai-ka-Pul.' 'Ammi', says Sadia, 'remembers taps and doors opening on their own in the house where she spent her childhood. This was attributed to Muslim jinns doing their *wazu*, ablutions, before offering prayers.' It is also said that one should never close a *taq* niche in the wall, because it blocks the passage for the jinns and angers them.

The jinn population is believed to be more than that of humans. During qawwalis at dargah courtyards a wide space is always left empty for the jinns. It is said that they are extremely fond of Sufi music. Under their influence women go into the state of *haal* or ecstasy. Believe it or not even Queen Victoria went into haal on hearing Sufiana Kalaam. Did the jinns influence her also? Incidentally they tried to do so with Akbar, two of whose sons, Hassan and Hussain died as the jinns resented the emperor's decision to build Agra Fort on the ruins of a fortress haunted by them. But Akbar managed to cope with the menace.

Sunny-Ki-Mariam & Co.

THE celebration of the feast of Our Lady of Good Health at the Masihgarh Church, where a statue of the Virgin Mary is taken out with great solemnity after a nine-day novena, remind one of the countless women named after Christ's mother, whose Jewish name was actually Mariam. It continues to be a common name among Jews, Christians and Muslims too, some recent examples of which are Mariam Ahmed, daughter of a Pathan landlord of Achnera, Mariam Habib, ex-editor of *Pakistan Times* and Maryam, daughter of Mian Nawaz Sharif.

Mariam Zamani was the title enjoyed by Akbar's Rajput wife, which led to the erroneous belief that she was a Christian. Her maqbara is situated opposite the emperor's own tomb at Sikandra. Mariam Piyari was the saintly woman who was granted a mango orchard by the emperor for a Christian cemetery. It is now known as Martyrs' Cemetery because of the grave of Padre Santus (a seventeenth century Portuguese priest) which is revered by all communities, and of a dozen others martyred along with him by fanatics.

Pahar-ki-Mariam was the woman who haunted Paharganj bridge before New Delhi Station was built and Mariam Begum was the one who was seen walking up and down from Jama Masjid Chowk to the overhead Daryaganj bridge (now demolished). She was always in a hurry, all dressed up as though trying to catch a train. Begum had a bag slung on her shoulder, along with a thermos flask full of tea. Sometimes at night she was waylaid by vagrants who molested her but she was back on her beat in the morning. A comely woman despite her sixty-odd years, Begum was said to belong to Quetta that was devastated by an earthquake long before Partition and in which her husband, children and other relatives had been killed, along with thousands of others, including the wife of an Anglo-Indian teacher, whose dress was always kept hanging in the schoolmaster's bedroom as a reminder of the tragedy. It seems Mariam Begum was in a hurry to get away from the city thinking that another catastrophe was about to overtake her. One fine day she disappeared, probably having succeeded in catching the train that had been long evading her, or fell victim to a murderous vagrant.

Like Begum, there was Mariam Pagli who wandered about uttering only four words, *Devaria bula rahe hain.* It was conjectured as a reference to her brother-in-law, whom she had married after the death of her husband but who later ditched her resulting in Mariam losing her mind. At that time the film *Pagli* was making waves in the cinema halls of Delhi and street urchins trailing Mariam would think they were teasing the film heroine. Pagli would cook her meals in a discarded commode and sleep under a roadside tree to resume her trek in the morning. Where she disappeared after twenty years is not known. And who can forget Jennifer Kendal in the film role of Mariam of Shahjahanpur? But perhaps the most interesting of such women was Sunny-ki-Mariam, a Scheduled Caste convert who married a defrocked Franciscan priest. Sunny Domingo belonged to the family that once owned Masigarh area, where its early nineteenth century head, Mrs Domingo gave her ancestral land, granted by the latter Mughals to Bibi Juliana of the court of Aurangzeb.

Sunny-ki-Mariam would cause quite an uproar in the Christian locality with word going around, *Mariam khel rahi hai*. This was an allusion to the periodic fits she would get and behave like a maenad, shaking her head violently and flaying her arms and legs. In this state she also cursed and made predictions which surprisingly enough came true. Sunny looked askance at such incidents, keeping busy with his coaching classes, which were highly popular with students as he was very fluent in Latin and English, besides his mastery over mathematics. Mariam had borne him three sturdy sons, who became good footballers, and a very pretty daughter. Her neighbours attributed her fits to the influence of 'alien gods' as she bore weird tattoo marks on her forearms, nose and temples, which made them describe her as *Guddi hui*.

Sunny was also popular with the ladies and they always sought him out whenever an o*batana* (Ubtan ceremony – the dabbing with haldi and chandan paste) was held after it had been applied on a bride in an age when fairness creams were still not in vogue. The excited women would try to catch him unawares and when he managed to escape being smeared, set up a chorus of *Sunny Sahib-ki-Lulu*. The word *Lulu* gained currency after Mirza Jahangir, Bahadur Shah Zafar's younger half-brother, used it to taunt Archibald Seton while trying to shoot the British Resident at the Red Fort as he had rejected his father Akbar Shah's request to make him heir apparent in preference to Zafar.

Another strange practice of Sunny-ki-Mariam was plastering her courtyard with cow dung and mud paste every Thursday, saying Mother Mary would come visiting at midnight. She also kept a candle burning and a vessel full of pulao ready for her to eat (sic). When Mariam died there was an earthquake but her husband and children escaped miraculously after their house collapsed. All this come to mind on 8 September when Our

Lady's feast is observed, but there are only a few who remember the mercurial Sunny-ki-Mariam – buried near Father Santus' chapel in Agra.

Vineyard Of The Sadhu

IN Delhi's nooks and corners are hidden some amazing spots. One of these is the Angoori Bagh of Madho Das-ki-Bagichi. On a tip from heritage activist Surekha Narain, one too stumbled on it and got fascinated by its history (which combines myth and fable) after dodging the chaotic traffic of Chandni Chowk on a humid August day.

This Angoori Bagh came up after the one in the Agra Fort, which has been described thus, in *Hardy's Encyclopedia*:

> Facing the central pavilion of the Khas Mahal is a rectangular garden which is four feet below the level of the marble path of Khas Mahal and is known as Angoori Bagh. There are no original vines.
>
> Only a few patches of lawn with the fountain in between are all that remains of this once famous garden. It is 228 feet x 169 feet, divided by four marble paved foot-paths. It was laid out by Shah Jahan in 1667 AD In the centre of the garden, there is a tank with a fountain 28 feet long and 2½ feet deep which was said to have been used for bathing by the ladies of the harem. The upper crust of the garden comprises special soil brought from Kashmir for the express purpose of cultivating choice grape vines, like the ones from Chaman on the Baluchistan-Iran border, whose grapes were much in demand in pre-1947 days. Some say Shah Jahan laid a vineyard in the Red Fort too which was destroyed in 1857 and where Muhammad Shah Rangila made merry with the *houris* of his zenana.

But where was the need for an Angoori Bagh in

the fort when there was one outside it?

Madho Das-ki-Bagichi Angoori Bagh has a lot of hoary trees now but once grapes grew there in abundance and travellers could eat them to their hearts' content. The story goes that a woman ate so many that she became intoxicated and her amorous side manifested itself. She got intimate with some passers-by and gave birth to twins. Whether the two boys remained in the Angoori Bagh or went away somewhere else is not known but their mother stayed put, just like wine personified as a female lying in her lover's arms. This is what a mendicant sitting under a tree in the Bagichi stated between puffs of the drug in his chillum. However the pujari of the garden's mandir, Niranjan Das thought it to be a noonday idler's tale.

According to him, Madho Das was not a rich Seth of Chandni Chowk but a Sadhu from Rajputana who had come to meditate in Delhi. One day while sitting in the hot sun, a king and queen happened to pass that way. The pujari identified them as Akbar and Jodha Bai. Since the queen was a Hindu lady she took pity on the Sadhu and asked the king to get a shelter built for him. The king agreed and asked the sadhu how much land he needed. The Babaji said the length of his hair. 'Very well', said the king, 'take it'. The sadhu, who was Madho Das, stood up and started whirling (the pujari too stood up and demonstrated the action). Slowly his matted locks uncoiled and grew and grew, covering an area of 36,200 feet. The king was amazed but kept his word. Madho Das built an Angoori bagh and a temple on the land which is still very widespread. But it is not 36,200 feet for sure despite the pujari's assertion. His tale is flawed on another count: Akbar and his queen couldn't have come to this part of a wilderness in Delhi because the Mughal emperor hardly stayed in the city. He only stopped in it during his visits to Lahore and Kashmir and, since there was no Red Fort, he preferred to camp in the Purana Qila.

So how did he stroll with his queen (who incidentally was not named Jodha Bai but only known in history as Mariam Zamani) some three miles to where sadhu Madho Das had made his *dhuni* (puja smoke) spot? Could it be that the royal couple of the pujari's tale were Shah Jahan and his daughter Jahanara who had come out for a walk outside the Red Fort (but why in the afternoon?). This would mean that Madho Das-ki-Bagichi and its Angoori Bagh belong to the seventeenth and not sixteenth century.

Even so the Bagichi is certainly an interesting place and the pujari a good raconteur. According to him Madho Das lived to a grand old age but went back to Rajputana, where his samadhi is situated in Jaipur. The present head of the Bagichi's Digambar Akhara, Ramanand Acharya Bachan Dasji Maharaj carries on the tradition of Baba Madho Das. There are nineteen mandirs near the place where Madho Das was found by the royal couple braving the hot sun. The Bagichi has three akharas – Digambar, Nirmoli and Nirvani with fifty-six shops outside. It has electricity, water and gas connections and the pujari pays the monthly bills from donations and shop rent. There is also a fridge and an old sofa set on which this scribe was made to sit and coaxed to eat dal-roti prepared by the pujari. A celibate, he says contrary to the Evensong, *Come when the lamps are lit*, women are not allowed to enter the mandir after sunset. Talking to him is an exhilarating experience as he waxes eloquent on the Angoori Bagh, from which sprang the Bagichi, though he doesn't quote Omar Khayyam:

Ah, with the Grape my fading Life provide,
And wash my Body whence the Life has died,
And in a Windingsheet of Vine-leaf wrapt
So bury me by some sweet Garden-side.

And why should he recite such lines since Sadhus are generally not buried but cremated, not by the garden-side but by the river-side, and the Yamuna ghat is not very far from the Bagichi? However, those visiting Angoori Bagh might, like the fabled fox, very well exclaim that the grapes are sour.

Lost Aura of Jaipur Nights

AWAY from the colourful nights at the Maharaja's palaces and the havelis of the Thakurs, there were other places too where night had its charm. One has to go back some ninety years to recapture the scenario of Jaipur Nights and identify the spellbinder, Major James Alexander (Kaptan Sahib). The hotels and restaurants and Tourism Department create their own nocturnal ambience but the old aura is hard to replicate.

The Major certainly was of foreign origin but for all practical purposes he was a Rajput not only because he was born and bred in Jaipur but because four generations of his forebears had also served the State faithfully and he had imbibed the characteristics of the land of romance and chivalry. He believed that the Rajputs came of the same Aryan stock as did the races of Europe and he was proud of his lineage.

According to Thomas Smith, he had led his regiment at the Afghan War of 1919, where he and his men distinguished themselves and where he was also wounded but returned victorious. Major James Alexander was offered a Jagir by the Maharaja but he only accepted the land where his regiment, the Aam-Khas, and he had once camped.

Thus Major James Alexander had a rich background and an equally rich career not only of military exploits but one in which his men and he had figured so prominently in eliminating the dacoits and thugs who infested the State's countryside. A man of many parts, Major Alexander knew Hindi, Urdu, Persian, English and of course the Rajasthani local lingo too. Among his hobbies were grooming his mare, rearing chicken, fighting cocks and partridges, pedigree dogs, gardening and monkey-baiting. He was a solid man, as attractive in uniform and in turban and jodhpurs as in a formal suit. And of course he was jovial and popular. That naturally made him a great storyteller. His stories, if written down, would make him as well known as Tod and other such masters.

Major Alexander would be rounded up every evening especially in winter, and coaxed to tell stories for which he was well fitted. He had a whole lot of his own experiences which he related with relish, gesticulation and mirth so as to allure and charm all his listeners, comprising the whole household and the neighbours. As there was hardly any other means of entertainment in those good old days, storytelling was very popular and a good storyteller as Major Alexander was held in high esteem. He had a fine stock of his own experiences which he narrated with verve, and he possessed the gift of making his audience laugh and clap and also feel frightened and even shed tears, for he was also well versed in the history and folklore of Rajasthan. When in mood, he would relate a true historical story. One evening he sat as if possessed and warned his listeners to be attentive and patient for he spoke of the beautiful princess Krishna Kumari of Mewar and her sacrifice for a cause.

The virgin princess Krishna Kumari was in her sixteenth year and though years have passed, the incident is never related but 'with faltering tongue and moistened eyes'. There was rivalry for her hand, one of the wooers being no other than the Prince of Jaipur, whose cortege (about 3,000 men) encamped near the capital. At the same time the prince of Mewar advanced his own claim to the princess' hand on the plea that the Princess had already been betrothed to his predecessor. He vowed resentment if his claim was disregarded, so the contenders were Jaggat Singh of Jaipur and Raja Mann of Mewar.

The matter was coming to a head when the father of the princess, the Rana, declined to dismiss the Jaipur suit. The rival forces were on the move to settle the matter either way. The Rana's capital was besieged for six months but gallantly defended. At this stage emerged 'Ameer Khan one of the most notorious chieftains India has known'. It was his intention to make money in the bargain. However as hostilities became imminent, Nawab Ameer

Khan made the suggestion that to avoid bloodshed the only solution to the problem was that the princess should die.

The man approached declined to commit the heinous act. It was therefore left to the women of the harem to do so. The notorious cup was prepared, as it was for Socrates, and the lovely princess bowed tc the wishes of her father. The cup was handed over to her and with determined hands she drank the contents but to no effect. Another cup with stronger brew was prepared and given to her, which also she drank but still the poison did not work. It seemed providence was finding it too cruel to end the pretty princess' life.

The mother was in a bad state but the princess told her, 'I fear not to die, for am I not your daughter? Why should I fear death? We are marked out for sacrifice from our birth; we scarcely enter the world but to be sent out again, so let me thank my father that I have lived so long!' Thus did she speak while the nauseating draught was prepared for the third time stronger and more deadly. She took it with a smile and drank it up. Such was the end of the then most beautiful princess of Rajasthan.

The audience had listened with bated breath until the Major had ended the tale. A tear rolled down his ragged face and the whole gathering also broke into tears.

Major Alexander, whose thatched colonial-style bungalow was outside Ghat Gate, bang opposite the Central Jail, died in 1948 at a grand old age after elder brother, Felix Alexander, born around 1857. His sons and grandsons lived in the bungalow until their death, after which it was sold to a truck transport company, along with the attached garden, well, gharial, haunted imli tree and side buildings. A sad end to an old landmark and a remarkable family. The last of the descendants living in Jaipur, Andrew died a few months ago, while the rest have migrated, with Colonel Ronnie Alexander of World War II fame still surviving in Australia as a nonagenarian. He sometimes thinks nostalgically of the aura of Jaipur Nights when his grandfather, the 'Kaptan Sahib' and 'Kaptani' held sway at the 'Chapparwala Bangla' on Agra Road, where also lived their adopted son, Joey Francis and his family. Of them 90-year-old Maggie Francis, the sole survivor, is an inmate of Durlabji's Avedna Ashram, in which nights hardly have any aura about them.

The Inverted Lotus

MANY have admired Safdarjang's Tomb as the last flickering lamp of Mughal architecture but it was left to Dulcie Hamilton, a passing-by travel writer from Melbourne, to remark that it was like 'an inverted lotus, just the opposite of the latter-day

Baha'i Lotus Temple' (in an age when the Lotus symbol is politically abloom). Both structures incidentally have an Iranian link as the founders of the Baha'i faith, the 'Bab' and Bahaullah belonged to Iran while Nawab Safdarjang also had Iranian antecedents. For this reason his last resting place occupied pride of place in Jor Bagh, the Shia cemetery that extended up to it at one time and was second in importance only to the (Hazrat Ali) Qadam Shareef shrine set up by Qudsia Begum, wife of Muhammad Shah in the eighteenth century. Safdarjang was the Vazir at her husband's court and later that of her son. It should be no surprise, therefore, that the tomb took pride of place during the Muharram mourning for Imam Hussain.

The tazia processions that came from the Walled City made their first halt at the palace of Mahabat Khan, behind his contemporary Abdu'n Nabi's masjid in the present ITO area and the next one at Safdarjang's Tomb before finally ending at the Karbala. Mahabat Khan's mahal does not exist now but his grave is there in Jor Bagh. Another interesting fact that few know about is that Safdarjang's first Urs or death anniversary saw many Shia divines arriving in Delhi from Oudh and surprisingly enough, a qawwali was also held at the behest of his son and successor, Nawab Shuja-ud-Daulah who was reputed to have the longest moustache in the Mughal empire. He aided Ahmad in the third Battle of Panipat in which the Maratha confederacy led by the imperious Sadashiv Rao 'Bhau' lost. After that Shuja-ud-Daulah clout in the Mughal durbar increased with Shah Alam's (designated emperor by Abdali) arrival in Delhi from Allahabad.

Safdarjang's mausoleum, designed on the pattern of Humayun's Tomb, is a poor imitation. The three-storey tomb in fawn-coloured stone also bears a faint resemblance to Akbar's mausoleum at Sikandra, but lacks the magnificence of the latter. Even so it is an interesting monument, situated amidst a garden of 300 square yards, and enclosed by a wall at the corners of which stand octagonal towers and a central dome, rising above a sixteen-sided drum.

Arcaded pavilions, named Moti Mahal, Badshah Pasand and Jangli Mahal, have been constructed on the northern, southern and eastern sides, like the pavilions in the outer quadrangle of the Taj. It is believed that these were meant for the accommodation of nobles who visited the mausoleum. The tomb has a carved cenotaph in the central chamber within which is another chamber containing two unmarked graves, both with earthen mounds above them. In it lie buried Mirza Muqim Abul Mansoor Khan Safdarjang, and his wife Banu Begum. The monument was built by Shuja-ud-Daulah at a cost of Rs 3 lakhs with a lot of marble and other material being pinched from the mausoleum of the Khan-e-Khanan and other Mughal buildings.

Safdarjang was the head of the Shia Irani party at the court of Ahmad Shah (1748-1754). His opponents were the leaders of the Sunni Turani party headed by Imtiaz-ud-Daulah and Imad-ul-Mulk. Safdarjang, who had succeeded Burhan-ul-Mulk as Nawab of Oudh, died at Faizabad in 1754. His body was brought to Delhi, for though he had to leave the Mughal court in disagrace after trying to play kingmaker, he nevertheless pined for his days of grandeur in the Capital and desired to be laid to rest there. His mausoleum has a mix of Mughal, Rajput, Iranian and Egyptian architectural patterns jostling for space.

Even so it attracts a lot of tourists but these days the water channels, a notable feature, are dry which is a turn-off. The renovation work has been done only on some portions while others are still badly in need of repairs. When one visited the tomb recently under overcast skies, one wondered if yesteryear music mehfils could be revived and *tazia* processions made to converge on it either at Muharram or Chhelum for the *halim* dish break that used to replenish the fatigued akharas or sword and lathi-wielding squads in the past. One thing that Safdarjang couldn't have dreamt about is that 261 years after his death his memory would be enshrined not only in the maqbara but also in the airport, road, hospital and enclave named after him by a generous posterity which only has a nodding acquaintanceship with him.

Vintage Over The Years

TIMES Gone By in the Metroplus always takes one back many years to when Nawab Dojana of Matia Mahal was among the early car owners in Delhi, the earliest being Lala Chunna Mal of Chandni Chowk. Dojana House (later converted into a flatted complex) was the rendezvous of the hereditary rich in the early twentieth century. Among them was the Nawab of Basai Darapur, now better known for its ESI (Employees' State Insurance Corporation) Hospital, with the Nawab a forgotten entity.

We take the motor car for granted because everybody who is anybody has one these days. The lanes and bylanes of Old Delhi, where wooden *thela*s transported people once, have cars both old and new, in which purdah women go for even short-distance shopping or visits to relatives and acquaintances. In West Delhi's Hari Nagar, Subhash Nagar, and Mayapuri the galis are so cluttered up with parked cars that it is difficult to even walk through them. The vehicles, some as big as the egos of the buyers, have mostly been bought through bank loans and it's a moot point as to how many of these have been repaid.

Probably one of the reasons for the mounting number of unpaid loans could be traced to the easy option of obtaining them and then just forgetting about the repayment. However, vintage cars do not create any such problems. They are heirlooms mostly or acquired by vintage car lovers, for which banks do not as a rule have any provisions for giving loans. By the way, the latest research shows that Indians spend more time behind the wheels than the Chinese, Australians, Filipinos, Thais and Pakistanis, not to speak of Afghans and others of mountainous countries, and Sri Lankans. No wonder our roads are so jampacked, morning and evening, with road rage and accidents taking a heavy toll.

The first motor cars that came were a novelty, with people standing on the roadside and admiring them as they glided with greater ease than the horse-driven carriages. The two World Wars gave a big impetus to the car industry and sturdier and swifter cars were designed. Had it not been for Kaiser Wilhelm II and Hitler the motor car industry would perhaps not have made such rapid progress initially. Now we have beautiful cars as sleek as planes but it cannot be denied that the older models, no longer in daily use, have their own aura. It was to maintain that aura that the Vintage car movement began.

But before that, when the film *Chaudhvin ka Chand* was the craze in Shimla in the 1960s one remembers going to Lakkar Bazaar from the Ridge and then climbing up to Meadows Hostel of Massey Sahib. There one met a group of visitors from Delhi who had come in an old Ford. How the car had made it up to Shimla was a miracle because very few vehicles were able to reach the hill station. The next day the visitors – two girls, two boys and their parents, all members of the Brown family – drove to Chotta Shimla, where their third daughter was studying at St Bede's College. On the way back, the car was involved in an accident and the family had to spend Christmas Eve waiting for the vehicle to be repaired. They made it to Lakkar Bazaar late at night and got up in the morning, still tired from the exertions of the previous day. It was Boxing Day and in the afternoon they decided to drive back to Delhi. But fate was unkind again and the car rolled down a khud, with all six passsengers meeting their death. Their bodies were finally recovered and the mangled car, too.

A relative had the Ford also buried in a separate mud grave and for some years people who went to visit the Brown family graves also offered flowers at the spot where the Ford was buried. What a vintage tribute to an old car!

There used to be a Mulberry House in Delhi too, owned by a Sindhi family, who later sold it to a rich spinster, Joan. Daughter of a retired magistrate, she was madly in love with a Sunbeam (a car not manufactured now). She doted over it and rejected all suitors, dusting the car every morning and washing it also at times. Then something unthinkable happened. She fell in love with a master mechanic named Joshua, who too was crazy about cars. They got married and moved to Alwar, with the Sunbeam of course. But Joan died in childbirth, leaving behind a son, the only consolation of the unfortunate Joshua, along with the Sunbeam. What happened to it finally one doesn't know but Joshua passed his life servicing the Maharaja's cars, some of which were highly prized at Vintage rallies.

The Thakur's Sleek Beauty

SLEEK cars and pretty women are both prized by those who know their worth. There are some who prefer one but not the other; but there are others who like both and relish their friendship. A story one heard from an old car lover, George Bedoes always comes to mind whenever it's time for the Vintage rallies. Bedoes was crazy about cars and regarded them as beauties which lent colour and charm to drab lives. You sometimes found him standing alone on the kerb-side in Delhi, watching sleek cars and their sleeker occupants glide by. Here is the tale he was never tired of relating:

A Thakur lived in an old haveli. In his younger days he could not resist the charm of fast-moving cars and pretty ladies. It was always love at first sight but it hardly lasted more than a year because the Thakur did not believe in letting his emotions grow stale. One is not sure what the discarded one thought of it, but the Thakur cared two hoots and was ready for his next conquest after he had washed his hands off her. Sometimes he went without a car or beloved for months but his practiced eye would sooner or later spot his next charmer and the game of love began all over again.

While still a youth Rajinder Singh had fallen in love with a Baby Austin owned by an Anglo-Indian Lucy with grey eyes and light skin. Nicknamed 'Grey' after the colour of her eyes she was slim and pretty and naturally quite proud of her good looks. Both Rajinder and she were different in outlook but shared a passion for cars. He liked to attend the club every evening with her and the friendship soon changed to infatuation for the lady and the Austin owned by her.

How the Thakur got attracted to Lucy was a mystery to his friends. Their eyes met and they just started liking each other, so much so that Rajinder began spending every Saturday and Sunday afternoon at her house, perched on a hillock just near the boundary of his haveli. The haveli was originally owned by Dr Nadar, who was an economist of note. He had married a British teacher of exceptional beauty and when the two strolled arm-in-arm in Church Street, Fatehpuri some were inclined to remark, 'Beauty and the Beast'. This was probably because Dr Nadar was ebony-skinned and a man of monstrous proportions who walked hunchbacked and had a stooping left leg. His nose particularly was too obtrusive on his ham-like face and one literature student of the college he taught in was convinced that he seemed to be an incarnation of Dr Samuel Johnson, the eighteenth century wit and scholar. Be that as it may, the Thakur was too handsome to be compared to either Dr Nadar or Dr Johnson.

Late one evening the Thakur and Lucy were spotted kissing under a tree by another club-goer, making them the subject of gossip. A close watch was kept on their movements but they were not to be deterred. Now their intimate meetings took place after a visit to the club under the trees growing inside the Thakur's compound. A few months later Lucy met with an accident while driving on the outskirts of Delhi. Rajinder came to know of it an hour later and rushed to the hospital. Lucy had been seriously injured and a doctor operated on her immediately. Lucy's family decided to sell off the damaged Baby Austin and the person who bought it on first-come-first-served basis was the Thakur.

Post-operation problems set in and poor Lucy, after lingering for some time, succumbed to them. It was a tragic blow to the Thakur who became a completely changed man. Marriage did not help. His wife left him in a fit of jealousy, accusing him of having a roving eye. Thereafter there was nobody to control him. Later the Thakur remarried and begot a family. His love for cars, however, continued. He bought and sold them at whim, but the Austin remained as a reminder of his infatuation for Lucy. He lavished the same affection on it as he would have on Lucy had she lived.

A replica of the car in marble was made and installed in the front porch of Rajinder Singh's haveli, with visitors admiring it as a tribute to a departed beloved of the 1930s. The Baby Austin's counterpart was a Morris Minor owned by the Kashmiri Thakurs but the family was unwilling to sell it though the Thakur was keen on acquiring it. Eventually he thought Lucy's memory was best commemorated by the Austin without a rival. And there the matter ended.

The Thakur died at a ripe old age and after that his heirs sold the Austin to a vintage car lover. Whether it still survives is not known. But if it does with someone somewhere, it keeps alive the memory of the Thakur and his beloved. If that be the case, is the present owner aware of its history?

No More: Till The Cows Come Home

ONE doesn't see many cattle in Delhi these days except for stray cows blocking the roads in some areas. But things were quite different fifty or sixty years ago when Chaman and his brother kept buffaloes and cows. In Old Delhi one found

Muslim *gwalas* or milkmen in Chatta Lal Mian, and Hindu gwalas at Mori Gate but most of them lived near the jungle on the Yamuna bank. The population explosion has meant the end of the livestock-keeping business.

One remembers going to Chaman's shed early in the morning, walking all the way to Chatta Lal Mian, not far from Daryaganj's Tiraha Bairam Khan. Chaman was a dark, stocky man and his brother even stockier. Their mother was an octogenarian and Chaman's wife, a comely village woman with just a sari draped around her and her hair open, would be seen helping Sookhie Pehlwan (a thin youngster who behaved like a strongman) feed hay to the buffaloes and cows. The buyers' queue was pretty long in the morning and the two gwalas kept milking the buffaloes into buckets before pouring the milk into the pots and pans held out by the customers. Some just brought an aluminum glass or brass *lota* for a *pau* (250 gm) of milk. There was one balding man who kept staring at Chaman's wife, but she didn't seem to mind his dirty looks as she was too busy with her work. But Sookhie sometimes tried to shoo the chap away by blowing up his puny chest, hitting a lathi on the ground and asking Chaman to get rid of him first.

Chaman, however, was blissfully unaware of why Sookhie kept making that strange request, much to the annoyance of those who had queued up earlier than the ogler.

Talking of Delhi's cattle wealth, this is what the old gazetteer says: 'Cattle form an important feature of the agricultural economy of the district. An ordinary Jat will certainly have his yoke of oxen and a cow or buffalo or both. A cow gives eight or ten calves, one a year; and a buffalo will give fifteen or more. The cattle are milked at sunrise and again before sundown. Among the cattle the *bhoori* (grey-brown) buffalo is the best.' Hence the saying by one angry man to another, 'Have I carried off your bhoori buffalo?' (that you are being cross with me).

'Sheep and goats cannot feed when the dew is on the ground: they get worms in the mouth and feet,' the gazetteer says. Water was given to them twice a day in summer and once in winter. In buffaloes and cows Rora (a cholera-like disease) was a great scourge. 'To do away with it, a rope was tied from one house to another (of a gwala basti). A weed called *bhainsa-gugal* was then burnt like incense in a fire and its smoke was made to curl around all the animals which either stopped the disease from spreading or prevented its occurrence.

Both Hindus and Muslims observed this practice.'

From Delhi city the cattle were led to the Yamuna bank by hired graziers who were paid when they brought them back at *gau-dhooli* or dusk. Sometimes teenage boys helped them. But they could be a nuisance also as cases of bestiality by them were not uncommon. There was stringent punishment for this kind of sex crime against animals but few cases got officially reported. The offender was generally given a good beating and asked not to come near the herd again. One other unusual thing worth reporting is that buffaloes and cows were prevented from entering deep into thickets in which there was a pool of rainwater under a babool tree. The belief was that it was haunted and could harm both the cattle and the graziers. That's why probably herds were taken to pastures new after the monsoon. And that, incidentally, was also the time when Nawab Qudsia Begum hatched a plot with a milkman in mid-eighteenth century in the Red Fort to kill the Mughal Minister Haider Quli, whose haveli still exists in Chandni Chowk.

Now, besides the stray cows, one sees buffaloes crossing over from Hari Nagar to Subhash Nagar and causing a traffic jam sometimes. Earlier they were herded into a grassy ground between Mayapuri and

Subhash Nagar, where they grazed the whole day. But since the ground has now been converted into a park, the cattle are taken towards the open land near the nullah that passes through an under-developed Rajouri Garden area. Chaman and his brother are dead, so are his wife and sons. But the grandsons are around though they do not keep cattle or sell milk now. Thus have Delhi's pastoral connections ended and nobody, except cricket commentators, take recourse to the saying, 'Till the cows come home' when a batsman holds on.

Shashi Kapoor's Love For Jaipur

THE death of Shashi Kapoor after a long illness, which made him wheel-chair bound for some years, removed an old link with the film industry that started with *Aag* and *Awaara*. A part of this link was also connected to Jaipur, a city he loved because it fascinated his wife Jennifer Kapoor nee Kendal. This association began when Shashi was acting in 'Shakespeareana', the theatre group headed by the Englishman Geoffrey Kendal, who later became his father-in-law. Both Jennifer and her sister Felicity probably liked Jaipur because of its hills, which reminded them of the Scottish Highlands back home and the locale of Shakespeare's play *Macbeth*, with its weird scenes – The Three Witches, Banquo's ghost and the murder of Duncan the Meek by the cruel Lady Macbeth at their palace.

Both sisters were fond of shopping in Johri Bazaar whenever they visited the Rajasthan capital, especially when Shashi was shooting for a film. Sometimes he had a spare day when, after escorting the two dear ladies around the markets, where they bought the famed Jaipur print costumes, *dulia*s, precious stones and hand embroidered *jooti,* he would slip away to Sanganeri Darwaza for a good helping of *kalakand,* after which the *kachori*s tasted even better. Although a sparse eater (which once made Rishi Kapoor remark, 'Uncle if that's how much you eat, I'm prepared to keep you for life'), Shashi did have a sweet tooth which he whetted in Jaipur bazaars. He was also fond of biryani of the North Indian kind, to get which he used to cycle a long distance in Bombay to buy a whole lot for Raj Kapoor and Shammi Kapoor and their wives. What spurred him on to go on this trip was the handsome tip he got as a teenager. In Jaipur instead of the biryani of Ghat Gate he enjoyed the *korma-tandoori roti* better.

Shashi was also fond of chaat, which had its own flavour in Jaipur, but more enjoyable for him was the chaat of Chandni Chowk, sold by a vendor in the evening sitting right below the Central Bank building. He would lick it and then go to Parathewala Gali where delicious paranthas were just four annas each in the 1960s and made of lip-smacking desi ghee too. Talking about ghee one remembers a report which said that on a visit to Jaipur Shashi bought a whole pot of it near Hawa Mahal – a favourite destination for both Jennifer and Felicity who liked to drink the lassi sold there.

It's also worth mentioning that when *Mughal-e-Azam* was being shot, with the hills of Jaipur as a background for the early wars fought by Jahangir as Prince Salim (role played by Dilip Kumar), Shashi Kapoor was also there with his father Prithviraj Kapoor (Akbar in the film) whose advice was valued much for the fighting scenes, as in his youth Prithviraj Kapoor had acted in such films as *Sikandar* (Alexander). That experience helped Shashi when he was playing the role of the Pathan Sirdar who carries away Mary (Mariam), the Anglo-Indian lady (played by Jennifer) and her daughter, in the film *Junoon*, based on Ruskin Bond's story, *A Flight of Pigeons* and an earlier version, *Mariam, A story of the Indian Mutiny*, written by J F Fanthome, who was a teenager in 1857 and wrote from first-hand experience. Shashi Kapoor went all the way to Agra from Shahajanpur (where some of the scenes of *Junoon* were shot) to see the grave of Fanthome, who died on 17 April 1914 and was buried in the St Paul's Church cemetery there.

A favourite visiting spot for Shashi was Ram Niwas Garden and its Albert Hall Museum, where he and his wife had seen the mummy of the Egyptian priestess (some say princess). It reminded the couple of their sojourn in Cairo, where the museum has some wonderful Egyptian exhibits, including mummies of the Pharaohs. Incidentally it was from here that the Jaipur mummy was brought during the nineteenth century and presented on behalf of the Curator of the Cairo Museum to Sawai Madho Singh II.

Would you believe that Shashi Kapoor was planning to shoot a film in Ram Niwas Garden mainly because of the mummy which had attracted the attention of his wife? But then fate willed it otherwise, for Jennifer was stricken with cancer and died early in 1984, leaving Shashi heart-broken.

Another story worth narrating is about a pearl bought by Jennifer Kapoor from the evening gems' auction market in Chauraha. She presented the pearl to Shashi on his birthday, which falls in March (he was born in that month at Calcutta in 1938, over two months younger than this scribe). Had he lived up to March 2018, he would have been eighty. But even otherwise he was the longest-living member of the Kapoor family, few months more than Shammi Kapoor who too died at the age of seventy-nine. Now to get back to the pearl: Gossip says that when Shashi's sister-in-law, Felicity saw it she remarked that it was a gem worth dying for. Hearing this Shashi handed over the pearl to her without any hesitation. Maybe it is still with Felicity if old-timer Khalil Mian's tale be true.

Shashi and Jennifer had indeed visited Bagh Chorniwala, Khalil Mian's ancestral residence, near which elephants and camels were led up and down by their keepers, and on which the Kendal sisters took a joyride in Amber when their theatre group visited the city for a performance at the special request of Maharani Gayatri Devi, so fond of reading Shakespeare's plays. Shashi, of course, was overjoyed on seeing the two on elephant-back and the pictures he clicked must be still gracing the family album, unless Felicity Kendal took them away with her after Jennifer's death.

The passing away of Shashi Kapoor should therefore leave Jaipurwallas much sadder than people elsewhere. He was the handsomest Bollywood actor of the times with his dimpled smile, a trait he shared with Sharmila Tagore – who naturally liked him for it, along with Dharmendra and Sanjeev Kumar for their acting talent. Though surprisingly enough, she didn't mention Rajesh Khanna, who appeared in some memorable films with her, including the heart-wrenching *Amar Prem*, with its haunting *Kucch toh log kahenge Logon ka kam hai kehna*, so shrewdly cited by Smriti Irani in her defence when she was under attack as Human Resource Department (HRD) Minister. As someone rightly remarked, Shashi and Sharmila were made for each other. But for fate, it would then have been dimple – dimple all the way to Tiger Hill!

Bibi Juliana's Sarai

Saga Of Medieval Sarais

SARAIS were built by rulers, nobles and philanthropists in olden days when there were no hotels for travellers and pilgrims. Their counterparts were the *dharamshala*s attached to temples mostly. Sher Shah constructed many sarais and so also the

Mughals, Lodhis and Tughluqs.

Among the major sarais was Arab ki Sarai, attached to Humayun's Tomb, built by the emperor's first wife, Haji Begum which still exists. Jahanara's sarai in Chandni Chowk was a seventeenth century marvel. Sarai Juliana was built by a Portuguese lady attached to Aurangzeb's court, in Okhla, where a DDA (Delhi Development Authority) colony marks the spot. Sarai Kale Khan owes its inception to a noble of the later Mughal period and is now remembered because of the ISBT (Inter-State Bus Terminals) depot across the river. Badli Sarai on GT Road survives only as a gateway. Sarai Sohei is a ruin near IGIA (Indira Gandhi International Airport). Azimgarh Sarai (Sundar Nagar) and the Sarai of Sheikh Inayatullah (Mehrauli) are now merely names. Mor Sarai was where Hardinge Library now stands. Katra Sarai in Mehram Nagar, dating to 1660, is a ruined building and there's no trace of Bhooli Bhatiyari-ki-Sarai. Balika Chaman on Chelmsford Road, opposite New Delhi Station, was also a sarai but has become a women's hostel.

Dharamshala Ray Sahib Lala Laxmi Narain is on Church Road, Fatehpuri. It was built in 1906. Lala Pyarelal Dharamshala came up in 1921 in Bazaar Sita Ram. The Sabzimandi Dharamshala dates back to 1939. Kalkaji Dharamshala is in Kalkaji and Najafgarh Dharamshala, built in 1770, is near Temple Chowk.

There are no sarais in service now though some of the dharamshalas are still in use. The sarais had common room for guests and also a place for horses, camels and bullocks used by travelers. Some offered meals cooked by the *Bharbuja*. Sarais disappeared when dak bungalows and hotels started coming up and people needed better facilities. But hotel guests are still governed by the nineteenth century Sarais and Hotels Act.

According to Subhash Parihar who did research for his book *Land Transport in Mughal India* (on which this story is based), there were sarais after every five *kos* or eight *kos* (ten or sixteen miles). The actual word was caravansarais, the author observes:

> Along the Mughal Agra-Lahore Highway, caravansarais are known to have existed at least at the following thirty-seven stages : Bad, Mathura, Azamabad, Chhata, Kosi, Hodal, Palwal, Khawaja Sarai, Badarpur, Nizamuddin, Badli, Narela, Gannaur, Samalkha, Panipat, Gharonda, Karnal, Taraori, Thanesar, Shahabad, Kot Kachhwaha, Shambhu, Rajpura, Sarai Banjara, Sirhind, Khanna, Sarai Lashkar Khan, Doraha, Phillaur, Nurmahal,

Nakodar, Mahlian Kalan, Sultanpur Lodhi, Fatehbad, Naurangabad, Sarai Amanat Khan and Sarai Khan-I Khanan. Of these, almost complete specimens still survive at Mathura, Chhata, Kosi, Taraori, Shambhu, Rajpura, Sarai Lashkar Khan and Malian Kalan. Sarais have partially survived at Azamabad, Thanesar, Shahabad and Doraha. Only gateways are extant of the sarais at Palwal, Badarpur, Badli (Azadpur), Gharonda and Sarai Banjara. Although sarais built by Akbar are known in other parts of the Mughal Empire, none of the sarais along Agra-Lahore Highway dates earlier than the period of Jahangir.

Architecturally, most of the extant sarais along the route follow more or less the same plan. These are invariably square or rectangular structures enclosed with a high battlement curtain wall (the largest of the surviving sarais at Chhata covers a square of some 210 m). Each corner of the enclosures is strengthened with a bastion, making them resemble forts so closely that local inhabitants still think them to be forts and call them so. Even some European travelers mistook these sarais for forts.

The access to each sarai, but for those at Mathura. Thanesar, and Sultanpur Lodhi which have only one gateway each, is provided through two splendid gateways, wide enough to permit large or heavily laden beasts such as camels to enter, set in opposite sides. These portals are so large as to accommodate a large number of rooms of various shapes, arranged in one, two or three storeys. A resident staff of caretakers and guards might have been permanently housed in these rooms of the gateways.

The central courtyard of a sarai is always open to the sky and along the inside walls of the enclosure are ranged single-storeyed small rooms to accommodate travelers. From amongst the extant sarais, the sarai at Shambhu has the minimum number of rooms, eighty-eight, whereas the sarai at Chhatta has the maximum, 148.

Every sarai was provided with a mosque for public worship. James Forbes writes that each mosque has a mulla to assist the pious Muslims in their prayers. The quarters adjoining the mosques or in its basement, found in some sarais, eg at Doraha, Shambhu, Azamabad etc. were, most probably, meant for the residence of these mullas. Often a splendid *hammam*, still surviving in the sarais at Doraha and Nurmahal, also formed a part of a sarai. One or more wells to supply drinking water were dug inside a sarai. Only two sarais along the route, one at Badarpur and the other at Nizzamuddin were provided with a *katra* (a walled enclosure for storing travelers' goods) each.

Pietro della Valle (1623) describing a sarai at Ahmedabad, namely Darzi Sarai or the 'Taylor's Inn' generalises that, 'this sarai and those in other Great Cities of India, are not, as in Persia and Turkey, one single habitation, made in the form of a great Cloister, with abundance of lodgings round about, separate from one another, for quartering of strangers; but they are whole great streets of the City designated for strangers to dwell in, and whosoever is minded to hire a house; and because these streets are locked up in the night time for security of the persons and goods which are there ....'

Tavernier also mentions two galleries in a sarai at Benaras, where merchants sold 'cottons, silken stuffs, and other kinds of merchandise'. James Forbes also saw in some sarais, two ranges of apartments for the convenience of merchants, forming a street from one gate to the other. He adds that the 'sarais with four gates contained a double range of these apartments' forming an avenue to each entrance. But no such compartments are seen in any of the sarais along the Agra-Lahore Highway.

The plan for a sarai having been standardised, it was the architectural and decorative treatment of their gateways where the architects exhibited their creativity. These magnificent portals display the stylistic development of Mughal gateways over a period of about one century and serve as a gauge of style. And in the absence of epigraphic or literary evidence, the architectural style of these gateways helps us fix the chronology of a sarai.

Broadly speaking, these gateways of the sarais along the route can be classified into two types. The first type follows the well-known Buland Darwaza in essence, i.e. in these the sides of the high central façade containing the archway, have been turned at an angle. The sarai at Fatehpur Sikri, built by Akbar used this type of gateway. Along the highway under survey, this type of gateways may be seen in the sarais at Nizamuddin, Shambhu and Nurmahal. In the second type of portals, the broad façade of the gateway is in a single plane and is flanked by an octagonal tower, usually covered with a dome or a *chhatri*, giving the ensemble the impression of solidity.

The institution of sarai did exist in India, in one form or the other, ever since ancient times. Ernest Mackay identifies a large building at Mohenjo-daro as 'some kind of hostel for pilgrims or travelers.' There is ample evidence suggesting the existence of sarais during the Sulanate period. Sultan Alauddin (1296-1316) directive that no one should drink, sell, or have anything to do with wine was proclaimed through the streets and wards, bazaars and sarais of the capital. An inscription of the time of Muhammad bin Tughlaq (1325-51) from Bhadgaon (Maharashtra) records the construction of a sarai at the place by Sunbul, the *Mehtar-i-Sarai* or inn-keeper, in 1328.

Afif clearly mentions the erection of monasteries and inns for the accommodation of travelers by Sultan Firoz Shah, where travelers from all directions were receivable as guests for three days. The sarais of the Sultanate period were situated in cities or towns and not along highways. The credit for providing sarais along highways first goes to Sher Shah Suri (1540-45). He showed an avid interest in the promotion of trade and travel throughout his empire. He is credited with having built sarais at the termination of every two kos (approximately 8 km), to facilitate travel. His name is so deeply attached to the institution of sarai that common lore would have us believe that every sarai in India was built by Sher Shah as in Iran every sarai is attributed to the Safavid Emperor Shah Abbas I (1589-1627). Sher Shah's son Islam Shah tried to emulate his father, building additional sarais. But all these pre-Mughal sarais are known from only literary and epigraphic sources. None of the actual structures is known to have survived.

The largest number of brick and stone sarais were built during the Mughal period. All the surviving sarais along the Agra-Lahore route date from this period. Abul Fazl records that Akbar once 'ordered that in the sarais on the high roads, refuges and kitchens should be established, and that articles of food should be kept in readiness for the empty-handed travelers so that when they had undergone the fatigues of journeying and had sat down to rest they might put food in their mouths without trouble'.

Jahangir, in the first year of his reign, issued twelve decrees to be implemented and observed throughout his realm and one of them was that, 'On roads where there were thieves and highway bandits and where the roads were somewhat distant from habitation, the jagirdars of that region were to construct a caravanserai and mosque and dig a well to encourage habitation in the caravanserai'. That this order was fully complied with is proved by dozens of surviving sarais of his period. An equal number of sarais survive from the period of his successors, Shah Jahan and Aurangzeb. Aurangzeb himself celebrated his victory over Dara Shikoh in the battle of Dharmat by erecting a sarai on the site of conflict.

Besides emperors themselves the other members of the royal household, queens, princes etc. also financed the erection of sarais. Jahangir's mother, Mariam-uz-Zamani, built a sarai along Fatehpur Sikri-Ajmer route, at Bayana, in 1613-14. Jahangir's consort, Nurjahan is known to have erected a number of sarais along various Mughal Highways. Francisco Pelsaert records Nurjahan's fame for erecting expensive sarais, in all directions of the empire, intending thereby to establish an enduring reputation. Her sarai at Nurmahal is a unique specimen of Mughal architecture along the Agra-Lahore Highway. However, in patronizing the erection of sarais her interest extended beyond mere charity. For example, her sarai just outside Agra, situated at the end of the lucrative Patna-Agra trade route, gave her complete control over tariffs levied on goods, coming from eastern India into Agra and further north.

Another wife of Jahangir, Khas-Mahal, who was a daughter of the noble Zain Khan, also built a sarai at Nizamuddin, Delhi, in 1642-43. Another well-known female builder of Mughal sarais was Jahanara, the eldest daughter of Shah

Jahan, respectfully called Begum Sahiba. Her most renowned sarai was Begum Sarai at Delhi, not extant now. Bernier and Manucci both speak highly of this sarai, the latter designating it as the 'most beautiful sarae in Hindustan' Bernier adds that 'This place is the rendezvous of the rich Persian, Usbek, and other foreign merchants'. Manucci also tells us that in this sarai 'put up none but great Mughal and Persian merchants'. She herself wrote of her sarai: 'I want to build a sarai, large and fine like no other in Hindustan. The wanderer who enters its courts will be restored in body and soul and my name will never be forgotten.'

Nawab Fatehpuri Begum patronised a sarai near her mosque in Chandni Chowk. Nawab Akbarabadi Begum built a sarai as a part of her mosque in Faiz Bazaar. Aurangzeb's wife, Nawab Bai, is known to have built a sarai at Phardpur, some ninety kilometers northest of Aurangabad. Other than royal ladies, the Brahmin widow of Shaikh Abdul Rahim Lakhnavi is known to have kept the name and fame of her husband alive by building sarais and other buildings of public use.

A clear picture of the working of the Mughal sarais is provided by various European travelers in Mughal India. Niccolao Manucci (the Venetian who lived in India from 1656 up to his death in 1717) records that each sarai 'might hold, more or less, from 800 to 1000 persons, with their horses, camels, carriages, and some of them are even larger'. Peter Mundy writing about Sarai of Nurmahal (near Agra) writes that in it could stand 500 horses, and conveniently put up two or three thousand people. The other travelers, who could not get rooms, most probably, pitched their tents in the courtyard of a sarai.

Each traveler was provided with a cot but he had to carry his own bedding. Provisions like flour, rice, butter, and vegetables could be bought inside the sarai or in its neighbourhood. Forster records that 'the necessary sum is delivered into the hands generally of a girl, who procures the materials…' but there were servants in each sarai who could prepare food for small payments. They were called *bhatiyaras*. Manrique considers the attendants in a sarai very obliging and better than European stablemen and innkeepers. Forster was pleased to see that the woman keeper of the sarai at Shahzadpur provided him a supper even at the risk of not being paid. Musicians, magicans, physicians, barbers, tailors, dhobis and women of pleasure were also found at the sarais, besides those selling grass for the horses.

Manucci records that 'in every sarai is an official whose duty it is to close the gates at the going down of the Sun. After he has shut the gates he calls out that every one must look after his belongings, picket his horses by their fore and hind legs.... At six o'clock in the morning, before opening the gates, the watchman gives three warnings to the travelers, crying in a loud voice that everyone must look after his own things. After these warnings, if anyone suspects that any of his property is missing, the doors are not opened until the lost thing is found. Still thieves sometimes broke into a sarai. The anecdotes of impostors and cheats who defrauded the lodgers in sarais form the theme of many a folk tale'.

The decline of the sarais in the nineteenth century coincided with the end of Mughal rule. That was unfortunate and the British who tried to replace sarais with Dak Bungalows only succeeded partially in filling up the void created by their disappearance.

Glossary

Aarati—worship with a lamp
Aazaan—call to prayer
Adaab—courtesy
Agarbatti—joss stick
Babalog—children of the colonial rulers
Badmash—rogues
Banka—a Marathi soldier
Bhabi—sister-in-law
Bibikhana—women's quarters
Bisarjan—immersion in a waterbody
Chador—a stretch of cloth that is offered in prayer
Chakor--bird
Charas—a kind of intoxicant
Chuhlah—open clay oven
Churail—a witch
Dargah—a place of worship where a saint is buried
Darhi—carpet
Dastangoi—story teller
Dastarkhwan—feast
Degh—vat, cooking pot
Dhaki, Dholi—drummer
Dholak—drum
Dhoti—wraparound
Fateha—obesience

Firangi—white man, foreigner
Gali—bylane
Ghayal—wounded
Ghoonghat—veil
Hamam—bath
Haveli—a large house
Hookahwallah—the man who prepares the smoking pot
Houries—fairies
Inquilab zindabad—long live the revolution
Jheel—lake
Kashphool—flowers of a variety of grass
Khadim—caretaker
Khadi—handwoven cotton
Khana—food
Khansama—orderly
Khullar—a mud cup
Kotha—house, a prostitute's house
Kotwali—police chief
Majhi—boatman
Mali—gardner
Mansab—a measure of land
Maqbara—grave
Mazar—grave
Mela—fair
Mian—husband
Mithai—sweets
Mohajir—outsiders
Mohalla—an area
Muezzin—a man who calls Muslims to prayer from the minaret of a mosque
Mujra—a musical event
Naach-gana—dancing-singing

Niqab—veil
Parganah—a land measure, district
Patua—a pot
Purohit—priest
Qaumi nara—slogans for freedom of country
Qawwal-Qawwali—Sufi singers and Sufi music
Rohu—fish
Samadhi—grave
Shayar—poet
Shayari—poetry
Shehnai—musical instrument
Shikari—hunter
Shradh—death rites
Tawaif—a call girl who sings and dances
Thaal—a plate
Thana—police station
Thela—a pushcart
Thumka—beat
Topee—hat
Urs—a festival to commemorate the dead
Vahanas—animals on which deities ride
Zamindar—landlord
Zenana—women, women's quarters